HRD and Learning Organisations in Europe

'Lifelong learning' is moving from buzzword to reality for ever more workers. Firms increasingly need their workers to be active, self-directed learners who contribute to innovations and improvements of processes, products and services. Companies that explicitly encourage and support worker learning, from a strategic perspective, are called 'learning organisations'.

This book is the result of a European study into the changing views and practices of professionals in the field of human resource development within such organisations. It investigates such questions as:

- How do HRD professionals regard their own role in the light of the growing importance attached to learning?
- How do they stimulate worker motivation for learning?
- How do they cooperate with line managers and employees?
- What road blocks do they face in changing HRD practices, and how do they try to overcome these?

Focusing on Europe, the book contains authors and research from Finland, the UK, Germany, the Netherlands, Belgium, France and Italy. Theoretical explorations of the learning organisation and the changing face of HRD complement nearly 30 case studies of HRD functions.

Saskia Tjepkema works as an HRD consultant for Kessels & Smit, *The Learning Company*, and as a researcher and teacher for the University of Twente, Faculty of Educational Science and Technology. **Jim Stewart** is Professor of Human Resource Development at Nottingham Business School. **Sally Sambrook** is a lecturer in Human Resource Management at the School for Business and Regional Development at the University of Wales, Bangor. **Martin Mulder** is Professor of Education and Head of the Department of Educational Studies in Wageningen University. **Hilde ter Horst** is Managing Director of MM&I, a company specialising in consultancy on and development of multimedia training materials and organisational learning. **Jaap Scheerens** is Professor of Education at the University of Twente.

Routledge Studies in Human Resource Development
Edited by Monica Lee
Lancaster University

HRD Theory is changing rapidly. Recent advances in theory and practice, in how we conceive of organisations and of the world of knowledge, have led to the need to reinterpret the field. This series aims to reflect and foster the development of HRD as an emergent discipline.

Encompassing a range of different international, organisational, methodological and theoretical perspectives, the series promotes theoretical controversy and reflective practice.

1 Policy Matters
Flexible learning and organizational change
Edited by Viktor Jakupec and Robin Usher

2 Science Fiction and Organization
Edited by Warren Smith, Matthew Higgins, Martin Parker and Geoff Lightfoot

3 HRD and Learning Organisations in Europe
Edited by Saskia Tjepkema, Jim Stewart, Sally Sambrook, Martin Mulder, Hilde ter Horst and Jaap Scheerens

Also available from Routledge:

Action Research in Organisations
Jean McNiff, accompanied by Jack Whitehead

Understanding Human Resource Development
A research-based approach
Edited by Jim Stewart, Jim McGoldrick and Sandra Watson

HRD and Learning Organisations in Europe

Edited by Saskia Tjepkema, Jim Stewart,
Sally Sambrook, Martin Mulder, Hilde ter Horst
and Jaap Scheerens

London and New York

First published 2002
by Routledge
11 New Fetter Lane, London EC4P 4EE

Simultaneously published in the USA and Canada
by Routledge 29 West
35th Street, New York, NY 10001

Routledge is an imprint of the Taylor & Francis Group

Typeset in Garamond
by HWA Text and Data Management, Tunbridge Wells
Printed and bound in Great Britain by
Antony Rowe Ltd, Chippenham, Wiltshire

British Library Cataloguing in Publication Data
A catalogue record for this book is available from the British Library

Library of Congress Cataloging in Publication Data
A catalog record for this book has been requested

ISBN 0–415–27788–4

Contents

List of illustrations

Figures

Tables

List of contributors

Daniel Belet is Managing Director of BLV Learning Partners, a French research and consulting organisation in the field of leadership and organisational development, and Associate Professor at the University of Bordeaux.

Antje Buschmann is a Research Assistant at the Institute for Personnel Management and Leadership Studies at Chemnitz University of Technology (Germany).

Dirk Buyens is Professor at the Ghent University and partner, head of the HRM Centre and Academic Dean at the Vlerick Leuven Gent Management School (Belgium).

Andrea Cavrini is General Director of Almaweb-Graduate School of Information Technology, Management and Communication of the University of Bologna (Italy).

Hilde ter Horst is Managing Director of MM&I, a company specialising in consultancy on and development of multimedia training materials and organisational learning.

Martin Mulder is Professor of Education and Head of the Department of Educational Studies in Wageningen University.

Katja Neubauer is a Consultant, Corporate Development for the Deutsche Messe (Germany). Until 2000, she worked as a research and teaching assistant at the Institute for Leadership and Personnel Studies, Chemnitz University of Technology.

Peter Pawlowsky is a Professor for Personnel Management and Leadership Studies and Director at the Research Institute for Labor Economics, Chemnitz University of Technology (Germany). He is co-founder and vice-president of the Society for Knowledge Management in Germany.

Rüdiger Reinhardt works as Project Manager at the Competence Center 'Knowledge Communication' and as Senior Lecturer at the University of St Gallen (Institute for Media and Communications Managemement) (Switzerland).

Sally Sambrook is a Lecturer in Human Resource Management at the School for Business and Regional Development at the University of Wales, Bangor.

Jaap Scheerens is Professor of Education at the University of Twente.

Jim Stewart is Professor of Human Resource Development at Nottingham Business School.

Saskia Tjepkema works as an HRD Consultant for Kessels & Smit, *The Learning Company*, and as a researcher and teacher for the University of Twente, Faculty of Educational Science and Technology.

Massimo Tomassini is Senior Researcher at ISFOL (Italy), and is a member of several European research networks.

Tapio Vaherva is Professor of Adult Education and Dean of the Faculty of Education at the University of Jyväskylä (Finland).

Sigrid van Schelstraete is Senior Consultant at TMP De Witte & Morel (Belgium). Until 1999 she worked as scientific staff member at the HRM Centre of the Vlerick Leuven Gent Management School.

Hetamari Woods works as an HRD Consultant for Nokia Finland.

Karen Wouters works as a Scientific Staff Member at the HRM Centre of the Vlerick Leuven Gent Management School (Belgium).

Foreword

This book is based on the results of a European study into 'The role of HRD within organisations in creating opportunities for lifelong learning'. The project, carried out by an international team of researchers, aimed to capture HRD concepts and practices throughout seven European countries: Finland, Germany, United Kingdom, The Netherlands, Belgium, France and Italy.

The partnership was a very fruitful one, and working on the project proved to be a learning opportunity for all involved. Therefore, the researchers would like to thank the European Union for funding this project. We hope the results live up to their expectations.

Equally crucial in bringing this project into being were the HRD practitioners and line managers (and their companies) who participated in this project. They were willing to lend us a 'look behind the scenes' by giving interviews or filling out our questionnaires. We were impressed by their enthusiastic stories, their strong views on the HRD field, the openness with which they discussed differences between 'current practices' and 'ideals', and the creative solutions they came up with to innovate their HRD practices, and we want to thank them very much for their contribution.

For the reader, it is important to note that the practices described in the case studies date from 1998. Given the dynamic nature of businesses and HRD practices, probably many of the facts have changed: mergers took place, new businesses were started up, department and company names have changed, etc. But the stories told in the case studies, are still relevant and recognisable today for both academics and HRD practitioners. We hope they will find them useful in further exploring and developing the field of HRD.

On behalf of the research team,
Saskia Tjepkema

1 Introduction

This book presents the results of a European study into the changing role of HRD, as the concept of the learning organisation becomes relevant for a growing number of firms. The background, objectives, research questions and the underlying research project are described in this chapter. An overview of the structure of the book is also provided, to help guide readers through the chapters.

New challenges for HRD

As innovation and flexibility in meeting customer's needs are now among the core challenges for many firms, 'learning' is becoming more of a strategic organisational challenge. This new significance of learning for the business is highlighted in concepts such as the *learning organisation* and *knowledge management.*

Also, with the decline of lifetime employment and the rapid speed of change, it is necessary for individual workers to learn continuously throughout their working lives in order to keep up with changes and to remain attractive for employers. So, *lifelong learning* has become a challenge at the individual level too.

Lifelong learning has become, and will remain, an important topic for Europe, as the continent develops into a 'learning society' (Gass, 1996; Brandsma, 1997). Work organisations are becoming important partners in this learning society, as they provide ever more opportunities for continuous learning for their employees, with the objective of optimising organisational learning.

This new emphasis on 'learning' poses challenges for human resource development (HRD): how can this particular activity support the development of companies towards learning organisations, and – in doing so – create opportunities for lifelong learning for employees?

Some of the main challenges facing HRD are:

- Establishing firm linkages between strategic goals at the company level, and HRD policy, thus making sure that HRD efforts support the achievement of business objectives.
- Finding new ways to support those individual and collective learning processes that take place during work, or are closely linked to work, on a just-in-time basis. Instead of focusing primarily on providing training programmes to work

on specific, clearly identified skill gaps, HRD departments have to pay more and more attention to other types of learning interventions, such as creating a learning climate in the workplace.

- Creating learning partnerships, in which HRD professionals, line managers and employees all fulfil an active role in setting learning objectives, creating learning opportunities and supporting learning processes as an on-going and integrated part of daily organisational life.

With a growing number of publications on HRD's role in organisational learning by fostering the learning of employees, the changing nature of HRD is gradually becoming more clear. However, many uncertainties remain for HRD professionals, especially in terms of how to enact their new roles. There is little practical literature, and very few instruments to help HRD practitioners in this regard. Meanwhile, many interesting initiatives are being undertaken by HRD practitioners throughout Europe in facilitating employee learning on a continuous basis, on- and off-the-job, and thus support the strategic learning processes of the organisation as a whole.

Background and objectives of the study

The study on which this book is based was conducted during 1998 and 1999. The main aim was to investigate HRD's changing role, focusing on the challenges faced by HRD departments in so-called 'learning-oriented organisations'. Learning-oriented organisations are defined as companies that strive to enhance opportunities for employee learning with the aim of evolving towards a 'learning organisation'.

The first objective was to look more closely at the ways in which the new role of HRD in fostering employee learning was interpreted in European organisations. Though several influential publications with a European origin have appeared in this field, literature on concepts such as the learning organisation and fostering workplace learning has traditionally been dominated by American and, to a lesser degree, Japanese perspectives and practices. Because the situation in Europe differs from that in those countries, it is useful to gain more insight into the European perspective. This was achieved by focusing fieldwork on several European countries, to gain an insight to the 'European dimension'. In this way the results offer a contribution to a European model for lifelong learning, which is becoming increasingly important as Europe develops into a learning society. This model will eventually address the role of individuals, governments, systems for primary education, vocational education and adult education as well as the role of work organisations in creating opportunities for lifelong learning. The results of this study will hopefully feed the discussion on the contribution that one of these parties – namely work organisations – can make to the emerging European infrastructure for lifelong learning.

The second objective, as important as the first, was to contribute to the further professional development of HRD in Europe. HRD currently faces many questions and challenges as a result of the organisational need for continuous learning and change. It is important that HRD meets these challenges. Competent and pro-active HRD professionals, who are able to assist organisations in the realisation of meaningful, strategic learning processes of employees, will help these organisations in securing their competitiveness. To further the professionalisation of the HRD field, both concepts and practices of HRD departments were considered in this study. The term *concept* refers to the ways in which HRD departments view their own role in creating opportunities for employee learning. *Practices* are the way in which HRD professionals try to bring their ideas into being, including the problems they face and the ways in which they solve them. By deliberately taking into account the practical considerations, the results of the study are twofold: an expanded knowledge base, and an extended range of useful working strategies and instruments. Thus, the results can serve both as:

- practical guidelines for HRD practitioners throughout Europe on how to facilitate employee learning and thus assist their organisations in securing their competitiveness in a continuously changing environment;
- a venture point for further research on the changing role of HRD in work organisations.

Thus, this book is aimed at both practitioners and academics (researchers, students, teachers) in the field of HRD.

Research questions and design of the study

The two key objectives were translated into the following research questions:

1 How do HRD departments in learning oriented organisations throughout Europe envision their own role in stimulating and supporting employees to learn continuously, as a part of everyday work (with the intention of contributing to organisational learning, and thus enhancing organisational competitiveness)?
2 What strategies do European HRD departments adopt to realise their envisioned role?
3 What factors inhibit the realisation of this new role? How do HRD practitioners cope with these factors?
4 What factors facilitate the realisation of HRD's new role?

To study these questions, a combination of qualitative and quantitative research methods was used. During the first phase of the project, conducted in 1998, data were collected by means of *case study research*. Four organisations were selected in each of the seven countries involved, resulting in twenty-eight case studies. The aim was to gain an in-depth understanding of the visions of HRD departments in these organisations, the strategies they adopted to bring these visions into practice, and the facilitative factors as well as the difficulties they encountered during this implementation process.

By definition, case study results are hard to generalise. In order to test out whether the case study findings were valid for a larger group of learning-oriented organisations throughout Europe, a *small-scale survey* was conducted across 160 companies throughout the seven countries in 1999. This constituted the second phase of the project.

The partnership

The study was funded by the European Commission, and carried out by an international group of researchers. The research project team consisted of partners from seven European countries – Belgium, Finland, France, Germany, Italy, the Netherlands and the United Kingdom – plus a member of the European Consortium for the Learning Organisation. The project management team consisted of researchers from the University of Twente, The Netherlands. Table 1.1 provides an overview of the partnership.

Each partner organisation managed data collection in its own country (the two Italian partners shared that responsibility for Italy). The project management team prepared drafts of all relevant documents, such as the data collection plan, data collection instruments, theoretical framework and the final report. The partners commented on those drafts, and their input was used to finalise documents. The partners met for two partner meetings, and otherwise communicated frequently through e-mail, telephone and letters. The role of ECLO in the partnership was mainly to help find suitable cases and to facilitate the dissemination of findings.

How to read this book

The book begins with a discussion of the conceptual framework underlying the study (Chapter two). This framework summarises important insights on HRD's role in learning organisations, based on literature and research. Then, a more detailed explanation of the research design is provided (Chapter three).

Central to this book are the case study reports from each of the participating countries (Chapters four to ten). These include cases from both the service and manufacturing sectors, with a rich diversity of types of organisation. The case studies are organised by country, so it is possible to read results for one country only. Each case study includes a brief description of the type of case organisation, so, it is also possible to read only those case studies from a particular sector, such as IT or manufacturing. Especially noteworthy HRD practices are highlighted throughout the case study chapters in separate text boxes.

The results from both the case study research and the survey are then summarised (Chapter eleven). Conclusions are drawn with regard to each of the research questions. A reflection on and discussion of the findings concludes the book (Chapter twelve).

Table 1.1 The partnership

Country	Organisation	Research team
The Netherlands (project management)	University of Twente, Faculty of Educational Science and Technology	Prof. dr. J. Scheerens Prof. dr. M. Mulder Ms. S. Tjepkema, MSc Ms. H. ter Horst, MSc
Belgium	Vlerick Leuven Gent Management School	Prof. dr. D. Buyens Ms. S. van Schelstraete, MSc Ms. K. Wouters, MSc
Finland	University of Jyväskylä, Department of Education	Prof. dr. T. Vaherva Ms. H. Woods, MSc
France	BLV Learning Partners	Dr. D. Belet
Germany	University of Chemnitz-Zwickau, Faculty of Economics Department of Personnel and Management	Prof. dr. P. Pawlowsky Dr. R. Reinhardt Ms. K. Meinicke, MSc Ms. A. Buschmann, MSc
United Kingdom	Nottingham Trent University, Nottingham Business School, Department of HRM	Prof. J. Leopold Prof. J. Stewart Dr. S. Sambrook
Italy	Isfol Scienter	Dr. M. Tomassini Dr. A. Cavrini
International	ECLO	Dr. M. Kelleher M. Alen, MSc

2 Learning organisations and HRD

Saskia Tjepkema, Hilde ter Horst and Martin Mulder

This chapter outlines the main theoretical concepts underlying this study. The chapter starts with a reflection on the need for organisational learning and an exploration of the concepts of the learning organisation and the learning-oriented organisation ('Lifelong learning, organisational learning and learning-oriented organisations'). Then there is a discussion of the theoretical basis on the changing role of the Human Resource Development function as a consequence of the concept of the learning organisation ('Human resource development in learning-oriented organisations'). As this book has a specific European outlook, the question is also posed as to whether the approach to HRD within Europe differs from that in the US and Japan (A European outlook on HRD? Comparison with US and Japan').

Lifelong learning, organisational learning and learning-oriented organisations

Currently, lifelong learning is an important topic on the European agenda. The idea of learning throughout the whole lifespan is not new. The notion has already been in the spotlights during the 1970s, when concepts such as 'lifelong learning', 'recurrent education' and '*education permanente*', were coined. During the 1980s, the discussion was continued on a smaller scale. Recently, the theme of lifelong learning has gained renewed attention (Brandsma, 1997). The most visible manifestation of this attention is the fact that the year 1996 was proclaimed as the official European Year of Lifelong Learning. This has rekindled previous discussions and instigated a new flood of publications, conferences and public debates.

Lifelong learning and the development of a learning society

Lifelong learning is defined by Brandsma (1997: 10) as:

- a process of personal development from employed and unemployed people that takes place continuously;
- a process that can contain both informal and formal activities;

- a process that makes demands upon structures in which lifelong learning takes place/can take place in creating the conditions that facilitate learning and learning to learn.

Lifelong learning is a process with many objectives, which the OECD describes as follows:

It is geared to serve several objectives: to foster personal development, including the use of time outside work (including in retirement); to strengthen democratic values; to cultivate community life; to maintain social cohesion; and to promote innovation, productivity and economic growth.

(OECD, 1996: 15)

The significance of lifelong learning gives rise to the need to develop a so-called learning society, which provides an infrastructure that supports learning throughout the whole lifespan. A learning society refers to mobilisation of not only the public education and training systems, but of all sectors in society, such as public authorities and individuals in creating opportunities for learning (Gass, 1996). Companies also play an important role in creating a learning society, as work grows to become an important source of learning (Pawlowsky and Bäumer, 1996). To an increasing degree, organisations deliberately set out to create learning opportunities for employees, believing that they need 'learning individuals' in order to realise 'organisational learning'.

Organisational learning

Current business realities of many European organisations place ever more demands on their ability to respond quickly and adequately to changes in their environments, by improving existing products and services or by innovation (Carnevale, 1992; Nonaka, 1991). As a result of the ever-increasing rate of (technological) change – induced by developments such as globalisation and the current 'explosion of knowledge' – organisational capacity for learning was pinpointed as the key ability for organisations in the 1990s, and beyond. New managerial concepts such as the learning organisation (Senge, 1990), the intelligent organisation (Pinchot and Pinchot, 1994; Quinn, 1994), the knowledge-creating company (Nonaka and Takeuchi, 1995) and knowledge management (Drucker, 1995; Leonard-Barton, 1995; Pawlowsky and Bäumer, 1996) reflect the search for ways to improve organisational capacity for learning.

There are several classifications of organisational learning processes (e.g. Fiol and Lyles, 1985; Bomers, 1990; Pascale, 1990; Swieringa and Wierdsma, 1992), practically all of which are based on the typology of Argyris and Schön (1978). This typology distinguishes between two types of learning: single loop and double loop learning. Figure 2.1 (Argyris, 1992) depicts both processes.

An organisation's governing variables are, for example, its mission statement, and its (tacitly held) assumptions on the best way in which to achieve the organisational goals. Organisations undertake actions based on these governing variables. These actions have certain consequences. Here, Figure 2.1 distinguishes between two possibilities. On the one hand, the results can be as expected, in which case there is a match between the intended outcome and the actual outcome. On the other hand, it is possible that the results of an action are not what the organisation had expected, in which case there is a mismatch between expectations and outcome.

Single loop, double loop and deutero-learning

In the theory of Argyris and Schön (1978) such a mismatch is the starting point for an organisational learning process. The organisation has to find out how to change its actions in order to achieve the intended outcome. This learning process can occur at two levels. First the level of single loop learning: this means the organisation makes small adjustments in its actions, but doesn't radically change them. To take a simplified example: imagine a chef who discovers hotel guests find the cake he just baked is too sweet. The next time the chef bakes a cake, he adds a little less sugar to the mixture than in the original recipe. In an organisational context a renewed version of a known product is a good example of an outcome of a single loop learning process.

However, making small adjustments at the action level is not always enough to solve the problem. Sometimes the reason for the mismatch is located at a deeper level: the organisation's governing variables. Then a double loop learning process is required in order to reach the intended outcome. To return to the example of the hotel chef: suppose he finds out the guests don't like sweet cake at all, but would prefer some savoury dish instead. In this case he discovers that one of his basic assumptions – that guests like sweet cake – is not accurate and needs adjustment. Instead of simply changing his cake recipe, he now has to seek an entirely new dish to make (and an entirely new recipe). In the case of organisational learning the outcome of a double loop learning process could be, for example, the introduction of a completely new product, or introducing an existing product in a totally new market.

Double loop learning processes thus have much more far-reaching consequences than single loop learning processes do. To illustrate this point, single loop learning is

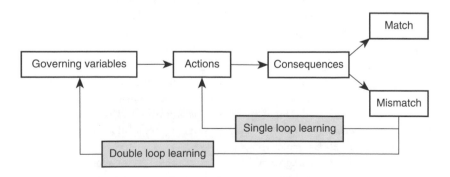

Figure 2.1 Single loop and double loop learning

often compared to keeping a ship on course by making small adjustments (Morgan, 1990), whereas double loop learning resembles the process of changing a ship's course. Single loop learning leads to incremental changes in organisational functioning, whereas double loop learning results in renewal or innovation of existing practices, services or products. Therefore, both kinds of learning processes add to each other. Imai (1986) drew up Figure 2.2 to illustrate the supplementary character of both types of learning processes.

Next to the processes of single loop and double loop learning Argyris and Schön (1978) have determined a third level of organisational learning, which they labelled 'deutero-learning'. This refers to the capacity of organisations of learning how to carry out, and how to optimise, their (single and double loop) learning processes. In other words, it refers to 'learning how to learn' (Senge, 1990; Swieringa and Wierdsma, 1992).

Organisational and employee learning

An organisation as such is an abstract notion, and so is its learning capacity. The ability of an organisation to learn is embodied in its employees. Employee learning thus is a necessary prerequisite for organisational learning (Kim, 1993).

For learning at an organisational level, organisations depend on the learning of their employees. In a sense employees embody an organisation's capacity for learning, since they embody the capacity to:

• acquire or create new knowledge for the organisation (e.g. by learning from daily work experiences, studying new technological advancements or learning about work practices used by other companies);
• disseminate this knowledge to others within the organisation;
• apply the new knowledge in improved or renewed work practices, products and services.1

In this respect, Honold describes a learning organisation as:

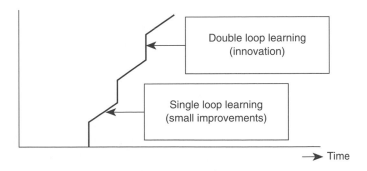

Figure 2.2 The relationship between single loop and double loop learning

one whose members are continuously deliberately learning new things. They apply what they learn to improve the product or service quality, the processes involved in making the product or providing the service, the quality of the environment in which employees work and the performance of members of the organisation.

(Honold, 1991: 56)

However, employee learning in itself is not enough to ensure learning at an organisational level. In order for an organisation to learn, employee learning should not be limited to individual learning. Adequate (bottom-up) communication is important in this respect, and a certain amount of empowerment of employees within the operational core. The first allows learning experiences from employees at different organisational levels to be transferred to other levels. The latter creates opportunities for employees to use their learning experiences in order to make improvements in the workplace (Pascale, 1990; Senge, 1990).

Learning organisations and learning-oriented organisations

The high current rate of change in the economic and technological environment of many organisations has given rise to the development of a new managerial concept: that of the learning organisation. This concept provides general ideas on how to design and manage organisations in order to survive in a highly changing environment.

Learning organisations

A learning organisation can, in simple terms, be described as an organisation that:

1 responds to (and anticipates) changes in its environment by learning on a strategic level (by single loop and double loop learning); moreover, it deliberately aims at improving its ability for learning (deutero-learning); and
2 in order to learn on a strategic level, makes use of the learning of all employees, therefore this employee learning is enhanced at all hierarchical levels.

In addressing the first point, one of the most distinguishing features of 'a learning organisation' is that it operates in an environment marked by a high rate of change. A learning organisation *accepts both this environmental turbulence and the fact that it cannot predict which changes will occur*. In the words of Pedler, Boydell and Burgoyne (1991): a learning organisation is marked by an acceptance that things don't stay the same for long.

Though this may seem a trivial matter, this attitude differs considerably from the tacit assumption most organisations hold – that the environment will not change profoundly and certainly not in a way that cannot be predicted. Seen in this light, the acceptance of change as a part of everyday organisational reality means a notably different strategic outlook from more traditional organisational models.

As a consequence of this acceptance of change, a learning organisation does not work according to a long-term detailed strategic plan. Instead, it has one overriding clear goal (often referred to as the organisational 'mission'), which serves as a general guiding principle for the course the organisation takes. It does not set out a specific 'route' by which it wants to reach this goal. In other words: a learning organisation knows where it wants to go, but does not plan in advance exactly how to get there.

Swieringa and Wierdsma (1992) use the metaphor of the 'traveller' and the 'tourist' to describe this attitude of a learning organisation with regard to strategic planning. The tourist typically travels according to a meticulously-planned schedule, in which every step of the journey is laid down in advance, whereas the traveller only has a broad idea of where he wants to go, and determines the exact route along the way. In doing so, he reacts to unforeseen circumstances. For example, if the weather is particularly nice in one location, he may decide to spend a few days extra there.

A learning organisation can be compared to a traveller. It knows where it wants to go (the 'mission') but plans how to get there step-by-step, constantly responding to changing circumstances. A clear picture of where the organisation wants to be in the long run, is indispensable. Without that, the company can easily lose its sense of direction as a result of the many incremental changes that are being made (Morgan, 1990; Senge, 1990).

Operating as a 'traveller' means there is a constant demand on the ability of the organisation to learn how to anticipate to changes and respond to unexpected situations in such a way that it can still reach its final goal. Thus, the organisation's capacity for learning becomes vital to its continued existence. That is, in short, the main reason why a learning organisation strives to continuously enhance its learning abilities at every level, in order to be able to react quickly and adequately to changes that might occur (Ansoff, 1987; Bomers, 1990; de Geus, 1988). A learning organisation is primarily an organisation that is capable of enhancing its own abilities for learning, it is capable of learning to learn (Senge, 1990; Swieringa and Wierdsma, 1992).

The second element in the definition above concerns *the role of employees*. As was mentioned earlier, for learning at a strategic, or organisational, level, organisations depend on employee learning, where employees embody the capacity to:

* acquire or create new knowledge for the organisation (e.g. by learning from daily work experiences, studying new technological advancements or learning about work practices used by other companies);
* disseminate this knowledge to others within the organisation;
* apply the new knowledge in improved or renewed work practices, products and services.

This notion affects the view of the added value which employees have for an organisation. Metaphorically speaking, the idea of the employee as a 'hired hand' makes way for the idea of the employee as a 'hired head'. Organisations need their employees to learn, in the sense of acquiring new knowledge and skills and using these to improve existing work practices, products or services, or to jumpstart innovation. Learning, therefore, becomes part of everyday work. As Sugarman describes it:

in place of the old model, which was first learning, then work, we now have the new model: first learning, then work-which-includes-continuous-learning. We are not just learning to do the work better; we are building the organisation's knowledge base and revising its tools, processes and products, as we work.

(Sugarman, 1998: 65)

And as this is the case, and employee learning takes on a strategic meaning for organisations, organisations seek ways to facilitate employee learning on an on-going basis (see, for example, McGill and Slocum, 1994; Winslow and Bramer, 1994). This can be achieved, for example, by managers acting not as a boss but as a 'coach', or by creating rich jobs that trigger learning.

This description does no more than provide a general image of what a learning organisation is. It doesn't present a clear, tangible picture of such a company. This is mainly due to the fact that the concept of the learning organisation is not an organisational model in the sense of a blueprint. The concept is more adequately described as a metaphor or an ideal type (see, for example, Leys, Wijgaerts and Hancké, 1992), a way of looking at organisations whereby the process of organisational learning, and not the primary work process is at the centre of attention. This makes it very difficult to assess whether or not an organisation is a 'learning organisation'. Consequently, there is little insight into the number of companies that can be labelled as such. However, it is clear that the management concept has gained a strong foothold. A considerable number of companies are experimenting with (parts of) the idea of the learning organisation. A logical starting point is the enhancement of employee learning.

Learning oriented organisations

Organisations which focus on creating opportunities for employee learning, with the long-term goal of becoming a learning organisation, can be labelled 'learning oriented organisations' (a term coined by Leys, Wijgaerts and Hancké 1992), organisations which:

* create (on-the-job as well as off-the-job) facilities for employee learning;
* stimulate employees not only to attain new knowledge and skills, but also to acquire skills in the field of learning and problem-solving and thus develop their capacity for future learning ('learning to learn').

Tjepkema and Wognum, 1996

The number of these so-called learning-oriented organisations is as yet unknown, but given the popularity of management concepts such as the learning organisation, the intelligent organisation and knowledge management, the group could already be quite large. In any case, the number in general is estimated to be growing rapidly.One could say that becoming a learning-oriented organisation is the first stage in the growth process towards a learning organisation. Becoming a learning organisation requires changes in organisational structures (e.g. process-oriented structure instead of functional, the introduction of teams), culture (e.g. learning culture) and management styles (e.g. from hierarchical styles towards a coaching style). Becoming a learningoriented organisation, means making the first steps towards these changes.

Especially in larger organisations, with a higher degree of specialisation, the HRD function traditionally plays an important role in employee learning. Its role changes considerably when their organisation becomes a learning-oriented organisation, intent upon stimulating and supporting employee learning on a continuous basis. In the next section this changing role of HRD is discussed.

Human resource development in learning-oriented organisations

As organisations develop into learning-oriented organisations, this has a profound impact on the relationship between work and learning. Whereas learning used to be primarily equalled to training, it now becomes predominantly associated with learning from experience, and self-directed learning. Similarly, learning is no longer regarded as a classroom activity, but primarily as something that takes place on-the-job as a continuous, on-going activity. On the one hand this changing view of learning has far-reaching consequences for line management, which is expected to manage the workplace as a place fit for learning (for instance by fostering a learning climate, and by coaching employees). On the other hand it considerably affects the role and tasks of human resource development (HRD) professionals, who are involved in the delivery of training activities for the organisation.

A new role for HRD

Since concepts such as knowledge management and the learning organisation are primarily managerial concepts, there is a considerable amount of literature with practical guidelines on the new role of line management as a leader, a facilitator of learning processes and a coach (e.g. Senge *et al.*, 1994; van den Broeck, 1994). The role of HRD in this process, however, receives much less attention in the leading management literature on organisational learning. Yet, it is becoming the theme of a growing number of publications in the (more specialised) field of HRD.

The role generally attributed to HRD practitioners in these publications is that of *consultant* to line management on how to facilitate and stimulate employee learning in the workplace, and how to link this learning to organisational needs and goals. Their work field broadens considerably, and the word 'trainer' (as they are sometimes called) is therefore really no longer an adequate label for their function. The new role of HRD practitioners will be that of a strategic learning facilitator, performance consultant or even change agent (Laiken, 1993; McLagan, 1996; Watkins and Marsick, 1993; Onstenk, 1994; Pearn, Roderick and Mulrooney, 1995; Robinson and Robinson, 1995; Stahl, Nyhan and d'Ajola, 1993). In some organisations, HRD professionals operate as change agents, starting and supporting the change process towards a learning organisation. Of course, such proactive HRD practitioners fulfil a different role from HRD professionals in companies where management has the leading role in the change process, and where HRD is a more reactive function. In general, the field of HRD seems to be moving from a reactive, isolated business function to a more strategic factor in today's companies (Garavan, Heraty and Barnick, 1999; Barham and Rassam, 1989).

Though the empirical basis for the new role of HRD departments is still very limited, some general working principles have been established, which reflect HRD departments' visions on their own new role in learning-oriented organisations and their tasks. The description below is based on a study of literature on HRD and organisational learning (Tjepkema, 1993a), and the findings of two small Dutch studies (using the case study approach) that were used to verify and add to the theoretical assumptions derived from that literature review (Tjepkema, 1993b; Tjepkema and Wognum, 1995). Both research projects entailed only six case studies, so the possibilities of generalising the findings are very limited. But the results did provide the conceptual framework for the current study.

General vision of HRD in learning-oriented organisations

Generally, HRD functions in learning-oriented organisations appear to focus deliberately on the broader field of learning instead of on training (which is but one form of learning). One of the first priorities of training departments that deliberately choose to aim towards 'facilitating learning' instead of 'delivering training', is to change their name in order to reflect this new vision. Thus, the 'training department' changes into, for instance, the 'centre for organisational learning and change' or the 'learning and development centre'. It is also common for these departments to (partly or completely) abolish the departmental structure, and place (some of the) HRD officers in the line organisation. Thus, an HRD 'department' in a learning organisation may look completely different from a training department in the traditional sense. Note that in this report, the term HRD department is used to mean 'all HRD professionals in the organisation' (whether organised in a departmental structure or not). The term HRD function is also used in a similar manner.

The vision of HRD departments in learning-oriented organisations regarding their own role can be characterised by three basic principles. These three principles (focus on learning, learning as a shared responsibility and linking learning to work) are explained in the literature as well as by HRD departments working on the development towards becoming a learning organisation (see case study research by Tjepkema and Wognum, 1995).

Focus on 'learning' instead of training

Perhaps the most distinguishing working principle of HRD departments in learning-oriented organisations is the above-mentioned broadened view of their own area of work. It is not limited to training, but expanded to include facilitating and supporting other learning processes within the organisation, with the aim of contributing to meaningful organisational learning processes. In this respect, one HRD officer who participated in the study mentioned earlier, stated: 'organising courses is not our main goal, our main goal is to support and facilitate organisational learning'. As a result, the HRD department not only fosters formal learning, but also strives to enhance informal and even incidental learning. In addition, the department not only focuses on individual learning, but also aims to facilitate the collective learning of groups and organisational learning (see also Stewart, 1996). This working principle leads to a broadened range of interventions provided by the HRD department. Moreover, the purpose of these HRD interventions changes. The interventions are specifically aimed not only at gaining new qualifications, but also towards enhancing the learning capacity of employees.

Learning as a shared responsibility

The second working principle is that 'learning' is a shared responsibility of management, employees and the HRD department. The HRD department regards its own role in this respect as primarily supportive (e.g. the role of consultant). This implies a shift away from the, often implicit, idea that is, or used to be, typical for most organisations, namely that training is primarily the responsibility of the training department (see e.g. Barham and Rassam, 1989). Employee responsibility for learning and training has two aspects. On the one hand, employees are increasingly held responsible for managing their own learning processes. They are expected to regard working and learning as inseparable processes, and view themselves as 'continuous learners' (Watkins and Marsick, 1993). This means they have to ensure they keep up with the latest developments in their profession, and deliberately look for opportunities to make improvements in the workplace. On the other hand, employees also have a responsibility towards the learning of their colleagues. Increasingly, employees operate as teachers and mentors in formal and informal learning processes. The aim here is to stimulate the transfer and sharing of knowledge within the organisation.

Linking learning and working

Third, the processes of learning and working are considered to be very much intertwined. The employee is both a 'working learner' and a 'learning worker', where learning is regarded as a normal part of everyday work and working is seen as a rich source for learning (see McGill and Slocum, 1994). There is even a new term for employees which reflects this close connection between working and learning: the knowledge worker, people who possess relevant knowledge and apply this in order to improve processes, products and services (Kessels, 1995; Keursten, 1995; Nonaka and Takeuchi, 1995).

On-the-job learning is stimulated as much as possible. This does not mean, however, that there is no room for off-the-job training activities. These will remain important, because in some instances they are the most suitable method for acquiring new knowledge and skills. However, they are no longer the dominant way of organising learning processes. They fulfil a supportive role with regard to the learning (and training) which takes place on the job.

Tasks of HRD professionals

As training, and the support of employee learning in general, is becoming regarded as a joint task of line management, employees and HRD professionals, the tasks of HRD professionals change. On the one hand, a change of focus occurs in the way in which the HRD professional carries out his or her more traditional roles, such as the role of trainer, because of changes in the nature of training programmes (e.g. the focus on self-directed learning and on establishing close links between training and working; see: 'HRD interventions'). On the other hand, this joint responsibility for HRD brings some new tasks for HRD professionals. In ever more cases the actual (formal or informal) training and development activities are being carried out by line management and employees, whereas the HRD officers monitor the quality of these HRD activities and provide assistance and advice from a professional point of view whenever necessary. In other words, different HRD roles (consultant, trainer, needs analyst, …) are performed by different people (HRD specialists, managers, employees, …).

Basically, case study research indicates that the two tasks which can be considered to be most 'novel' for HRD professionals in companies which strive to become learning organisations, seem to be: consulting non-HRD professionals (such as line management, subject matter experts and other employees) on HRD specific matters and quality control tasks with regard to training activities carried out by line management and/or employees (Tjepkema and Wognum, 1995).

HRD interventions

'Facilitating employee learning' in the broadest sense is the overriding concern of HRD departments in learning oriented organisations. As such, this leads to a broadened range of interventions provided by the HRD department. The focus is on informal learning, and training activities are no longer HRD's main 'product'. Also, as already noted, the purpose of HRD interventions changes.

The interventions are aimed not only at gaining new qualifications, but also towards enhancing the learning capacities of employees. 'Development' activities (which are less formalised than training) particularly increase in number. Traditionally training, concrete and measurable learning goals are formulated, preferably in behavioural terms. The training is conducted, following a detailed plan, based on a careful analysis of the training need. By contrast, development activities are marked by more open-ended and roughly defined goals. The learners themselves carry the responsibility of reaching these goals, the 'trainer' merely performs the role of mentor, coach or facilitator. He guides the learning process, but doesn't completely control or design it. There is also no detailed structure, in which to fit the learning activities, only a rough outline. The activities are planned along the way. For this reason, these development activities are also known as semistructured training. Examples of development activities are: action learning projects, work meetings in which employees communicate some of their knowledge to their peers (e.g. the results of a project they have been working on) or work with an experienced colleague in another department for a while (as a form of internal apprenticeship).

Though training is only one of the offered activities, it remains an important one. In many cases training remains the most suitable approach for the transfer of knowledge and the teaching of certain skills. The training methods change, however. The trainee will take a more active role toward his own learning and training. The trainer explicitly teaches trainees how to learn, and how to shape their own learning activities. This may foster a general learning attitude. Also, training and work are more closely linked, not only by creating more on-the-job training, but also by using real-life problems in training activities (or simulating them). In this way, the transfer of learning is better protected.

In addition to these changes in the nature of HRD interventions, attention is being paid to fostering learning on the job in general, by creating a work environment favourable for learning. Examples of conditions which facilitate learning (and on which the HRD department can exert influence) are: creating a mentor system, job rotation, organising meetings between employees with similar expertise who work in different parts of the organisation, providing materials for self study – for instance in an Open Learning Centre – or providing job aids. However, the most important condition for learning in the workplace – a stimulating work environment, (with a healthy learning climate, for example) – remains mainly the responsibility of line management. HRD professionals can provide advice and assistance to line management in this respect. This brief sketch of HRD's vision, roles and HRD activities served as the vantage point for this study.

A European outlook on HRD? Comparison with US and Japan

The results from this study (see the following chapters) indicate that few differences exist between each of the countries participating in this study. There was no evidence of significant differences between HRD in Finland and in France, for instance, or between Germany and Italy. Whilst some differences were found, there were more similarities. At first sight, this might seem strange. An instinctive response to the question as to whether there are differences in HRD within Europe would be: 'Of course there are'. Not only do business contexts vary, but differences in national histories, cultures and traditions have led to different national jurisdictions and regulations in countries. The variation becomes apparent in cross-European diversity in areas such as rights to educational leave, differences in training taxes, fiscal deductibility of training costs, relationships between (vocational) education and HRD, and differences in school-to-work transition practices. However, when looking at the major theme of this study, HRD in the learning-oriented organisation, and especially HRD visions, similarities appear to be greater than the cross-European differences.

But is this to say that there is a specific European outlook on HRD in the context of the learning organisation? To shed some light on this issue, a review of literature on HRD in Japan and the US was conducted in an attempt to compare HRD views in those countries with those encountered in this European study2 (ter Horst *et al.*, 1999).

It proved difficult to say whether Europe has its own specific outlook on HRD when compared to Japan or the US. Based on the literature review, similarities in outlook between Europe, Japan and the US appear more significant than the differences. This may be caused by the fact that within the European study, data collection was restricted to large organisations only (see Chapter three). Our impression is that the literature about HRD in Japan and the US is also predominantly based on large organisations. As a result, the context of many organisations is comparable, as that is the global economy. If small- and medium-sized companies would be included in the study, the results might have been different, as many SMEs only work for regional or even local markets, which are more diverse in the sense that they operate in varying regional and local economies. Below, we'll look a little closer at the results of the literature study, comparing 'Europe' to the US and Japan (ter Horst *et al.*, 1999).

Concerning the general *HRD visions*, similarities outweigh differences between the US, Japan and Europe. This is also understandable, as important functions of HRD are to contribute to employee development, improving job performance, problem solving, organisational performance improvement, and career development. HRD departments in Europe as well as the US and Japan see themselves more and more as strategic partners. Supporting the business and contributing to achieving business goals are, to an increasing degree, highlighted as major HRD objectives.

Differences in approach can be found when considering the *roles of HRD professionals*. Both in Europe and the US this role, generally speaking, changes from trainer to consultant. Moreover, a more active role is expected from managers and employees. Managers are given more responsibility for employee learning and employees are expected to take responsibilities for their own development process. For HRD professionals, this means they will have to support them in doing so, in order to ensure quality of HRD interventions. Some of this support may consist of providing learning resources. This is in essence a rather *practical* role. Having managers fulfil an active role in HRD also gives HRD practitioners room to give advice (consult) on HRD issues, which can be considered to be a more *strategic* role, since it provides HRD professionals with the opportunity to help managers link training to corporate needs and to use opportunities for informal learning at work (instead of only training). It also provides them with room to work on other more strategic tasks such as monitoring competencies, helping managers in their new role, offering new HRD concepts and promoting learning.

In Japan, however, line management, and not the HRD function, is the major partner in employee development. The manager is fully responsible not only for employee development but also for creating a learning culture, for example. Just as in Europe and the US, Japanese employees are expected to take on an active role regarding their own development process. But it appears that this has been normal practice in Japan for a long time, and is not a new development.

An HRD function, as it exists in European and US companies, seems non-existent in Japan. Large organisations in Japan do have a training department, which merely focuses on providing training and/or training materials. But an HRD department with HRD professionals that also fulfil other tasks (rather than 'traditional' training tasks), such as supporting a learning culture, supporting knowledge management etc. seems to be very rare in Japanese organisations.

With regard to *HRD strategies*, most of the differences between US and European firms on the one hand, and Japanese businesses on the other, can be found with regard to HR approaches. First, forms of training appear to vary. In Japanese organisations *formal on-the-job training* (supplemented with informal learning on-the-job) is most common, whereas US and European companies tend to focus on *formal off-the-job training*, in combination with *informal learning on-the-job*. The focus on formal learning-on-the-job in Japanese organisations can be explained by the major guiding concepts in this country, such as lifetime employment and seniority-based practices. Second, in Japan, a strong emphasis is placed on group processes. In contrast to this, in America the emphasis is on individuals. Europe can, in this respect, be characterised as focusing on both individual and group development.

It has to be said, that although we did compare 'Europe' as a whole to Japan and the US, these are in themselves nations within which the differences between companies are also large. So, the reflection on similarities and differences between Europe, Japan and the US, is based on an overall view, and based on (gross) generalisations about the situation in these nations. Of course there is no such thing as a European, US or Japanese HRD model, but it was an interesting exercise to compare HRD practices in these different countries, and although it has not yielded a 'European HRD profile', it has provided some extra background context against which to interpret the insights of this particular study, which was European in nature.

Notes

1 Together, these activities make up what is also known as a 'knowledge cycle', or 'organisational learning cycle' (Dixon, 1994; Pawlowsky and Bäumer, 1996)
2 Literature was searched in several databases on the basis of key words such as training, HRD, learning organisations, innovation and competitiveness in Japan and the USA. In addition to this, new literature was found in the lists of references of the respective publications ('snowball method'). Finding useful publications about HRD in Japan and the US proved to be not so easy. First of all, there is the language barrier when studying Japanese literature. Second, there is much literature about HRD in the respective nations, but not much that has been written about specific cases or is based on research. Third, much of the literature is not up-to-date. The literature used for this review was mainly restricted to descriptive and analytic publications about the position of HRD in the nations studied. The sources varied widely in quality. The emphasis was placed on referenced and high quality publications. Research literature was used whenever possible.

3 Methodology

Saskia Tjepkema

The theoretical framework of HRD's role, as outlined in the Chapter 2, has very limited empirical validation, since it is based only on a literature study and two small national case study research projects. Moreover, it is unclear whether the framework is valid for the European situation, since much of the literature on which it is based is of American origin, and empirical data were only collected in the Netherlands. Therefore, to clarify the European outlook on HRD in learning-oriented organisations (the main objective of this study), data were collected in seven European countries, using a combination of qualitative and quantitative methods.

In the first phase of the project, case study research was the main method. The aim was to gain an in-depth understanding of the concepts of the HRD departments, the strategies they adopt to turn these into practice and the facilitative factors as well as the difficulties they encounter during this implementation process. The design of the case study research is described in the section on 'Case study design and realisation'.

In the second phase of this study, a survey was conducted with a larger group of organisations, to ascertain to what extent the case study findings are representative of organisations throughout the seven EU countries that participated in the study. The second section describes the design and implementation of this survey.

Case study design and realisation

Research questions

The questions guiding data collection were:

1 How do HRD departments in learning-oriented organisations throughout Europe envision their own role in stimulating and supporting employees to learn continuously as a part of everyday work (with the intention of contributing to organisational learning, and thus enhancing organisational competitiveness)?
2 What strategies do European HRD departments adopt to realise their envisioned role?
3 What factors inhibit the realisation of this new role? How do HRD practitioners cope with these factors?
4 What factors facilitate the realisation of HRD's new role?

Selection of cases

For the case studies, it was decided to select companies with over 500 employees from the population of learning-oriented organisations in the seven participating countries. The reason to limit the study to larger organisations is that these often have a more clearly discernible HRD function than small- and medium-sized enterprises (SMEs). To select suitable case studies, preliminary research was conducted in each country. On the basis of studies already conducted (e.g. Leys, Wijgaerts and Hancké, 1992; Stahl, Nyhan and d'Ajola, 1993; Tjepkema and Wognum, 1995), it was possible to operationalise the concept of the learning-oriented organisation, to identify characteristics against case studies could be selected.

The next step was the selection of possible case organisations. A variety of methods was used, such as scanning recent literature for case descriptions, scanning conference announcements and using personal networks of the researchers. After a comparison at project level (e.g. to see if the cases complemented each other well), the selected organisations were then approached for a telephone interview. For the interview, a checklist of selection criteria was constructed, which was used by all partners.

Characterisation of case study organisations

The aim of the initial telephone interview was to establish whether the organisations were willing to participate in the project and whether they met the most important selection criterion: can they be seen as good examples of learning-oriented organisations? For instance, do they value employee learning, provide facilities for (informal) employee learning, value and support the acquisition of learning skills? Other important criteria were whether the HRD tasks were carried out in a pro-active way (either by managers, HRD professionals or others), whether there was a clear vision on the role of HRD (professionals) in the organisation, and whether the organisation undertook interesting and innovative initiatives to support employee (and even organisational) learning. The aim was not to create a representative group, but to select 'good examples' of learning-oriented organisations with a pro-active HRD function, since it is from such examples that the most interesting lessons can be learned. In case study research, this is a more fruitful approach than to select representative organisations. Also, it was impossible to create a representative group, given the small size of the sample.

Following this procedure, a total of twenty-eight cases were selected: four cases in each of the seven participating countries (Belgium, Finland, France, Germany, Italy, the Netherlands and the United Kingdom). As far as possible, each partner selected two cases from the service sector and two from the manufacturing sector, to enable a comparison between these two types of companies. To further facilitate comparison, the researchers tried, as far as possible, to select cases between 500 to 1,000 employees. Sometimes it was not the whole company that was selected as a case, but one division or a single establishment. This proved to be difficult for some companies, so some of the cases are larger than 1,000 employees. A short description of the twenty-eight cases is provided in Table 3.1.

Table 3.1 Overview of case organisations

Country	Case organisation	Core business
Belgium	1. DVV	Insurance
	2. Siemens Atea	Telecommunications
	3. Alcatel Bell	Telecommunications and multimedia
	4. ISS Cleaning service	
Finland	5. Vaisala	Meteorology
	6. Valmet paper machinery	Paper machinery manufacturing
	7. Okobank Group, central cooperative	Financial services (banking)
	8. Outokumpu Zinc	Metal production
France	9. Motorola	Production of telecommunication equipment and electronic components
	10. Auchan Bordeaux	Retail (hypermarket)
	11. Accor	Hotel and tourism services
	12. GT group	Road transport
Germany	13. Bosch Siemens Hausgeräte	Domestic appliance manufacturing
	14. Hoechst Schering AgrEvo	Chemicals production
	15. Gesellschaft für Technische Zusammenarbeit	Consultancy (in technical areas)
	16. Sony Germany	Marketing and sales electronic devices
Italy	17. Barilla	Food industry
	18. Bayer	Chemical pharmaceutical industry
	19. Lever	Cosmetics manufacturing
	20. Datalogic	Bar-code manufacturing
The Netherlands	21. Akzo Nobel, BU Salt	Mineral extraction and production
	22. Ericsson Telecommunication, R&D department	Telecommunication
	23. BAC (IT centre Internal Revenue Service)	IC-T products and services
	24. KIBC, BU Utility Building	Construction industry
United Kingdom	25. Royal Mail, Nottinghamshire, operational unit	Postal services
	26. Rolls-Royce Aerospace, Airline Business Operations	Aero engine mangufacturing
	27. Royal Scottish Assurance	Financial services (insurance)
	28. Wolverhampton & Dudley Breweries	Brewery (beer production and retail)

Data collection

After having selected suitable case organisations, all partners collected data and compiled a case report for each organisation. Data collection, conducted in 1998, involved a variety of methods to enhance reliability of the findings (a process commonly known as triangulation; see Yin, 1984). To gain insights into the ways HRD departments view their own role in the firm (research question 1) researchers conducted:

- an in-depth interview with the head of the HRD department (as the person who maps the vision and sets out the general course of the department);
- a study of relevant documents (such as mission statements, HRD policy and plans).

The interview as well as the document study focused on the vision of the HRD professionals with regard to their own role in the organisation (what contribution does the HRD function want to make, how would it like to make it, how do the HRD specialists regard the cooperation with line managers and employees, etcetera).

To gather information on the strategies the departments adopt to realise the proposed role (research question 2), and the facilitative and inhibiting factors with regard to this process (research questions 3 and 4) researchers conducted:

- in-depth interviews with the head of the HRD department and (some of the) HRD professionals;
- interviews with approximately five line managers and approximately five employees;
- a study of relevant documents (such as instruments, function descriptions, information on training methods etc.).

The purpose of these interviews and the document study was to gain insight into the strategies HRD professionals employ to realise their envisioned role: how do they seek to enact their vision? These strategies might contain, for example, experiments in new methods for HRD strategy formulation, changes in the approach to training, changes in the way the department is organised (for example, by positioning HRD officers close to line management).

It was considered important to interview not only HRD professionals on the proposed strategy of the HRD department, but also line management and employees, for two reasons. First, line management and employees are likely to notice the effects of the new strategies of the training department. Second, from what is now known on HRD departments in learning-oriented organisations, training and development is not only a task of HRD officers, but also of line management and employees. Therefore, it was necessary to gain insight into the way they view these (relatively new) tasks.

Interviews

Four key variables can be recognised in the research questions: the organisational context (learning-oriented organisation), the vision of the HRD function, strategies employed to realise the envisioned role and influencing factors. All of these variables were worked out in topic lists, which were used by the researchers to conduct the interviews. The theoretical framework, as described in Chapter two, was used as a basis to guide the questions. As described earlier in this section, four types of respondents ('roles') were interviewed for each case:

- HRD managers;
- HRD practitioners;
- line managers;
- employees.

Document analysis

Interviews constituted the most important means for data collection. However, it was also important to analyse relevant documents. The main objective was to verify if answers to questions regarding the vision of the HRD department and strategies the department adopt to realise these visions are actually laid down in formal documents. Documents were also used to collect further information of interest for the research. Examples of relevant documents are: mission statements; organisational policy and plans; HRD policy and plans; training plans; information on training methods; information on responsibilities towards employee/organisational learning; job descriptions; and evaluation reports.

Data analysis

For a thorough analysis of the data, first a within case analysis was conducted by all partners, prior to writing the case study reports. Second, a cross case analysis was performed, both per country and overall, by the project management team. For these analyses, the matrix technique described by Miles and Huberman (1981) was used (see also Yin, 1984). The partners provided matrix reports of their cases to the project management team, in addition to their written reports.

Survey design and realisation

Respondents

The primary respondents for the survey were HRD directors/HRD managers: those with a strategic/managerial role in the HRD function. Because of their overall view of the HRD function, they were able to answer all the questions (on vision as well as on strategies). In case of very large organisations, the HRD function at the division level or a large establishment was selected, not the HRD function at the corporate level. In order to optimise response rates, respondents were approached by phone first, to ask whether they were willing to fill out the questionnaire (a 'warm approach'). If respondents agreed to participate in the study, questionnaires were subsequently sent by mail. The Italian partners considered a telephone survey more appropriate for the situation in their country. Therefore, in Italy, the survey was conducted by telephone, using the same questionnaire as in other countries.

Questionnaire

The questionnaire addressed the same topics as the case study research:

- organisational context;
- vision of HRD function on own role;
- strategies to realise envisioned role;
- inhibiting and facilitating factors.

The questionnaire also included some descriptive questions (on the organisation, HRD function, respondent etc.). The project management team drew up a first draft of the questionnaire, using the results of the case studies, topic lists from the interviews and other HRD surveys. Project partners were asked to provide feedback and ECLO asked twenty-six of its corporate members to fill out the questionnaire as a pilot test. On the basis of the pilot and feedback of the partners, the questionnaire was finalised.

Sample

As in the case study research, the survey was aimed at HRD departments in large (500 employees or more) organisations, which can be considered to be learningoriented organisations. The primary objective of the survey was to verify case results. Therefore, it was important to select organisations according to the same selection criteria, namely:

- there is reason to assume the company can be regarded a learning oriented organisation (or aspires to be one);
- the company has an HRD function;
- the company has at least 500 employees.

Large organisations were chosen because these usually have a specialised HRD unit with an explicit view on its own role within the firm. Though this may also hold true for some smaller companies, the survey was conducted in large companies only, in order to facilitate comparison of results. The desired number of organisations participating in the survey was approximately 140 (twenty per country). Of course, this is a rather limited number, but the number of learning-oriented organisations was estimated to be relatively small at the outset of this study. Although the total population of learning-oriented organisations with a pro-active HRD department is estimated to be small, this situation is somewhat different for each of the participating countries. As some of the partners found it easier than expected to find suitable organisations who were willing to participate, for some countries the number of respondents was higher than planned. The questionnaire was eventually completed by respondents from 165 companies during 1999. Table 3.2 provides an overview.

Characterisation of survey participants

As mentioned above, the survey was directed at companies with over 500 employees. In order to achieve a large enough sample, a number of somewhat smaller organisations

Table 3.2 Number of questionnaires from each participating country

Country	Questionnaires	
	Number	%
The Netherlands	17	10
Belgium	39	24
Finland	19	12
Germany	27	16
France	22	13
United Kingdom	20	12
Italy	21	13
Total	**165**	**100**

Table 3.3 Organisational size

Size	Companies	
	Number	%
0–500 employees	41	25
501–2500 employees	39	24
2501–5000 employees	23	14
Over 5000 employees	56	34
Missing data	6	4
Total	**165**	**101***

Note: * over 100% due to rounding

were also selected, although there were no 'small' companies. Also, researchers checked whether the company had an HRD function (another important selection criterion). Table 3.3 provides an overview of the size of the companies participating in the survey.

The most sizeable group of participating companies consisted of particularly *large* firms (over 5,000 employees). In such cases, a large establishment was usually asked to participate in the survey. About a quarter of the companies were relatively *small* (under 500), and another quarter were of *average* size (between 500 and 2,500). The rest (fourteen per cent) consisted of between 2,500 and 5,000 employees.

Most companies participating in the survey (thirty-eight per cent) had a *division structure*, and about a quarter (twenty-six per cent) had a *functional structure*. Other organisational forms were also represented in the sample, but only by very small portions of organisations. Table 3.4 provides an overview. It is worth noting the relatively large number of missing values (or data) (seventeen per cent): either respondents failed to complete this question, or answered it in a way that could not be analysed.

As with the case studies, the aim was to create a sample in which *manufacturing and service sectors* were more or less equally represented. Table 3.5 shows that service organisations were slightly over-represented: half of the survey participants come from service companies (fifty per cent). Over a third of the companies were from manufacturing industries, or combine production and trade (thirty-seven per cent). A small proportion of companies are from the trade industry (seven per cent).

Table 3.4 Organisational structure

Structure	Companies	
	Number	*%*
Divisional organisation	62	38
Functional organisation	42	26
Network organisation	11	7
Project organisation	6	4
'Chain organisation'	1	1
Team organisation	1	1
Mix	14	9
Missing data	28	17
Total	**165**	**100**

Table 3.5 Organisational sector

Sector	Companies	
	Number	*%*
Manufacturing industry (production)	57	35
Service organisation for profit	58	35
Service organisation non-profit	25	15
Trade (buy and/or sell)	11	7
Industry and trade	4	2
Other/missing data	10	6
Total	**165**	**100**

Table 3.6 Organisation of HRD function

Organisation of HRD	Companies	
	Number	*%*
Centrally-positioned HRD department	65	39
Local HRD department(s)	12	7
Centrally-positioned HRD department and local HRD department(s)/Central and local HRD	8	5
Shared function of HRD staff and (line) managers	22	13
Shared function of HRD staff and competence managers	7	4
Shared function of HRD staff and external consultants	1	1
Shared function of HRD staff and corporate university	3	2
(Central or local) HRD practitioner(s)/consultant(s), not in separate department	7	4
HRD tasks are performed by line managers, no specialised HRD staff	3	2
Other/missing data	37	22
Total	**165**	**99***

Note: * under 100% due to rounding

An important question when considering the context of HRD is the way in which the HRD function is organised. Results for this question are presented in Table 3.6.

When considering the way in which the HRD function is organised in the companies participating in the survey, it becomes obvious that the most common organisational form is a *centrally positioned HRD department* (thirty-nine per cent), *(a) local HRD department(s)* (seven per cent) or *a combination of the two* (five per cent). A rather considerable portion of the companies organises the HRD function in a *form other than a separate department*. In those cases, HRD is most often a shared function of HRD staff and (line) managers (thirteen per cent). In relatively few companies, HRD is shared between HRD staff and either competence managers (four per cent), external consultants (one per cent) or a corporate university (two per cent). Sometimes HRD practitioners carry the responsibility for HRD alone (four per cent), and in some other cases, this responsibility lies with line managers, no specialised HRD professionals are employed in those firms (two per cent). Unfortunately, a rather large proportion of companies did not (adequately) answer this question. The percentage of missing values is rather high (twenty-two per cent).

4 Cases from Belgium

*Dirk Buyens, Sigrid van Schelstraete and
Karen Wouters*

This chapter describes the results of the case study research in Belgium. Four organisations were studied: the insurance company DVV, the telecommunications firms Siemens Atea and Alcatel Bell and the cleaning service ISS.

The first four sections contain full case descriptions (based on data from 1998), including for each case:

*   background information on the organisation, such as core businesses, number of employees, and current (learning-oriented) strategies;
*   vision of the HRD professionals on their (new) role in the learning (oriented) organisation;
*   strategies they employ to realise these roles.

The next section describes factors that (negatively or positively) influence the achievement of these envisioned roles. General conclusions and a summary are provided in the final section.

DVV – insurance company

The company

Facts and figures

DVV (De Volksverzekering, or People's Insurance) is an insurance company active in the retail and corporate sector. It has a comprehensive product portfolio of policies for, among other things, car, accidents, fire, illness and life insurances. The organisation is built around a network of agencies, each of which operates autonomously, and the company employs 1,300 people.

The centralised HRD department, called DVV Academy, has a staff of thirty working in the field of recruitment and selection, training and development, HRM-consulting, compensation and benefits, organisation and management development and knowledge management (see Box 4.1).

Box 4.1 Changing the HRD department at DVV

DVV has chosen to begin the introduction of the learning organisation at the HRD department. In doing so, the mission of HRD is expanded from just training personnel to being a *model* for the entire corporation. To make the change clear to all employees in the firm, the HRD department was renamed 'DVV Academy'.

Based on the theoretical concepts of the learning organisation, the structure was changed. DVV has integrated the main HR tasks, such as recruitment, career policy/ promotion, rewards, training and education, and organisational development. A centre of knowledge consists of the central library, intranet and the internet website. All articles, books, papers, training courses, yearbooks, that may be of use to most employees are accessible through those media. The objective of DVV Academy is to provide facilities for learning, not to impose a system. The accent is placed on self-commitment and motivation.

Business strategy

DVV's current organisational strategy is characterised by client intimacy, multi-access distribution, growth and innovation. Company objectives are formulated using the balanced score card technique, meaning that the strategy shows a wide range of objectives in different areas. Until a few years ago, DVV found itself in a very stable environment, with hardly any competition. But in 1995, things changed. First of all there was the 'Cauwenberghs Law', which made it possible for customers to annually review their insurance policy. As a consequence, competition between the different insurance companies increased enormously. Second, the frontiers of European countries were fading away. This was perceived as an opportunity for the large insurance companies from other countries to also become active in the Belgium market. This resulted in a highly competitive insurance market. From that moment, DVV needed to become more innovative and client-centred. Therefore, strategic changes such as total quality management, business process re-engineering, activity-based costing and a new management information system were implemented.

In order to sustain and support these changes, DVV strives to increase its potential for organisational learning. The company quotes knowledge management guru Peter Drucker, where he states:

> We are entering a knowledge society in which the basic economic resource is no longer capital of natural resources, but is and will be knowledge and where knowledge workers will play a central role.
>
> (Source: DVV internal documents)

In DVV's view of the concept of the learning organisation, creating and stimulating a work environment in which employees are intrinsically motivated for learning, and in which learning takes place spontaneously, is a very important issue. Employees are seen as a competitive advantage, and they are expected to be open to change.

Change processes

In order to create a learning environment, DVV uses competence management as one of its change strategies. Traditionally, individual development was seen as a positive contribution to the development of the organisation. In the concept of the learning organisation, the organisation does not focus directly on the development of personal competencies, but places an emphasis on creating a learning environment. Next to competence management, DVV is also working on a new organisational culture. The organisation wants to change from a bureaucracy to a culture based on enterpreneurship, teamwork, and a stimulating learning environment. Overall, it can be said that within the context of becoming a learning organisation, competence management and creating a learning culture (learning environment) are currently keystones for DVV.

HRD within DVV

HRD objectives and people involved in HRD

The HRD department of DVV, called DVV Academy, consists of thirty HRD professionals working in the field of recruitment and selection, organisation and management development, knowledge management and training and development.

The general aim of the DVV Academy is 'to support and facilitate the human factor in the organisation, from start till leaving the company' (source: internal DVV documents). Implementing a learning culture, working on a learning environment and using competence management are current objectives, derived from this goal.

These objectives imply a different role for HRD professionals. They act not only as trainers and designers of learning situations, but also become internal consultants. Their tasks include:

- supporting organisational processes and initiating new innovative concepts;
- introducing the concept of the learning organisation;
- realising the desired cultural change in the organisation;
- acting as a role model for the whole organisation (see Box 4.1);
- working on learning-oriented organisational problems in close co-operation with line managers;
- providing advice to employees on issues related to learning and development;
- implementing and organising competence management;
- co-ordinating and organising training activities;
- developing tools and learning methods.

With these tasks in mind, DVV Academy focuses on supporting single loop learning (improving existing processes and services) as well as double loop learning (changing basic assumptions, beliefs and objectives). But their task is only of limited duration. The fundamental responsibility for HRD lies with line management. Eventually, the DVV Academy will disappear, and line management will be completely responsible for learning and development. The current role of the DVV Academy is to prepare managers for this future situation. They provide them with examples, advice and tools, and organise management development programs. The idea is that the Academy disappears when DVV has reached the goal of becoming a learning organisation. In that ideal situation, the HRD professionals will work as consultants, spread over the different departments.

HRD strategies

In this context, it is interesting to note that in terms of HRD activities, no significant change in training programmes has been made. DVV still organises standard training programmes for employees who are interested. The only change is that the Academy now organises some additional learning elements such as continuous evaluation, use of internet and intranet, and conferences. In order to determine the success of these initiatives, DVV is using evaluation instruments at different levels in the organisation. At the top level, the company is working on an organisational business plan. In this business plan, the direction for organisational development is described. At the departmental level, management works to develop balanced score cards. Competence management (see Box 4.2) is used as an evaluation instrument on a more individual level. Other specific initiatives they undertake are image building, installing a new function-classification system and introducing a new remuneration system based upon responsibilities, competencies and the realisation of objectives. By using these instruments, DVV also wants to measure whether HRD's role has changed successfully. But they realise that measuring the success of being a learning-oriented organisation is difficult and takes a long time.

Box 4.2 Competence management at DVV

Within the context of the learning organisation, HRD focuses on the development of the organisational environment as a learning context. Competence management is an important strategy, used to evaluate people applying for a particular job and for furthering development of people in their present jobs.

The competence profile is a document used to examine whether particular individuals have learning needs and, if so, how these needs (= negative score) can be turned into reserves (= positive score). Wherever needs are identified, specific training courses can be used to meet these needs.

In DVV, competencies are considered as organisational characteristics, not (only) individual ones. The cumulative evaluation of people's competencies can also be used to measure whether the company is more competent than before, meaning that it has more 'reserves'.

Siemens Atea – telecommunications company

The company

Facts and figures

Siemens Atea (established in 1892) is a company in the field of telecommunications for public and private networks. It provides products and services for communication with voice, text, images and data. Siemens Atea is also working in research, development and engineering within all important domains of telecommunications. For example, it is an active partner in establishing the Belgian GSM network. Siemens Atea employs around 1,550 people.

Of these, eighteen people work in the centralised HRD department, primarily in the field of personnel management and administration, and training and development.

Business strategy

As with DVV, innovation and customer orientation are important driving forces for Siemens Atea. Until ten years ago, Siemens Atea had only a few markets and clients. But in the turbulent world of information and communication, it becomes necessary for Siemens Atea to direct its products and services to a larger, more international market. To become internationally attractive, Siemens Atea is trying to develop itself from a 'follower' organisation (reactive) into a more creative and innovative enterprise (pro-active). The company's mission illustrates this aim:

> turning the power of telecommunication into an advantage for our customers and for each individual in the society, and producing and selling our products, systems and services in the market of telecommunication in a profitable way.
> (Source: Siemens Atea internal documents)

Innovation, creativity and customer orientation are important elements of the new company profile. However, the organisational strategy consists of two more elements: (1) being excellent, and (2) having enthusiastic and motivated employees. According to Siemens Atea, employees are the most important actors in the 'war of competition'. Their knowledge, competence and sense of enterpreneurship are the most valuable factors for realising a pioneer's role in the world of telecommunication. Employees need to be creative and pro-active, take initiative, and have a well-developed sense of responsibility. Siemens Atea's vision is that:

> every employee, on his own level and in his own speciality, wants to improve continuously, learn and is able to look further than his own task. The transfer of knowledge is organised efficiently and making mistakes is accepted as part of the learning process.
> (Source: Siemens Atea internal documents)

Change processes

In order to become a learning organisation, Siemens Atea has defined concrete change strategies such as (1) actions to improve client satisfaction, (2) actions to increase employee satisfaction and motivation, and (3) improvement of the market position (for example by using centres of competence and centres of excellence). Central to these change strategies is the role of the individual. Employees are the key actors in the change process. Therefore, Siemens Atea uses competence management as the key instrument in, directly, developing its employees and, more indirectly, developing the organisation as a whole.

HRD in Siemens Atea

HRD objectives and people involved in HRD

The organisation of the HRD function in Siemens Atea has much in common with the situation within DVV. For example, both companies have a centralised HRD department. In both organisations, HRD professionals fulfil a steering role in the change process towards a learning oriented organisation, they work pro-actively, are responsible for the relationship between organisational and departmental strategies, are working with competence management, and need to take responsibility for implementing a learning culture. In the future, the responsibility for learning in both companies will lie with line managers. The HRD department fulfils a more supportive role by offering methods and techniques. The main difference between the two organisations is that Siemens Atea wants to keep the HRD department as a centralised department where DVV eventually wants to spread HRD responsibilities towards line management across the different business units in the organisation. In both organisations, the HRD professional wants to become an internal consultant for management and employees.

HRD strategies

HRD management within Siemens Atea strongly supports the vision of a learning organisation. Their expertise is used in the change process of becoming a learning organisation. HRD professionals are working towards a more pro-active policy. This means developing long-term training programmes and experimenting with new technologies. This introduces a new way of learning: virtual classes. Employees can follow courses irrespective of their actual location at that moment. By making training as accessible as possible, Siemens Atea is trying to make it easier for employees to start learning. Other learning facilities include: Atea VideoNetwork, coaching, teleclassing, training programmes inside and outside the organisation, teambuilding programmes, knowledge databases, an education paper with an overview of available courses and a library. The HRD department finds it important to provide the employees with what they want and need, and use an 'internal client satisfaction' evaluation instrument in an attempt to measure the opinion of the employees about learning in Siemens Atea.

Stimulating employees motivation and sense of responsibility for their own learning is an important issue (see Box 4.3).

Box 4.3 'Jeff's law' at Siemens Atea

Jeff, an HRD practitioner in Siemens Atea, has developed a paradigm to anchor new ways of thinking into HRD systems of the organisation.

The fundaments of 'Jeff's law' are people's life expectations, not in terms of the length of a human life, but in terms of what people expect *from* life. People who have clear and challenging life expectations have a high degree of learning tension. This tension enables them to process high amounts of information which results in a high learning ability.

Jeff's Law further states that people with a high degree of learning tension do not usually stop at the point of learning: they possess so much self-empowerment that they can transform this learning ability into an ability to change. They use this power to change their environment in order to realise their life expectations.

Hence, a clear sense of life expectations and self-empowerment are capabilities that need to be developed by everyone who works in an environment characterised by change and an enormous amount of knowledge and information. People need to be motivated to develop their learning abilities and willing to invest in themselves in order to find their way in such a context. Therefore, Siemens Atea feel it is important to invest in developing these abilities in their workforce.

Alcatel Bell – telecommunications company

The company

Facts and figures

Alcatel Bell is in the business of designing, developing and installing telecommunication and multimedia tools, systems and services. Examples are networks, cable transmission, radio-communication, satellite communication, and the installation and maintenance of networks. Around 118,000 people work for the Alcatel Group worldwide (80,000 in Telecom), with the Belgian branch of Alcatel employing 4,700 people.

The HRM department has seventy employees. The department is partly centralised (remuneration, recruitment and selection) but the HRD staff is decentralised. Next to these HRD professionals there is a separate (centralised) training department, referred to as Alcatel University. Alcatel University has a staff of seventy: seven training consultants, about forty training engineers, fifteen training co-ordinators and eight people in logistic support.

Business strategy

The mission of Alcatel Bell is

being an expert in all domains of the telecommunication, and having a leadership position as a world wide supplier of quality products and services.

(Source: Alcatel Bell internal documents)

Bundling individual competencies plays a key role in realising this aim:

Our company can not be a drifting ship on the turbulent waters of a stormy world market. To sail the right course, all individual talents and competencies need to be bundled. Only a strong team, driven by motivation and enthusiasm, will be able to beat the competitor.

(Source: Alcatel Bell internal documents)

As with DVV and Siemens Atea, key issues for Alcatel Bell are customer orientation, innovation, and participation and motivation of all employees. These are considered necessary to address the growing demand for integrated solutions for systems and services, liberalisation and globalisation of markets, high development costs against a short life span of products, and increasing competition.

In Alcatel Bell, knowledge is seen as the essential competitive advantage. The company operates on the idea that the most important prerequisite for becoming an expert and market leader is the ability to continuously generate and use unique and differentiated knowledge in its products, processes and services. Because of the fast evolution of technology, knowledge ages very quickly. Generating new knowledge by permanent training and development is an important issue for the organisation. Equally important is *using* the available knowledge. Knowledge resides within individuals: the challenge of the organisation is to get the right knowledge at the right moment in the right place.

Change processes

To structure the processes of knowledge creation and sharing as much as possible, Alcatel Bell uses Nonaka and Takeuchi's (1995) theory of knowledge management (in which every hierarchical layer plays a role in the process of creating and using new knowledge). Several change strategies (Hi-Speed programme) are introduced for becoming a learning organisation: (1) working on innovative high-speed solutions; (2) client orientation; (3) employability and (4) team spirit.

Currently, attention is directed mainly to employability as a change strategy. Alcatel Bell strives to make the organisation attractive to young employees by providing them with the opportunity of employability. A third of the employees is under thirty years old, mostly high-potential employees with great opportunities in the labour market. Alcatel Bell is dependent on them – they are one of the company's biggest assets – so it is very important for the organisation to remain attractive for these employees. Alcatel Bell is trying to increase its attractiveness by creating a flat organisation with less hierarchical layers, stimulating managers to operate as coaches, and by working on a culture of which 'learning to change continuously' is a key feature.

HRD in Alcatel Bell

HRD objectives and people involved in HRD

In Alcatel Bell, knowledge management is seen as the most important change strategy for becoming a learning organisation. In this process, HRD professionals are responsible for:

*   communicating the principles of knowledge management to employees (mostly through training);
*   guiding the change process in the daily work situation;
*   supporting employees in generating and sharing knowledge;
*   helping employees to use their emotional intelligence as effectively as possible;
*   analysing gaps between individual performance and organisational needs;
*   organising and providing courses, training and self-directed learning.

HRD professionals have a steering role in the organisation. Their responsibilities are strongly related to stimulating and supporting new knowledge creation.

Training and development is seen as a shared responsibility of management, employees and HRD professionals. Managers need to inform, advise and stimulate employees to continuously enhance their knowledge and skills. Employees need to make optimal use of training possibilities in order to perform successfully in their present and future job. HRD professionals offer training opportunities, tools and techniques, give advice and facilitate necessary learning processes.

HRD strategies

Employees in Alcatel Bell are provided with permanent education, function-related training, self-directed learning, on-the-job training, coaching and personal development plans:

> The HRD initiatives are directed to active support of the organisational goals, and they offer help in existing problems at the organisational level, in the career development of the individual, and in the direct working practice of the job.
> (Source: Alcatel Bell internal documents)

A key word behind all of these strategies is *employability*. By actively increasing employability, employees will be able to function within a broader range of jobs. For example, job rotation is used to increase employability. As a consequence, more training is needed.

Another HRD initiative that serves to increase employability is to ensure that every employee achieves a minimum number of training hours. More specifically, every employee needs to follow twenty hours of classroom training, twenty hours of on-the-job training, and ten hours of Bell Permanent Training (see Box 4.4). A second important group of strategies, employed by the HRD department, is related to increasing the creation and sharing of knowledge. In creating new knowledge, HRD activities include workshops, courses, and on-the-job training etc. However, HRD professionals have only a small role in this. They provide management with possibilities for training and development. Management is responsible for implementing these in the different units of the organisation.

Concerning the transfer of (new) knowledge, HRD professionals stimulate employees to work in teams, to share experiences with each other, to invite people from outside for their expertise etc. Another way of sharing knowledge is mentorship. In the first six months, a more experienced employee will coach every new employee. In this way, much knowledge and experience can be shared. A third initiative for sharing knowledge is the opportunity for employees to rotate between different business units. In this way, knowledge does not stay with one unit but can be spread across the whole organisation.

In order to determine the success of these initiatives, Alcatel Bell uses evaluation instruments at different levels in the organisation. At the top level, the company tries to measure the efficiency of training activities. On a more departmental level, employee satisfaction sheets are used. The HRD department also wants to use information on job rotation as an indication of the success of training activities and the way HRD professionals are implementing these activities. Statistics on training hours are used on a more individual level. It is the responsibility of HRD professionals to stimulate and motivate employees for participating in a certain number of training hours.

Box 4.4 20–20–10 project at Alcatel Bell

The 20–20–10 project in Alcatel Bell is part of a greater project called the Hi-Speed change process, focusing on creating timely, innovative 'high speed' solutions, and improving market and business development for Alcatel. Employability of personnel is considered a prerequisite for realising the objectives of Hi-Speed.

The basic idea of the 20–20–10 project is that every employee must follow a minimum number of training and education hours, more specifically: twenty hours of class room courses, twenty hours on-the-job-training and ten hours Bell Permanent Education.

The most important objective is to stimulate supervisors and employees to increase their employability using training programmes. For blue-collar workers, a separate education programme will be defined. Because of differences between both groups of employees, there will be substantial differences between both programmes.

A second objective of the project is motivating and stimulating line management to engage in career counselling, which should result in career interviews between the management and their employees. During these conversations the following topics should be covered: required competences for the future, training and education plans, strengths and weaknesses, ambitions and a development plan.

ISS – cleaning service provider

The company

Facts and figures

ISS is an international cleaning service. It describes its own core business as 'managing and delivering a wide range of high quality services which add value for their customers and meet the need for clean, efficient and comfortable environments for people at work and at leisure'. Their market focus is on hospitals, airports, food hygiene and general cleaning. ISS Belgium employs 3,100 people.

Only one person is responsible for HRM in general, two more work specifically in the field of HRD. Top management is responsible for outlining and implementing HRD policy.

Business strategy

ISS's current organisational strategy is called AIM 2002. AIM stands for *A*mbition, *I*nnovation, and *M*otivation. ISS wants to transform itself from the world's biggest cleaning company into the leading and most innovative customer-driven service enterprise. Reasons for this change are primarily competitive markets and the need to stay attractive for (potential) employees. In order to achieve these goals, the company uses the principles of the learning organisation.

In ISS, employees are seen as the company's most important asset. But ISS encounters problems retaining employees. The cleaning sector traditionally has a high rate of employee turnover. ISS's challenge is to make the work and the organisation as attractive as possible. As within Alcatell Bell, the company uses the concept of the learning organisation to make the organisation attractive to work for.

Change processes

The company's main change strategies are: (1) decentralising the organisation in such a way that business units are closely connected to different clients (customer orientation); (2) making jobs in ISS more interesting; and (3) continuously developing employees at all levels. Thus HRD is integrated in the general strategies and change initiatives at ISS.

HRD in ISS

HRD objectives and people involved in HRD

In total, twelve employees are active in the field of HRD. Their role consists primarily of providing adequate training possibilities. Two of them are responsible for the administration and logistic support of training programmes. Responsibility for defining and implementing the concept of the learning organisation lies with top management, who defines HRD policies. Finally, line management is responsible for HRD in the daily work environment. ISS did not change very much in the organisation of the HRD function with the aim of becoming a learning organisation. As before, line management is still responsible for employee learning.

However, some changes in HRD policy and activities were made. One of the current strategic objectives is making jobs in ISS more interesting and rewarding for employees at all levels. This includes a shift towards full-time jobs for their service workers. In 2002, the company wants eighty per cent of all employees to be 'professional, full-time workers with specialist knowledge in adapting leading edge methods to secure delivery of the ISS quality standard' (source: ISS internal documents). Changes in HRD policy also include an increasing focus on continuous development and long-term career development. Through training programmes, the company is trying to increase employee satisfaction. Employees are able to gain promotion, and assert a stronger influence and assume greater responsibility over their own work. A final change in HRD policy is related to recruitment and selection. Unemployment and job switching are significant for ISS. To reduce the number of employees that do not like or fit their jobs, the company needed to change the recruitment and selection process. So, ISS started job centres where potential employees are invited to be assessed. An important new element of the selection is showing potential employees an introductory video that describes the future job as realistically as possible. In this way, candidates are able to decide whether or not they would like to work in those circumstances. Overall, HRM and HRD strategies are closely linked.

HRD strategies

Accompanying the described shift in HRD policy, a shift in HRD activities can be observed. Some new initiatives include:

- training programmes to upgrade unskilled operators to semi-skilled employees;
- career development programmes for middle and top management;
- the use of intranet and internet as virtual supplements to training programmes;
- the use of intranet for documenting and distributing best practices;
- the five-star programme through which employees can become more competent and achieve a higher position in the organisation;
- induction courses, used to generate employee commitment to ISS.

Thus, it can be concluded that learning and development at ISS is used mainly for making the organisation attractive for employees. Training activities are a means to retain people in the organisation. A more concrete example of this is the use of certificates. When employees have followed twenty hours of training, they receive a certificate, which, for most of the uneducated staff, is the first they will ever have received. Consequently, most employees are very proud of this certificate. Receiving the certificate is an external motivation to learn. Another example is the annual employee satisfaction survey. This evaluation survey measures the opinion of the employees about learning opportunities in ISS. Actions are based on making ISS more attractive for them.

Factors influencing HRD's role and how HRD deals with them

The preceding sections have described visions and strategies of the four case organisations with regard to becoming a learning organisation, as well as HRD's role in this process. This section describes factors that affect the achievement (or lack of achievement) of HRD's envisioned role. Inhibiting factors, facilitating factors and strategies to overcome barriers are briefly discussed.

Inhibiting factors

All the Belgian case study organisations were found to be facing some inhibiting factors in the change process towards a learning (oriented) organisation. Table 4.1 lists the most significant.

Table 4.1 shows that an important inhibiting factor, mentioned by all HRD departments, is a lack of motivation and responsibility for learning on the part of employees. Apparently, employees first need to see some positive results from all new initiatives, before they can be motivated about the concept of the learning organisation. Lack of time (in all cases) and money (at Siemens Atea and ISS) to pursue new initiatives are also important inhibiting factors, as is a lack of understanding of goals, tasks and responsibilities of the HRD department (all cases).

It might well be that these factors are related. If there was more clarity regarding the added value of the HRD department, employees could be expected to be more motivated to engage in HRD activities, and more time and money might be made available. This also goes for the lack of motivation and support from management as experienced by DVV. The clarity of HRD's role can become clouded for several reasons. The most significant ones are the change in vision, change in organisational structure and changes in HRD activities, undertaken in order to support the development towards a learning organisation. Lack of communication between the HRD department and the organisation (employees, managers) sometimes serves to aggravate this lack of clarity. However, it is interesting to note the effort some HRD departments

Table 4.1 Inhibiting factors – Belgian case study organisations

Inhibiting factors	DVV	Siemens Atea	Alcatel Bell	ISS
Lack of motivation and responsibility for learning from employees	•	•	•	•
Lack of time for new initiatives	•	•	•	•
Lack of money for new initiatives	•	•		
Lack of understanding of goals, tasks and responsibilities of the HRD department/ lack of clear objectives and evaluation criteria for HRD department	•	•	•	•
Lack of motivation and support from management	•			
Insufficient learning culture (no tradition, systems and methods)	•			

make to measure client needs and satisfaction (see case descriptions). This might be regarded as a way to improve communication and clarify expectations.

Finally, it also seems that the 'newness' of this way of working has a negative influence. Not having a learning culture makes it difficult in DVV to realise goals such as employees taking responsibility for their own learning or increased knowledge sharing.

Conducive factors

When HRD professionals were asked to identify factors that support the development towards a learning (oriented) organisation, a large number of factors were found. Table 4.2 gives an overview of the most important ones.

The most important conducive factor seems to be positive results of new HRD initiatives (all cases). This factor corresponds with the inhibiting factor of 'lack of motivation' mentioned in the previous section. It seems employees first need to see some results to confirm the validity of the concept of the learning organisation. Once they receive this 'proof', they are more willing to support the activities of the HRD department.

A second conducive factor, that also mirrors an inhibiting factor, is active involvement of management (in Siemens Atea and ISS). Whereas lack of support from management stifles the change process, active support stimulates it.

A third significant conducive factor is having enough opportunities for training and development (all cases). With many opportunities it is easier for the HRD department to adjust its initiatives to the wishes and needs of the employees, and, in addtion, it makes it easier to develop new training activities.

The fourth significant factor was a pleasant work climate in the HRD department (in DVV and Siemens Atea). A possible explanation is that if HRD professionals are able to work together constructively and support each other, this helps them to cope with uncertainties in their new role, and to fulfil a pioneering role.

Coping strategies

The case study organisations adopt different coping strategies to reduce inhibiting factors and to enforce conducive factors. The most important ones have already been mentioned in the case descriptions (sections on HRD strategies). However, it is relevant

Table 4.2 Conducive factors – Belgian case study organisations

Conducive factors	DVV	Siemens Atea	Alcatel Bell	ISS
Positive initial results of new HRD initiatives	•	•	•	•
Active involvement of management	•	•		
Many opportunities for training and development	•	•	•	•
Very pleasant work climate in the HRD department	•	•		

to note here that DVV started networking with other organisations that work intensively with the concept of the learning (oriented) organisation. In Siemens Atea and Alcatel Bell, the position of the HRD professionals is an important aspect of the inhibiting and conducive factors. Specific attention is therefore being paid to clarifying the position of the HRD department in the organisation. It needs to be clear to all employees what roles, tasks and responsibilities belong to HRD professionals. And finally, in Alcatel Bell, communication is seen as the most important coping strategy. Through continuous communication, HRD professionals try to direct their initiatives towards the wishes and needs of management and employees.

Summary and conclusions

Organisational context

Four Belgian case study organisations were discussed: DVV, Siemens Atea, Alcatel Bell and ISS. Table 4.3 provides a short overview of the main features of each case, such as sector, number of employees, HRD function and the number of HRD practitioners.

   All four case study organisations were found to be dealing with strong(er) competitive markets and/or fast(er) changing technologies. As a result, improving and innovating their products, processes and services and becoming more customer orientated are important strategic issues.

   Employee learning or (in the case of Alcatel Bell) knowledge management is considered an important means to realise these objectives, therefore creating opportunities for learning is strategically relevant for these companies. For two case studies (Alcatel Bell and ISS) this is also important in order to ensure that the company attracts and retains employees.

Table 4.3 Overview of Belgian case study organisations

Company's name and sector	Number of employees	HRD
DVV, insurance	1,300	• Centralised DVV Academy and line management • 30 HRD practitioners
Siemens Atea, telecommunications	1,550	• Centralised HRD department • 18 HRD practitioners
Alcatell Bell, telecommunications and multimedia	4,700	• Decentralised HRD professionals and centralised Alcatel University • 10 HRD professionals • 70 employees in Alcatel University
ISS, cleaning services	• Total: 200,000 • Belgium: 3,100	• 2 HRD professionals and top management in Belgium • 12 HRD practitioners

All companies employ change strategies oriented toward creating a learning environment for their workforce, for example by creating a learning culture, as in DVV or by creating a decentralised organisation, as in ISS.

HRD's envisioned role

In all four organisations, the role of the HRD department was found to be changing from the more traditional role of providing training towards a more consulting department. The HRD professional is changing from a developer and trainer towards a consultant for management and employees. Perhaps ISS is the only exception. In DVV, Siemens Atea and Alcatel Bell, the HRD departments fulfil a steering role in the change process. In ISS, management fulfils this role, and the HRD professionals perform a more reactive and supportive role (logistics, organisation of training).

Important objectives for HRD professionals in DVV, Siemens Atea and Alcatel Bell include supporting the company in becoming a learning organisation, introducing knowledge management, creating a learning culture and providing managers with tools and techniques, with the objective of management taking responsibility for supporting employee learning. DVV is deliberately trying to prepare managers for this new role. In ISS, the HRD department strives for administration and logistic support of training programmes, and supporting the strategic objective of becoming an attractive employer.

Strategies adopted to realise HRD's new role

In some cases, the organisation of HRD departments was changed to support these changes in roles and responsibilities. In particular, the DVV Academy uses decentralisation to provide management with all the HRD tools needed and in Siemens Atea, an experienced 'learning organisation' manager is responsible for implementation of learning organisation principles.

There are also significant changes in HRD activities. Three companies (Siemens Atea, Alcatel Bell and ISS) use new HRD activities to support the change towards a learning organisation and/or support employee development. It is worth pointing out the use of HRD activities to make jobs more attractive in ISS and Alcatel Bell. This is in line with the strategic goal of both companies to retain employees (and thereby retain knowledge) for a longer time. Both regard this as an important prerequisite for becoming a learning organisation.

Influencing factors

Significant inhibiting factors, which negatively influence the HRD departments attaining their new role, include a lack of motivation and responsibility for learning from employees and lack of time and/or money to initiate new initiatives. Another important inhibiting factor is a lack of understanding of goals, tasks and responsibilities of the HRD department and, related to this, a lack of clear objectives and evaluation criteria for the HRD department. It might well be that these factors are related.

Important conducive factors include positive results of new HRD initiatives and the existence of broad facilities for training and development. It was also found that the active involvement of line managers sometimes has a positive influence on the role and activities of the HRD department.

Different coping strategies were adopted by the case study organisations to reduce inhibiting factors and to enforce conducive factors. Some of the key strategies include:

- clarifying the position of the HRD department within the organisation;
- networking with other organisations who work intensively with the concept of the learning organisation;
- communication between the HRD department and managers and employees in order to improve products and services.

5 Cases from Finland

Tapio Vaherva and Hetamari Woods

This chapter describes the results of the case study research in Finland. Four organisations were studied: the electronics producer Vaisala, the paper machine manufacturer Valmet, the Okobank Group and the metal producer Outokumpu Zinc.

The first four sections contain full case descriptions (based on data from 1998), including for each case:

- background information on the case organisation, such as core businesses, number of employees, and current (learning-oriented) strategies;
- vision of the HRD professionals on their (new) roles in the learning (oriented) organisation;
- strategies they employ to realise these roles.

The next section describes factors that (negatively or positively) influence the achievement of these envisioned roles. General conclusions and a summary are provided in the final section.

Vaisala – electronic measurement systems manufacturing

The company

Facts and figures

Vaisala develops and manufactures electronic measurement systems and equipment for meteorology, environmental sciences, traffic safety and industry. Its markets are global and its core customer groups are meteorological organisations, research institutes, defence forces, air and road traffic authorities, and industry. The company employs 774 people.

Vaisala has a centralised HRD unit, which employs five persons.

Business strategy

Vaisala operates in a narrow product market, where a rapidly changing business environment requires continuous changes. Key words in the organisation strategy are product leadership, client-centeredness, and operational excellence. Product leadership means maintaining a high product quality both by on-going product improvement and by developing new products. Vaisala is trying to achieve product leadership by maintaining and developing a close customer-oriented mode of operation and continuous research. Vaisala functions with small volume in distinct markets so a customer-oriented, flexible mode of operation is essential. Application knowledge must be excellent so that customers and their wishes and needs can be analysed closely: 'with Vaisala's products, customers should feel that they get added value' (source: Vaisala internal documents).

Change processes

In order to sustain and support these organisational strategies, Vaisala strives to increase its potential for organisational learning. One of the main change strategies is the continuous development of workforce competence.

In defining competence profiles, future competence and knowledge are analysed. Competence profiles are also expanded from the individual level to the team level. This fits with another important change strategy, working in teams. According to Vaisala's management, teamwork in particular makes competence in the organisation flexible and adaptable. In teamwork, not only is knowledge management essential, but also a 'learning' way of working. Management believes that a mode of operation which emphasises continuous learning will stimulate the development of individual change and adaptability, flexibile capacity, and team based multiple competence. The aim is twofold: to develop existing employees, and to recruit new skilled persons.

Another change strategy concerns the adoption of a process orientation. Vaisala has previously been a functionally oriented organisation but now its functions are viewed as processes. Its core processes are marketing, sales, product, delivery and after sales. Process thinking has brought a new teamwork and cooperation model to the organisation that presupposes that everyone in the organisation has broad-based competence and understanding.

HRD within Vaisala

People involved in HRD

Vaisala's HR department employs five people, including one specialised HRD manager, whose role is to create (together with others) directions for personnel development, development programmes and competence projects. The others fulfil a combination of HRD and personnel management tasks. The department does not have a very stable structure, as it is organised according to the changing circumstances. However, all HR professionals agree that, with the eye on the implementation of the concept of the learning organisation, their responsibility for learning and development has increased.

HRD professionals operate as internal consultants to line management. This connection between HRD and business is also found in the kinds of problems they are working on. According to the HRD manager:

> the majority of projects are like lines drawn in the water. It cannot be said that these are only personnel development projects. All developments have a clear connection to the development of the business.

According to the HRD professionals, their consultative and co-ordinating role is increasing continuously. Their aim is to provide consistent and innovative personnel development activities to different management areas. In larger learning processes, HRD professionals participate in strategic planning. But in smaller learning situations, HRD's role is to function as background supporter and organiser of development activities.

Line managers are fully responsible for the development of their people. Line managers are key persons in organisational development, because they have responsibility over the development of their staff and they also function as initiators of team development. HRD professionals are assisting them by providing them with ideas, inspiring and motivating them and helping them find the right tools and techniques.

HRD objectives

In general, HRD is moving towards an initiative role. At the beginning of the change process towards a learning organisation, HRD's task was to listen to the customers' needs and sell the meaning of HRD's role within the organisation. Now, HRD's role is to develop personnel development processes in such ways that these support business processes and bring about a shared framework into the company. In more concrete terms, this means HRD professionals should:

- Contribute to learning, competence development and knowledge management: HRD professionals need to be able to evaluate and engender a smart and suitable way of learning for every situation; contribute to competence development by avoiding competence gaps through sufficient competence mapping; and a significant role in knowledge management (ensure that information and knowledge is distributed between teams and across the organisation).
- Support managers: induce and motivate managers to take responsibility for learning; provide management with feedback about the multiple skill development in teams as well as about the atmosphere in the organisation; provide managers with ideas, tools, techniques and methods for learning.
- Support teamwork: arranging a right mix of people in teams; direct the team development process from above and support management in the recruiting processes for team players; support teamwork, provide tools, and ensure continuous learning.
- Maintain the organisational skill base: the HRD department has to make sure the company has the right personnel for the work in the next three to five years by recruiting the right personnel and analyse the organisational development needs. Demands have been changed. It must be assured that new employees are

suitable for both the professional competence and personnel features to be members of self-managing work teams. Vaisala needs competent personnel, committed to their work and developing themselves in the same direction as that of the organisation.

HRD strategies

Vaisala distinguishes between different levels of learning: individual, team, team superior, and the organisational level. The pressure point of learning varies according to the work tasks and work history. In production, team learning is emphasised but in planning, individual learning plays an important role. In the recruitment phase the individual is emphasised, although the aim is to create multiple-skilled teams. So special attention is given to team learning. According to HRD professionals, organisational learning probably receives the least attention. At the individual level, personal development plans are used. At least once a year, sometimes twice a year, development and target interviews are conducted between superiors and subordinates in which they assess whether progress has been made according to the goals set in the previous interview. Employees can also bring forward their personal development needs. Based on the results of this discussion, employees can choose to participate in specific HRD activities. But the development meetings are being taken towards the team level. At the same time as the individual discussions, the team analyses its competence level, and decides how to develop itself more to being a self-directed team.

As a consequence of the change process towards a learning organisation, learning situations have changed significantly. Vaisala's way of securing its personnel's competence and continuous development is to provide HRD activities which stimulate (informal) learning on-the-job, such as working on different projects, coaching, working in teams, job and task rotation, benchmarking, and self-directed learning. More and more projects and simulations are connected to the real work.

Formal training remains important (attending seminars, participating in the company's internal and external development programme). In terms of subject matter, issues of interaction skills, communication ability, competence management, and flexible cooperation are currently important.

Valmet – paper machinery manufacturing

The company

Facts and figures

Valmet is a paper machine manufacturer. Paper, board and tissue machines, stock preparation equipment, paper-finishing machinery and converting machines are important resources in Valmet. The company has production plants and service operations in all the main market areas in Europe, North America and Asia Pacific. The average number of employees in the whole Valmet group is 13,500. The subject of this case study was Valmet Paper Machinery where the number of employees is approximately 2,200.

Valmet Paper Machinery has a centralised personnel development unit which employs fourteen staff, each having different development tasks varying from recruitment and planning to development.

Business strategy

The main reasons for Valmet to change the organisational strategy are the increasing complexity of product technology, the multiplication of global business, tightening competition in narrow specialised markets, and the transference from profit-centered activities to a process-oriented way of functioning.

Valmet's organisational strategy includes the centralisation of business, order and delivery processes and the aim is controlled growth and maintaining profitability through all stages of the business cycle. Valmet tries to secure a leading position in technology, market share and profitability now and in the future through investments in research and development. International cliented-centeredness is one of the important strategies.

Valmet's clients are considered to be sensitive to economic trends. To diminish this sensitivity, Valmet attempts to build a wide international marketing and service network. Another organisational strategy is concentrating on the continuous development of the company's core competence: paper machine production. Valmet's aim is to be the world's leading paper machine manufacturer, as well as being innovative as well as competitive. Keeping up with the competitors presupposes speed. The firm's main aim is therefore to cut delivery times by half.

Change processes

One could say that the change process is mainly based on customers and competitors. The ability to react quickly to changes (and thus optimise speed and quality) pre-supposes ever greater flexibility and a learning ability from the personnel. Because of this, Valmet wants to invest in its employees. The company tries to make experts in the field stay in the organisation, and to be both motivated and entrepreneurial. For Valmet, this means that the continuous development of products takes centre stage and the personnel must have competencies to respond to current and future challenges. The learning-oriented way of functioning is consciously stressed in Valmet. However, according to managers, the development is in its early stages. The goal is to create an organisation in which 'everybody learns something, every single day' (source: Valmet internal documents). Competence management is used as a way to realise continuous personal development.

Centralisation of business, order and delivery processes is another part of the change strategy. For example, previously, machine parts were manufactured in various units. Centralisation of the manufacturing processes has been started. Valmet is trying to adopt a process-oriented approach:

> we are more interested in the good progress of the process, material and informa-
> tion flows, meaning that we manufacture a product for the customers with the

help of the process, measure customer satisfaction and also make procedures that improve the customer satisfaction in the next process.

(Source: internal documents Valmet)

HRD within Valmet

People involved in HRD

Valmet Paper Machinery has a centralised personnel development unit and its own school. The personnel development unit consists of fourteen employees, each having different development tasks varying from recruitment and planning to development. The unit's personnel is divided into development and training areas like language training, management training, work community coaching, team building and information technology.

HRD practitioners have an initiating and co-ordinating role although the role of line management in advancing issues is crucial. The HRD department is still acting more reactively than pro-actively. The HRD professionals are responding to the challenges and questions, introducing models and ways for developing personnel. They inform and activate line managers to develop their own personnel. This is one of their main tasks. Line managers are responsible for developing their own personnel. One of their goals should be to ensure a sufficient competence level among their employees in every unit. They should evaluate the personnel's training needs. After that, managers can consult the personnel development unit to think together about possible learning activities.

The change towards a learning-oriented organisation also brings different requirements for new employees. Things like the ability to function in international work tasks, flexibility, the ability for job rotation, linguistic ability, being able to work in teams, and also tolerance to uncertainty are emphasised. Employees are not only expected to learn, it is demanded of them. In reality, the possibilities for employees in basic product levels to get more training are limited, although it is emphasised that employees are responsible for their own development. When they do not have the right competencies for doing their job well in the next five years, they need to develop themselves. If not, they are no longer attractive to the organisation. This implicates a strong connection between training activities and business activities. In Valmet Paper Machinery, development interviews take place once a year. In these meetings, employees' needs and possibilities for development are evaluated. But, according to managers, these discussions do not yet create a connection between the organisational strategy and individual needs. Only personal learning possibilities are identified.

HRD objectives

The process of changing into a learning-oriented organisation has its impact on the role of the personnel development unit in Valmet. The unit's new mission is to realise and develop top expertise in all customers' core competence areas, and support experts in working in teams in an entrepreneurial manner. This will directly support the customer orientation of the company.

An important element of the department's vision is to recruit and develop personnel on the basis of long-term planning. According to HRD professionals, the training in the organisation is mainly directed towards fulfilling existing training needs. Their aim is to be able to predict what kinds of competencies are needed in the next five years. Evaluation of the actual personnel development is done through core competence mapping (mapping essential and strategic know-how at all organisational levels) and by asking customers whether they are satisfied with the products and services provided. In these kinds of evaluation, the part personnel development plays is hard to define. That is why HRD professionals are looking for more functional, clear, objective, personnel development strategy evaluation methods.

Another important element is to operate in a customer focused way. The department wants to function as a widely networked team and provide cost-competitive services, based on the customers' true needs. Furthermore, the department wants to use internal coaching and job rotation as tools for personnel development.

Initially, in the change process towards a learning-oriented organisation, the personnel development unit had been a reactive element. This means the directions were provided by the organisation's top management. Practitioners recognise that the personnel development unit needs to be part of the change process, and that concrete actions are required.

HRD strategies

Many actions of the HRD professionals are strongly connected to competence management. In Valmet, competence management is related to the transfer of knowledge, produced and adopted through networking, on a national and international level. The HRD department aims to transfer information that corresponds to the needs of the organisation. The HRD professionals select from external trends those that fit the organisation, discuss them with personnel to define individual and organisational needs, and also consider whether external information and expertise is necessary. Inside Valmet, there is not yet a systematic way of transferring information. One of the tasks of HRD professionals is to set up a clear and flexible information transfer system.

Besides competence management a second main topic is teamwork. HRD professionals have a supporting role in team learning. Recently, Valmet began working in functional teams, but the development is very slow and the speed at which it operates cannot be influenced greatly. The team defines the development speed itself and the progress cannot be faster than the level of the team's competence. The idea is that HRD professionals act as team coaches, providing teams with working methods and learning activities that fit with the level of team development. Unfortunately the HRD unit has not enough resources to realise that purpose.

When looking at the actual training possibilities, there is an attempt to adapt traditional training methods like classroom teaching towards more learner-oriented methods. The learners are given more responsibility over their own learning processes. They must take part and commit to training much more than before. This new training method is applied in team management, linguistic and international training. An example from German linguistics: Finnish participants who normally function in different work tasks have been sent, as a guest, to German clients. During this trip, speaking in Finnish was banned. In this way, the participants developed international relationships and interaction together with the improvement of their ability with the German language.

Technical product training is still provided in a traditional classroom manner. The technical development need of Valmet is very specialised. Therefore, this development is kept inside the organisation. Alongside the development of technology, Valmet has invested in work community development, teamwork and evolvement of managerial skills: 'because a good result does not come simply from high technology but also from the right way of functioning' (source: Valmet internal documents). The development programmes 'Valmet Leadership Programme' and 'Valmet Edge' are the essential corporation-wide management programmes that are being delivered in cooperation with the Swiss management consultancy and training institute IMD.

Besides participating in more or less traditional training programmes, employees are also encouraged to change work duties based on development. Attending projects, working in teams and self-directed learning are also considered part of personnel development.

Okobank Group (Central Unit) – financial services

The company

Facts and figures

The Okobank Group consists of 250 independent member banks and the Okobank Group Central Cooperative, the group's central institution. The Central Cooperative serves as the bank group's competence and service centre, creates member bank oriented services, steers and oversees the member banks' risk management, financial stability and liquidity, and safeguards the interests of the entire bank group. The Okobank Group holds nearly thirty per cent of the market share in savings and credits. The company primarily serves the interests of individual customers and wage earners. Its aim is to offer its private and entrepreneurial customers the most versatile asset management and investment services possible. The Okobank Group has an average of 10,000 employees.

The subject of this case study is the central unit of Okobank Group. It has approximately 1,700 employees and about thirty HRD professionals and trainers.

Business strategy

The aim of the Okobank Group is to become the leading retail bank in Finland. In this, a customer-oriented mode of functioning is essential. But the deciding factor in the banking competitiveness is the skill base of its staff:

The goal is to develop a customer's lifelong financial wellbeing and to increase the organisation's growth, risk management and profitability. Personnel development is essential owing to the increasing complexity of customers' needs. In order to serve the customers' needs efficiently in the future, demands are made on personnel to broaden their technical, professional and attitudinal development.

(Source: Okobank internal documents)

Okobank's organisational strategies are mainly based upon close cooperation with its customers and on skilled personnel. The central reason for the Okobank Group Central Cooperative to work towards a learning-oriented organisation is the tightening competition. Competition creates the need for a learning-oriented way of functioning. In order to answer the ever-increasing challenges of the environment, the personnel's reaction speed and readiness for change as well as the ability to learn need to be increased.

Change processes

The first change strategy for becoming a learning-oriented organisation is changing the organisational structure. Personnel's work duties are changing, competence areas and structures are analysed thoroughly, people start working in teams and a competence development unit and business development unit are created. The aim of the competence development unit is to develop personnel skills according to the values, vision and strategy of the bank. The competence development unit, together with a business development unit, forms a new strategy for the organisation. In line with the new competence development unit is the initiative of using personal development plans. In the near future each employee will have a long-term development plan, which will be based on both a personal development path and on organisational strategy. This represents both a personnel and business development necessity.

A second change strategy, which is closely related to competence development, is changing the direction from training towards learning in the workplace. In this way, learning is connected to everyday work processes. The emphasis is on the integration of training in the business. In this, the bank tries to support both the development of special skills and broader professional skills at the same time. Every employee has to understand the banking business as a whole and the connection with his or her own work. But more narrow expertise still remains important, because customers needs are becoming increasingly complex. As well as offering multiple ways of learning in the workplace and individual responsibility for broadening professional competence, improvement of the learning ability and motivation and creating a new leadership culture are important elements for the Okobank Group in working on the development of a learning organisation.

HRD within the Central Unit of Okobank Group

People involved in HRD

The Okobank Group Central Cooperative has a centralised competence development unit. At the time of this research, the number of HRD professionals is changing. Due to cost efficiency, training within the organisation will decrease, and attracting external services will increase. HRD professionals' tasks and responsibilities are and will be connected to co-ordinating development and consulting. Every person in the competence development unit has a defined area of responsibility, which are the development of employees with identified potential, professional competence, and teamwork.

Managers are responsible for the development of their employees. Regular development interviews were being designed. In these meetings, learning needs will be identified by the manager and the employee. Finally, each employee is responsible for his or her own development.

HRD objectives

Important elements of the HRD vision are:

- integration of HRD into business functions;
- integration of training into concrete work;
- analysis and co-ordination of external training;
- maintenance and constant development of existing competence inside the organisation.

To achieve this vision, the role of HRD professionals is starting to change. According to HRD professionals, their role has been changed already. Previously, they worked mostly as trainers, but nowadays their main work consists of organising and coordinating personnel development functions. They try to clarify what the customers of the competence development unit need, maintain the flow of training available, put development functions together, motivate and stimulate employees for learning, and create a learning culture.

Managers have another opinion of what HRD professionals are doing. According to them, the HRD unit is too far away from the business functions of the organisation. Due to this, the co-ordination between management and HRD is not yet clear and sufficient. Managers hope for more interaction, cooperation and new initiatives. They desire a more active approach and want support in their responsibility for learning and development. They hope for a more consultative role from HRD professionals.

Evaluation criteria regarding the HRD vision are unclear. Some diagnostic tools are under development. The functioning of the competence development unit is evaluated by manager's and customer's feedback and by development discussions. There is a need for clear and objective evaluation instruments.

HRD strategies

With regard to the HRD activities in the organisation, the main target of the Central Cooperative is to link HRD to business strategy and after that to make a close link between training and working. The firm tries to change the direction from training towards learning in the workplace. For the more traditional training programmes, it is moving from single courses to larger examinations that consist of different modules, which can be combined according to the real development needs. The amount of self-study, distance learning, pre-study material, teamwork, workplace learning and action learning is increased in the degree study programmes. The learners will have a personal tutor who will supervise, help and guide when needed. But there is a realisation that this change is not enough for achieving learning in the workplace. Expertise from outside is used to think about alternatives and possibilities for learning in the workplace in Okobank.

Outokumpu Zinc – steel production

The company

Facts and figures

Outokumpu Oy has four product groups: base metals, stainless steel, copper products and technology. The company has operations in thirty countries and employs approximately 14,000 people. Outokumpu Oy is organised into four business units: Corporate Management, Corporate Services, Industrial Holding, and Base Metals. Base Metals comprises the production of copper, zinc and nickel.

The organisation participating in this research is Outokumpu Zinc, which is part of Outokumpu Base Metals. Outokumpu Zinc employs about 750 people. There is a centralised personnel development unit, which employs altogether six persons.

Business strategy

Outokumpu Zinc recently found itself in a situation where it had both ageing personnel and an expanding business in which more resources were to be invested. From this situation, some intensive strategies were started with the idea of achieving competitive advantage. Key words in these strategies are improvement, innovation and client-centeredness.

Outokumpu focuses its business development for achieving profitable growth by emphasising those operations where the group has the best prerequisites for success: cost efficient production, a good competitive position and strong competences. The achievement of competitive advantage presupposes increasing quality awareness and also the creation of ever-closer customer relationships. The company's overall strategy is to produce zinc as cost efficiently and to as high a quality standard as possible at the same time when personnel development and the organisation's way of functioning is being systematically developed.

Change processes

The new organisational strategy is about bringing competitive advantage to the organisation. Traditional ways of achieving this are technology, cost efficiency and marketing efforts. Although the simultaneous emphasis on these three areas is still apparent, a fourth element is now included: organisational capability, meaning the systematic development of personnel competence and organisational ways of functioning. Outokumpu has started investing in the continuous development of the personnel competence and the systematic improvement of new employees. Also, the aim is to network local area enterprises.

Different means of rewards are also identified to motivate the personnel (challenges at work, responsibility over entities, and the possibility to have influence on their own development). The ultimate aim is to create a constantly developing team based organisation.

In short, the change strategies for taking the organisation towards a flexible and learning way of functioning are:

- in the field of organisation:
  - increasing the efficiency in the organisation's working capital;
  - perception of and widening the organisation's service network;
  - development of purchasing functions;
  - creating of a team organisation;
  - implementing a quality system for business processes.
- in the field of human resources:
  - identification of the personnel's core competence;
  - development of training systems for present and future personnel;
  - development of a new reward system.

HRD within Outokumpu Zinc

People involved in HRD

The centralised HRD department in Outokumpu Zinc is responsible for training, recruiting, personnel services and communications. Altogether, six people work in the department. They are – among other things – responsible for recruitment, personnel planning, providing training, and making training plans. HRD professionals' main responsibility is to ensure that the training supply covers all organisational levels.

Furthering professional training is line management's responsibility. Managers, employees and HRD professionals are all responsible for the development of organisational and individual competencies. Everybody has to take part in the analysis of training needs and in the formulation of personal development plans. Self-evaluations are essential in the development discussion, although the results have to be in line with the mission and vision of the organisation.

HRD objectives

HRD has been a driving force in the change process towards a learning organisation. It still plays an essential role in advancing and maintaining strategic discussions and decisions about the concept of the learning organisation. HRD's task is to add value by managing the right personnel development solutions and by co-ordinating the change process. The main challenge is to function in a more guiding way.

Although development projects particularly emphasise individual learning, collective development projects (team learning) are also essential. In individual learning, HRD professionals should co-ordinate and guide training programmes. In team learning, HRD professional's role is to plan, arrange and realise different development projects and to create pre-conditions for continuous learning. Their job is to ensure that all teams get the amount of training they need.

HRD strategies

In Outokumpu Zinc the HRD strategies are directed to recruitment, training, reward and changing the organisation's structure to support the development of competence and the advancement of teamwork. Outokumpu strives towards the creation of team organisation and the development of a new recruitment training system. The organisation has created its own training system (Zinc Maker Training) which matches both work practices in the company and a nation-wide training system. The Zinc Maker Training is closely linked to the recruiting process which gives participants (new employees) the basic qualifications for working in different tasks connected to the use and maintenance of production processes. For new employees, a new recruiting training system has been created through which it is possible to learn the basis for zinc production and also get a job in the organisation. For the development of the more experienced employees, the system of Steps of Growth has been created (see Box 5.1). By following training modules, employees can make promotion to a next level of competence, which is then checked with the manager. Agreements to proceed to a next competence level are written down in the development plan. New employees are also included in this system. They begin at the lowest level and according to their ability and motivation they move upwards in the system.

Based upon the new recruitment training system, a personal development plan is formulated for new employees. In the formulation of this plan, both professional interests and the company's needs are considered. The plan can be applied through both learning at work and through more traditional, professional training. Career planning is strongly connected with competence development. Based on the development of personal competencies, the employee has the possibility to move on to a next level in the organisation ('Steps of Growth'). This also means that the employee's personal development plan will be checked and improved, according to this career step. The development of competence is meant to show an increase in responsibility, salary and challenges at work.

This change in the training system also has its implications for recruitment and selection. Participants need to be interested in learning new things and have the

---

Box 5.1 Steps of growth at Outokumpu Zinc

Outokumpu strives to support the competence development of workers for an extended part of their working career. To realise this vision, the Steps of Growth system was implemented. This system distinguishes between five levels of work:

1 Basic operator: single task, limited applicability as a work group member
2 Multiple skill worker: more tasks, duties in other work groups
3 Zinc worker: through know-how able to function in special situations, professional qualification
4 Multiple field worker/specialist: possibility to work outside of teams, special skills
5 Zinc master: ability to work in demanding, expertise building tasks, specialised vocational degree.

Upon entering the organisation, a personnel development plan is formulated for the new employee, the aim of which is to direct competence development in work. In the formulation of this plan, both areas of professional interest and the company's needs are considered. Learning strategies adopted in the plan include both learning at work and traditional, professional training. Outokumpu strives to ensure possibilities for learning at work by hiring temporary employees. In this way permanent staff have more time to learn at work and also to broaden the borders of their job description. Whenever the worker's competence has developed to a degree where he/she can accomplish the level's work tasks, the employee has the possibility to move on to the next level. The development of the competence level also means that the employee's personnel development plan is checked according to this. The development of competence is meant to result in an increase in responsibility, salary and challenges at work. As a whole, the aim of Steps of Growth is to provide personnel development in such a way that it produces instant benefits to both individual and organisation.

---

motivation to constantly develop themselves. Outokumpu Zinc also strives to support the development of longer term working relationships. In order to realise all this, the organisation tries to be an interesting and meaningful workplace in which the personnel feel comfortable, can work in a motivated and profitable manner, commit to targets and stay with the company. According to the company:

> constant competitive advantage can only be achieved through a longstanding experiential learning process. A flexible learning organisation is the prerequisite for staying in the business. The world is changing so quickly that it is not possible to serve customers when having an inflexible organisation.
>
> (Source: Outokumpu Zinc internal documents)

Factors influencing HRD's role and how HRD deals with them

The preceding sections described the visions and strategies of the four case study organisations with regard to becoming a learning organisation, as well as HRD's role in this process. This section describes factors which affect the achievement (or lack of achievement) of the envisioned role of the HRD department. Inhibiting factors, facilitating factors and strategies to overcome barriers are briefly discussed.

Inhibiting factors

All the Finnish case study organisations were found to be facing some inhibiting factors in the change process towards a learning (oriented) organisation. Table 5.1 lists the most significant ones.

The first inhibiting factor is a practical one. The most striking is a lack of HRD professionals. The case study organisations all report that they have not enough HRD professionals, and/or not enough time to achieve the desired changes and fulfil the new tasks.

There are also inhibiting factors related to the difficulties of changing an existing situation, such as old organisation structures (Valmet, Okobank and Outokumpu) and a low sense of responsibility in employees for their own development (Valmet).

A final inhibiting factor, mentioned by Valmet, Okobank and Outokumpu is too large a distance between the HRD department, management and employees. Of course such a distance makes it difficult to realise the desired cooperation between these three parties.

Conducive factors

A large number of factors that support the development towards a learning (oriented) organisation were found. Table 5.2 gives an overview of the most important ones.

Whereas lack of HRD professionals presents a significant negative factor, the expertise of HRD professionals who do work in these companies is considered a positive influence by all organisations. Support from top management for the new developments is also important (Vaisala, Valmet and Outokumpu). Most case study organisations (Vaisala, Okobank, Outokumpu) also experience that where motivation for learning on the part of the employees exists, this helps the change process.

It is interesting to note that the internalisation of the meaning of lifelong learning and the importance of personal development are both also mentioned (Vaisala and Outokumpu) as conducive factors. This indicates a general awareness of the importance of learning, which might be seen as one of the most central requirements for the desired culture change.

Coping strategies

To reduce inhibiting factors and to enforce conducive factors different coping strategies are adopted by the case study organisations. The most important ones were already mentioned in the case study descriptions (sections on HRD strategies), but there are also some new ones.

An inhibiting factor was the small number of HRD professionals. One of the coping strategies in Vaisala is recruiting more HRD practitioners. Another solution

Table 5.1 Inhibiting factors – Finnish case study organisations

Inhibiting factors	Vaisala	Valmet Paper Machinery	Central Unit of Okobank	Outokumpu Zinc
Lack of HRD professionals/lack of resources	•	•	•	•
Old organisational structures interfere with new ways of functioning		•	•	•
Employees do not have enough responsibility over own development (for example, their manager decides who participates in which training activity)		•		
The distance between the HRD department, management and employees is too large		•	•	•

Table 5.2 Conducive factors – Finnish case study organisations

Conducive factors	Vaisala	Valmet Paper Machinery	Central Unit of Okobank	Outokumpu Zinc
HRD professionals have great expertise in the field of learning and development	•	•	•	•
Personnel development is clearly supported by the (top) management	•	•	•	
Employees are very motivated to learn	•		•	•
The meaning of lifelong learning has been internalised as a part of everyday work (learning culture)	•			•
The importance of personnel development is widely understood in the organisation	•			•

for this problem is to delegate more responsibility for training and development to line management. In order to do that, special training programs will prepare managers for their future tasks. Also a more clear definition of work, roles and areas of responsibility are made in Vaisala. In this way, the company tries to reduce the possibility of doing work twice.

In Valmet and Outokumpu, showing the added value of the HRD department is an important strategy to cope with negative forces. In Valmet HRD professionals try to constantly emphasise visibility and meaning of HRD functions in the organisation. For example, a common language is created by active participation of HRD professionals and others in different types of cooperation. Also HRD's position in the organisation will be clarified clearly to the personnel. One aspect of this is accountability of the HRD unit. The services of the personnel development unit must be profitable. The fact that first results can be shown, makes it easier for HRD professionals to sell their products and services in the organisation.

Showing added value is also important in Outokumpu Zinc. By supporting the continuous development of the individual's own competence, the HRD professionals hope to show their added value to the organisation. Both employees and managers must see the value of the change towards a learning-oriented organisation, and the value it brings to the workplace. This will motivate them to learn.

Summary and conclusions

Organisational context

Four Finnish case study organisations were discussed: Vaisala, Valmet, Okobank Group and Outokumpu Zinc. Table 5.3 provides a brief overview of the main features of each case, such as sector, number of employees, HRD function and the number of HRD practitioners.

All four organisations were found to be facing strong(er) competitive markets and/or fast(er) changing technologies. As a result, improving and innovating products, processes and services, and becoming more client-centred are important strategic issues for all. And employee learning is considered essential to reach these goals, for instance because it improves organisational flexibility (Valmet) or helps to increase client service (Okobank).

Competence development or competence management is therefore considered an important means for realising the new organisational strategies in all four cases. It can be said that all these firms also pay attention to increasing learning in the workplace. Next to stimulating individual learning, all organisations also change their organisation structure as a means to realise the new strategy (e.g. by adopting a process orientation and/or implementing teamwork).

Table 5.3 Overview of Finnish case study organisations

Company name and sector	Number of employees	HRD
Vaisala, measurement equipment manufacturing	774	• Centralised HRD unit • 5 employees
Valmet, paper machinery manufacturing	2,200	• Centralised personnel development unit • 14 employees
Okobank Group Central Cooperative, banking services	1,700	• Centralised competence development unit • 30 employees
Outokumpu Zinc, steel production	750	• Centralised personnel development unit • 6 employees

Envisioned role of HRD

In all the companies, HRD is considered a shared responsibility of managers, HRD professionals and employees. The HRD professionals usually fulfil a consulting role, and provide training and learning opportunities, and resources and tools. Line managers are responsible for development of their employees. An active role from employees is expected with regard to their own development.

With regard to the objectives of the HRD departments, it can be observed that in all four case organisations HRD departments aim for a strategic contribution to the organisation, for instance by keeping the skill base of the company up to date or by supporting strategic programmes such as the implementation of teamwork. In one case, Outokumpu Zinc, the HRD department even fulfils a leading role in the entire change process towards a learning organisation. Another common objective is providing learning opportunities, in particular by integrating learning and working.

Strategies adopted to realise HRD's new role

Concerning the strategies employed by the HRD departments to reach these aims, it can be said that the use of personal development plans is becoming more and more common. This is in congruence with the strong emphasis on personal responsibilities of employees for their own development. All four cases use both formal training methods as well as methods which provoke and support informal learning on-thejob to fulfil development needs, which is in line with their intent to integrate learning and working.

Influencing factors

The most striking inhibiting factor experienced by the Finnish case organisations is a lack of HRD professionals to realise the desired changes and fulfil the new tasks. Other inhibiting factors are related to the difficulties of changing an existing situation, such as the old organisation structures and not enough responsibility of employees for their own development.

While a lack of HRD professionals presents a significant negative factor, the expertise of HRD professionals who do work in these companies is considered a positive influence. Support from top management for the new developments is also important. Most case organisations also experience, next to a lack of responsibility, motivation for learning on the part of the employees which helps the change process.

To reduce inhibiting factors and to enforce conducive factors different strategies are adopted by the case study organisations. Most noteworthy are:

- recruiting new HRD practitioners and delegating more responsibility for training and development to line management, in order to solve the lack of specialists;
- showing the added value of the HRD department; both employees and managers must see the value of the change towards a learning-oriented organisation, and the value it brings to the workplace, in order to be motivated to learn or support others in learning.

There is also the problematic issue of language – and whether there is yet a common language (or discourse) between researchers and practitioners. Whilst the project has focused on the role of HRD practitioners in learning-oriented organisations, it has become apparent that many practitioners do not adopt the term HRD and do not speak of their organisations as being learning-oriented. However, their roles are indeed characteristic of what is commonly described as HRD, and their organisations do indeed display many of the features associated with learning (oriented) organisations, at least as they were defined for the purposes of this project. The issue of language and terminology is an important one, not least in advancing theory *and* practice. There are obvious dangers in theory building being too far ahead of practice, which can be a consequence of esoteric and obscure language. Meanings and definitions must, therefore, be further explained and shared if academics and practitioners are to learn from each other and together.

To finally conclude, this two-year study, involving almost 200 organisations across seven European countries, has found empirical evidence of a changing role for HRD professionals and an increasing responsibility for HRD activities amongst managers and employees. A key reason for pursuing the learning (oriented) organisation concept is to enhance competitiveness. With these factors in mind, there is a need for HRD professionals to ensure the development of a strategic role, to clarify their functional role, develop the new skills required of these changes, and more clearly demonstrate their value and contribution to organisational success.

6   Cases from France

Daniel Belet

This chapter describes the results of the case study research in France. Four organisations were studied: the semiconductor plant, Motorola, the retail organisation Auchan, the hotel and tourist service chain Accor and the road transport firm, GT Group.

The first four sections contain full case descriptions (based on 1998 data), including for each case:

- background information on the organisation, such as core businesses, number of employees, and current (learning-oriented) strategies;
- vision of the HRD professionals on their (new) roles in the learning (oriented) organisation;
- strategies they employ to realise these roles.

The next section describes factors that (negatively or positively) influence the achievement of these envisioned roles. General conclusions and a summary are provided in the final section.

Motorola – semiconductor plant

The company

Facts and figures

Motorola is a well-known American manufacturer of electronic components and telecommunications equipment. Its main French facilities include a manufacturing and research unit for semi-conductors, a manufacturing unit for automotive electronics and a corporate telecommunications research centre. The case focuses on the semiconductor plant in Toulouse, which employs 2,700 people.

In Motorola's decentralised global organisation, each business unit formulates its own HRD policy. The HRD function in Toulouse is jointly operated by the Toulouse HR department and Motorola University. The HR department has a staff of seven, plus thirty-two internal instructors. Motorola University is staffed by two regional representatives.

Business strategy and change processes

After experiencing tremendous growth between 1992 and 1995, the Motorola group at world level experienced some difficulties and was losing its leadership position, especially in the area of telecommunications. In order to recover its position, Motorola is now in the middle of a change process, which includes changing the organisational structure, looking towards new markets, working on quality improvements and innovation of new products.

Central to the corporate strategy of Motorola is the will to invest in employee development through training and other HRD activities. Motorola considers the concept of knowledge transfer as the heart of all renewal, mainly through continuous learning efforts at all levels of the organisation. A learning organisation is mainly seen as a *network* permitting exchanges of experiences at all levels, with a corporate culture stressing human investment, knowledge transfer and the importance of continuous training for everybody. This learning orientation is considered as the most effective means to attain the objectives central to the corporate strategy: total customer satisfaction, excellent quality and product innovation.

To support the development towards a learning organisation, Motorola set up the Motorola University in order to assist business renewal and growth by creating and sharing knowledge not only within the company but also with customers, suppliers and other stakeholders. Motorola believes this will help them to acquire, and to maintain, competitive advantage as a world leading organisation :

> Motorola University is our training arm dedicated to create and deliver learning solutions for our strategic business and personal development challenges, including those for our customers and suppliers that affect our business.
>
> (Source: Motorola internal documents)

HRD within Motorola

People involved in HRD

As explained, HRD is a shared responsibility of the HR department from the Toulouse unit and Motorola University (which is represented by two HRD professionals). The HRD department acts as the lead unit, defining training plans in line with the corporate strategy and monitoring implementation. The representatives from Motorola University provide those training services and courses requested by the HR department.

The role of the total HRD function appears increasingly to prioritise training efforts according to the need of the company strategy, and to fulfil a 'pedagogical' role towards line managers who are responsible for employee development. The HRD function is helping the managers in their new role as HRD actors. An active role is expected from employees in discussing with the line manager training needs, training efforts and evaluation of training results (see Box 6.1).

Motorola University provides consulting services to both employees and managers in defining individual learning needs, learning options and individual development

---

Box 6.1 Individual development plans in Motorola

Motorola introduced individual professional development plans in the organisation. The aim of these plans is to achieve the best possible fit between the economic needs of the company and the professional development wishes of the employees.

The individual development plan is a deliverable of a managerial procedure according to which every manager must have a quarterly meeting with all their direct subordinates. Both employees and managers share the responsibility of achieving the individual professional development plan. Manager have an advising role and a supporting role. They also provide, in co-operation with the HRD function, tools which help the employees to achieve the agreed goals.

The HRD department has an accompanying role in the broadest sense. It supports in clarifying the process, its goals and the importance of the process for the company to all employees and managers. The HRD department also monitors the implementation of the process in the organisation and analyses the process and results.

More specifically the HRD department focuses on supporting the managers in their role. Specific training activities for example are directed towards the attitudes and behaviour of the manager.

Individual development plans have proven themselves as a very efficient tool to foster internal communication and for the top management to follow the personnel perceptions. It has also obliged all managers to devote time to their leadership function. This appears very consistent with the company's managerial philosophy which emphasises the strategic importance of personnel from the operating core.

---

plans and individual integrity entitlement (a document commenting upon the relationship between employees and their managers concerning professional development).

HRD objectives

HRD's main aim is to contribute effectively to the corporate strategy. The main HRD policy theme is centralisation of all training efforts in order to get a more overall and accurate view, and better strategic control of the training investment. Motorola believes that at the heart of renewal lies the concept of knowledge transfer. For this reason, Motorola's HRD function focuses on continuous training for employees and it has developed several tools (e.g. individual professional development plans) which stimulate regular discussions of each employee with their supervisor about his or her training needs, recommended training efforts and evaluation of training results.

The HRD department also supports employee development through other forms of learning, such as teamwork to improve procedures and work processes and through a new reward system.

HRD strategies

The training policy seems to evolve from a catalogue approach towards a more strategic approach with a strong involvement from line management. When looking at concrete

HRD activities it can be said that the main activities for the training department are defining training policy in line with the corporate strategy and controlling the implementation of the policy.

Three main activities are presently emerging:

1 Supplying line managers with as much information as possible about their employees and supporting them in their role of monitoring and improving the professional competencies of their subordinates.
2 Participating in a global project aiming at managing job and professional competencies on the Toulouse site. Key competencies have been worked out for all jobs, including technical as well as behavioural competencies.
3 Professional development of managers. Motorola is making efforts in the development of, especially, young managers for their new role. This activity needs to be continued to ensure the company remains attractive to the best engineers. This is very important in order that Motorola can stay at the leading edge of technology and product innovation.

Motorola University provides a catalogue of training courses (classified as either cross-sector or sector-specific courses). The department also supports other learning activities such as project teams. It also tries to improve knowledge transfer by supporting technical specialists in delivering courses and practical training.

One other activity worth mentioning is a 'business training consulting group' which has started with the aim to work together with the change drivers, to understand their critical business issues and to help them design adequate learning interventions.

Motorola's HRD department has implemented evaluation strategies based both on individual evaluation of training by employees and through quarterly exchanges between individual employees and their managers. This joint evaluation of the real impact of the training or professional experience is an important tool for evaluating HRD activities.

Auchan – retail organisation

The company

Facts and figures

Auchan is a large chain of supermarkets with stores in eleven countries. The Auchan group is a fast-growing company which has established a leading position in the supermarket retail trade. It operates a wide range of brands and types of stores.

The case focuses on the Bordeaux–Lac hypermarket, which is one of the largest stores in France. This store has about 800 employees including a variable number of temporary workers.

Each hypermarket is a very autonomous unit run by three or four senior managers – the general manager, the control and finance manager, and the human resource manager – who are jointly responsible for the financial results of the hypermarket.

The HRD manager and five HRD practitioners represent the HRD department for the Bordeaux–Lac hypermarket.

Business strategy and change processes

Auchan sees itself as a learning company (even if they don't use this word often) because of their comprehensive corporate training system, which has been created as a major part of the business development strategy. The company has made the professional development and excellence of its employees a key component of its corporate development. The underlying philosophy is that Auchan wants to provide the best service to the clients, and that this can only be achieved by having professional employees. Since the mid-1980s the company has worked on the development of a comprehensive training system for all types of personnel and for all types of jobs within the supermarket.

An additional and very important process for Auchan is the development of a strong corporate culture which is built upon training for employees, transfer of supermarket business know-how, the idea that every employee is responsible for his or her own mission and sharing the benefits of the company progress with all the employees.The company has also implemented a new leadership strategy which emphasises continuous improvement.

HRD within Auchan

People involved in HRD

The HRD department in Auchan's hypermarket in Bordeaux has five staff. Three of these are involved in the store's HRD activities, while the others work on identifying training needs and planning training sessions. The professional staff are supported by thirty-two specialised employees who deliver training on a part-time basis, mainly outside the store. The HRD function has an open 'training space' with equipment not only for training sessions, but also for self-study, so employees can learn in their own time on a voluntary basis. The co-operation of HRD practitioners, managers and employees is considered important. The department managers, as well as more experienced employees, play a significant role as trainers for both newcomers and existing personnel (see Box 6.2).

HRD objectives

Auchan's main objective is to get excellent employees at all levels and in all jobs to deliver high quality services and products to the customer. HRD policy appears to be one of the main strategies to achieve this corporate objective. Auchan's HRD policy stresses ten major points, including :

- allowing for personal development;
- giving respect to each employee;

Box 6.2 Managers as trainers at Auchan

Experienced and well-performing employees are selected at Auchan and trained to become trainers for new starters. An important aim of the employee/trainer system is to motivate newcomers to learn and develop.

The training is twofold, focusing on becoming a trainer as well as becoming manager, and lasts for ten months. Managers mentor the employees during this course. After completing the course the best employees are given full responsibility in their training function. They are also involved with updating the training materials. In order to fulfil their new tasks the trainers can make use of all kinds of specific pedagogical tools like books, exercises etc. They also get a dedicated training room with all modern training equipment.

This training role for the best employees has a strong and positive effect on them and is often a key to promotion.

The HRD department of Auchan, which is part of the larger HR department, has been heavily involved in the design of all the training programmes and in other training and personal development procedures. Also they are involved in the follow up courses of all training sessions at both collective and individual levels.

This 'employee/trainer' system has a strong impact on employee motivation. Employees regard it as a reward and an acknowledgement of their professional achievements and competences. Evaluations up-to-date confirm the succes of this training. Not only trainees are enthusiastic, but trainers and managers are also positive.

- training and developing the professionalism of everybody;
- facilitating individual progress through promotion and easy access to information through two way communication.

These policy points all focus on personal and professional development of all employees as well as on developing and arranging learning opportunities in order to support employee development.

HRD distinguishes between three learning levels.

1 Learning at individual level refers to various training sessions adapted to any level and job and informal learning supported by a supervisor, mentor or tutor.
2 Group learning refers to teamwork and problem solving workgroups.
3 Learning at the organisational level refers to a strong learning culture emphasising the necessity to capitalise on good practices, know-how and experiences and to share these among each other and with other stores.

HRD strategies

Activities performed by the HRD group are diverse, from organising training activities to supporting all kinds of informal learning, with the aim of supporting knowledge sharing.

The Auchan group HRD function has produced several catalogues of training and courses on various themes including corporate matters, as well as technical and professional issues. The catalogues relate to all jobs. All kinds of training methods and tools are used such as books, videos and CD-ROMs. As already mentioned, the Auchan Bordeaux–Lac hypermarket has an open training space where individual or group learning can take place.

Additional activities include, for example, the encouragement of each store to formalise and capitalise on its best practices in order to disseminate them throughout the group, and to share knowledge and know-how at the internal business school for managers. A mentor coaches managers and this has proved to be very successful for both the development of managers and for integrating the company culture. Another activity is called the 'product month'. Future managers spend a month in the kind of department they will be appointed to, under the supervision of an experienced manager.

Managers also have an evaluation meeting with their supervisor once a year. Managers have targets to reach and these are discussed during this meeting, after which new targets are identified.

Accor Group – hotel and travel service provider

The company

Facts and figures

The Accor Group is a world leader in the hotel, tourism, travel and service industries in 142 countries. The company runs a network of 2,600 hotels ranging from luxury brands to simple leisure hotels. It also operates a world-wide network of travel agencies and a European network of car rentals.

In 1985 the Accor Academie was set up for the hotel and tourism activities. This internal academy is a good illustration of the dynamic HRD strategy conducted within the organisation. The focus of the case study lies with this corporate academy, which employs fifty-five people.

Business strategy and change processes

The Accor Group has three major strategic orientations: re-allocation of resources in the hotel sector, a re-launch of development policies in most business activities and a re-engineering programme called ACCOR 2000, which includes modernising information flows.

The Accor Group is a service organisation and all employees are in direct contact with the clients. Therefore, Accor considers adequate employee behaviour and professional services delivered to the customers the main sources of added value to the company. In addition, the world-wide dimension of the business activities of Accor requires common professional standards and values. The Accor Group wants to capitalise upon successful experiments and ideas in order to profit as much as possible from the potential synergies which come from such a huge and diversified service group.

The main strategy to achieve this standardisation and synergy was the building of a 'service university' called the Accor Academie. This academy employs a range of internal and external trainers/consultants who provide training sessions for groups of employees (especially managers). Other tasks include initiating inter-professional synergies, conveying group values and, in a general sense, helping to meet the present and future challenges of the company.

The academy also provides consulting services for change strategies, such as sharing internal competencies and know-how, project management development and the analysis of the best performing types of professional manager.

HRD within the Accor Group

People involved in HRD

The Accor Academie has a staff of internal and external trainers/consultants. They are responsible for running training sessions and for consulting services. The development of their consulting roles stresses their responsibilities as professionals in management development and organisational learning. Activating and utilising the professional competencies of the participants in the training sessions is emphasised, especially within established workgroups, in order to share know-how.

HRD objectives

The Accor Academie's main aims are to create and implement training sessions for all groups of employees, especially for managers, to initiate inter-professional synergies, to convey group values and to help the company meet present and future challenges.

The Accor Group has put the emphasis on the second issue. It aims to support collective learning with horizontal links, collective production of know-how, free flow of information and communication, collective commitment to the corporate strategy and reflection about failures and successes in a supporting learning environment.

HRD strategies

The Accor Academie has its own training accommodation with all necessary modern facilities and equipment. The department offers training courses in five main fields: management and human resource management; sales and marketing of services; new information technologies; professional techniques and financial management, and corporate culture training. Currently, the focus is on three crucial business areas: new technologies, sales and marketing, and technical issues and maintenance.

The academy also plays a major role in projects aimed at knowledge creation and sharing. For instance, it supports the project 'Accor 2000 succeeding together' which is carried out with the aim to improve professional processes, methodologies, learning tools and methods in order to improve the quality of the company services. But the Academy also supports related projects and activities, such as:

- sharing internal competencies and know-how in a project concerning management development;
- analysis of the best performing types of professional management;
- scanning the most advanced technologies which can help business effectiveness and dissemination of best practices.

Other change strategies include, for example, tutorship programmes for non-qualified young people (see Box 6.3) and coaching managers to deliver project based training sessions.

The Accor group has also developed evaluation grids for managers to support them in their scheduled meetings with employees. These grids contain information on professional competencies development, success/failure analysis, know-how dissemination, and reflection on action etc. The HRD function uses the results of these meetings as crucial indicators.

Box 6.3 Tutorship programme for young people at Accor

The Accor Group has signed an agreement with the French Ministry of Labour to train (and then recruit) young people without formal qualifications. Internal tutors from Accor act as trainers.

The Accor Group has developed its own tutorship training programme for the internal tutors all over the country. It consists of ten days of training per year. The tutors are managers with at least five years of experience in the job and one year of experience in the same department who volunteer, with the agreement of their managers and the HR department.

The training programme focuses among other things on communication, welcome behaviours, contracts, pedagogy, evaluation systems, dialogue techniques, roles and responsibilities of the tutor. Training methods used in the course are for example speeches, pedagogic games, videos and role games to test the tutor in concrete situations.

The staff providing these courses are usually senior consultants and trainers of the Accor Academie who have been trained in training tutors.

The role of the Accor Academie has also been to develop the programme entitled 'Academy Within the City'. All the trainers have participated in the design and development of pedagogic tools and methods. Collaboration within the state employment agencies has been set up to implement this programme throughout the country. The academy also supports the trainers.

This tutorship programme seems to be successful. More than 1,200 tutors have been trained by the Accor Academie. The tutor's qualification has been recognised by the French Ministry of Education. The tutors can also become consultants for the professional training in these fields, delivered in the specialised technological schools, or move from one hotel brand of the group to another hotel brand.

GT Group – road transport firm

The company

Facts and figures

GT Group is a transport company that specialises in renting out lorries and commercial vehicles with drivers to several industrial manufacturing companies. The GT group is located near Bordeaux, but has business activities all over France. The company is structured in several units across eight regions. The company is well known in France for its social image and its innovative character. Some 1,000 employees work for the GT Group, 765 of which are drivers.

The managing directors of the eight regional units are specifically in charge of human resource management, while the parent company is responsible for central services such as administrative tasks concerning personnel management. As with Motorola and the Accor Group, the GT Group has an internal school, in this case known as the GT Institute. The HRD function is performed by the four staff members of the GT Institute and by the managers who support and control teams of drivers.

Business strategy and change processes

GT Group's superiority in the management of drivers with 'social lease-back' (a system of taking over customers' lorries and drivers) as a core competence, declined some years ago when some clients didn't renew their contracts. After an in-depth reflection about the evolution of the French road transportation industry it was decided to launch a collective learning process, focusing on logistics.

This process was necessary to inform employees about the changes in the market, uncover weaknesses and misunderstandings within relationships between the GT Group and its customers and discover new business opportunities for GT. In addition the company wanted to better understand and formulate the perception of the company towards the market in order to decide which core competencies should be developed by GT to improve its position in an increasingly competitive market. Although GT already had a long experience in enhancing professional development of employees through continuous training, the new learning challenge was to reinforce collective enquiries, with the intention of continuously redesigning services to ensure their relevance to rapidly changing customer needs. It was also decided that organisational changes were necessary to improve the competitive position of GT. Rather than structuring the activities through operational regional subsidiaries, specialised entities in different transportation activities were created. To achieve these major changes a new role was expected from managers and the GT Institute was launched.

HRD within the GT Group

People involved in HRD

The GT Institute has a full-time staff of four. The Institute is now independent of the GT Group; formally it is not a part of the HRD department of the GT Group. The institute is not only working for the GT Group, its main client, but also for GT's competitors. The expansion of clients led to a rapid growth of training activities. The HRD function is performed by the GT Institute and by the managers who support and control teams of drivers. Management and the HRD function work in strong cooperation to make a policy to meet the new challenges. GT managers are not directly involved in the GT Institute which has its own staff and trainers, although synergies between the GT Institute and the GT Group are obvious. The GT Institute assists operational managers in their HR tasks.

HRD objectives

GT Group did some research on GT's core businesses with the aim of redefining its mission, to meet the customer's wishes and future requirements, and to acquire new competencies in the field of logistics in order to diversify and strengthen its offerings to the market.

The GT Group focuses on the changing needs of the customers by working on the professionalism of employees. A new and active role is expected from managers. The HRD function is focusing on all employees but especially on management because they have to be the driving force for changes in the GT Group. Management and the HRD function worked in close co-operation on a policy to tackle the new challenges. The most important issues for HRD are fostering individual and collective learning (internally) and the expansion of training activities for new clients in the transport industry and other industries (externally).

HRD strategies

The HRD function at GT is actively involved in a learning process for managers in order to support them in making the transformation to managers of a strategic business unit, with all of the associated responsibilities including marketing, logistics and HRD. An important activity of the HRD function is the GT Institute. At its launch, the institute had two main goals: clarifying training competencies available within GT and increasing awareness in employees and customers of the importance of permanent employee learning. Currently, employees are intensively trained in the first two years and afterwards every three years compulsory courses have to be followed. The GT Institute is providing courses at two levels: individual competence assessment and specific collective courses. Individual competence assessment refers to a systematic analysis of behavioural attitudes, learning style and managerial capacities from employees. Based on this analysis the institute supports employees in defining an individual development project. Examples of collective courses include quality management, running meetings, and train the trainers.

Factors influencing HRD's role and how HRD deals with them

The preceding sections described the visions and strategies of the four case study organisations with regard to becoming a learning organisation, as well as HRD's role in this process. This section describes factors which affect the achievement (or lack of achievement) of the envisioned role of the HRD department. Inhibiting factors, facilitating factors and strategies to overcome barriers are briefly discussed.

Inhibiting factors

All French case study organisations were found to be facing some inhibiting factors in the change process towards a learning (oriented) organisation. Table 6.1 lists the most significant ones.

As the table shows, there is large variety in the constraints experienced. None of the inhibiting factors were experienced by more than two cases. Production and time constraints sometimes inhibit learning (Motorola and Auchan). The compulsory training system provides an inhibiting factor for Motorola and Auchan, as does the fact that the content of some courses is outdated. Both factors have a negative influence on the motivation of the employees in their involvement in training activities.

Other inhibiting factors concern the workforce, such as the lack of motivation on the part of some employees or managers, who do not consider employee development to be a priority (Motorola and Auchan). An inhibiting factor for the Accor Group concerns the multicultural aspects of this global company. This sometimes makes learning from each other difficult. Though variety can also kindle learning, differences can also present difficulties. For the GT Group, the unbalanced structure of the age profile is an inhibiting factor. It causes problems like the unwillingness of a large number of drivers to adapt to new technologies and methods, and the lack of opportunities for employees with potential to move up the hierarchy.

Conducive factors

HRD professionals were also asked to identify factors that support the development towards a learning (oriented) organisation. A large number of factors were found. Table 6.2 gives an overview of the most important ones.

Table 6.1 Inhibiting factors – French case study organisations

Inhibiting factors	Motorola	Auchan	Accor Group	GT Group
Production and time constraints	•	•		
Compulsory training system	•	•		
Some courses are outdated		•		
Lack of motivation of employees or management	•	•		
Multicultural aspects			•	
Unbalanced structure of age pyramid				•

Table 6.2 Conducive factors – French case study organisations

Conducive factors	Motorola	Auchan	Accor Group	GT Group
Support of top management	•		•	•
Clear training system/procedures	•	•		
Understanding/sharing of corporate objectives by all employees	•			
Learning by increasing contact with customers				•
Impact of training on competency development and impact on remuneration		•		
Experienced people involved as trainers		•		
Professional HRD staff/Academie			•	

As the table shows, the most important conducive factor seems to be support from top management (Motorola, Accor, GT Group). Paradoxically, clear training procedures were also mentioned as a positive factor by the same companies that considered the training system as an inhibiting factor. Motorola finds training procedures, such as individual professional development plans very useful in encouraging, monitoring and evaluating professional training of employees. For Auchan the structured and sophisticated training system has a positive impact because it allows employees to develop and allows new members to integrate within the company quickly.

A few conducive factors mentioned are concerned with employee involvement and commitment to the company. Motorola mentioned the understanding and sharing of the corporate goals by all units in the company and by all employees. For example, everybody is aware of the fact that quality improvement programmes are necessary for the development of the company. This helps motivation for learning. The GT Group reports that increased contact with customers fosters employee learning. At Auchan the impact of training on competence development and remuneration has a positive influence. Also the system of experienced people training other employees seems to be very effective (see Box 6.1).

It is interesting to note that, for the Accor Group, the unique position of the academy and the prestigious image of this corporate university makes it easier to cope with negative factors. The professional HRD staff, the facilities of the academy and the openness of this educational institution to various outside partners and visitors are part of this image.

Coping strategies

With regard to strategies employed to cope with inhibiting factors, it was found that in all French cases, attention is being paid to communicating clearly to employees why change is necessary, why learning plays an important role in the change process of the organisation and that learning takes place not only by following courses but also by learning from each other. This involvement and understanding of employees is considered to be very important to achieve the desired changes.

Summary and conclusions

Organisational context

Four French case study organisations were discussed: Motorola, Auchan, Accor group and GT Group. Table 6.3 provides a short overview of the case organisations characteristics like sector, number of employees, HRD function and the number of HRD practitioners.

It was found that the main reasons these four organisations invest in employee development are the desire to realise continuous improvement and/or innovation (Motorola, Auchan, GT Group) and to achieve better customer service (Motorola, Auchan, Accor Group). It needs to be recognised also that a lack of vocational education or training in France in certain occupations is a major reason for Auchan and the GT Group to invest in training for their employees.

As a change strategy to stimulate employee learning, knowledge sharing and innovation, training programmes are important for all four organisations. Two cases, Motorola and Accor have also implemented their own corporate university, to link HRD closely to business strategy. These universities have broader tasks than providing training: among other things they also give advice, support knowledge creation and sharing within the company and support change programmes.

Envisioned role of HRD

HRD functions from all companies emphasise the importance of continuous learning and development of all employees as an essential part of the corporate development process. Major HRD issues are:

Table 6.3 Overview of French case study organisations

Company and sector	Number of employees	HRD
Motorola, semiconductor plant in Toulouse	2,700 employees	• HR department and Motorola University • HR department: 7 employees • Motorola University: 2 employees
Auchan, hypermarket in Bordeaux, retail organisation	• In France: 15,000 employees • In Bordeaux: 800 employees	• HR manager and HR department • 1 manager and 5 HRD professionals
Accor Group, hotel, tourism, travel industries		• Accor Academie • 55 trainers and HRD professionals
GT Group, road transport	1,000 employees	• Managing directors of units and GT Institute • 4 HRD professionals in GT Institute

- involving employees in making changes to improve products, services, work methods etc.;
- investing in a learning culture and promoting a positive attitude to learning;
- consulting in tracking training needs and in developing employee development plans;
- providing training;
- providing advice to management on employee development issues.

Double loop learning, for example, preparing the organisation for fundamental change, is considered to be important but more difficult to realise. Evidence that HRD functions are trying to support double loop learning is that all organisations try to link HRD strategy to the corporate strategy in order to support organisational development.

The main activities of HRD professionals can be split up into two categories: training and consulting. Training often take place outside the workplace in a separate training space or institute. Consulting activities are said to be becoming increasingly important.

The involvement of management has also become more significant, especially within Motorola and Accor. They have become new actors in the HRD function. In the GT Group managers were already important actors in the HRD function. The main task of the members of the GT Institute seems to be providing training, not consulting.

The most important aims for HRD functions seem to be to support the corporate strategy by working to improve professional development of all employees, and to look for future developments and needed HRD interventions to prepare the organisation for change. There is much attention devoted to linking training strategy to corporate strategy. For instance, in Motorola a current objective is to centralise training policy, so it can be managed more closely. This should result in a closer link to the general corporate policy.

Strategies adopted to realise HRD's new role

Employee development is supported mainly by offering a wide range of training, but more informal learning methods (such as tutoring, mentoring) are also used.

Management development receives specific attention in three cases (Motorola, the Accor Group and the GT Group), because managers are considered important actors in the development towards a learning organisation. Promoting knowledge sharing (by concrete activities or by stimulating a learning culture) is also an important activity for all HRD functions, most notably for the Accor Group and Auchan.

Influencing factors

In terms of becoming a learning organisation, a large variety of constraints were found, but none of the inhibiting factors was experienced by more than two cases. Some factors are practical, such as production and time constraints, a compulsory training system or an outdated content of some courses. Other inhibiting factors concern the workforce, particularly the lack of motivation on the part of employees and managers, who do not consider employee development as a priority.

The most important conducive factor seems to be support from top management. Paradoxically, clear training procedures were also experienced as a conducive factor by the same companies who considered the training system an inhibiting factor.

With regard to strategies employed to cope with inhibiting factors, communication was found to be very important. All case study organisations pay attention to communicating clearly to employees why change is necessary, why learning plays an important role in the change process of the organisation and that learning takes place not only by following courses but also by learning from each other. This involvement and understanding of employees is considered to be very important in achieving the desired changes.

7 Cases from Germany

*Peter Pawlowsky, Katja Neubauer, Rüdiger
Reinhardt and Antje Buschmann*

This chapter describes the results of the case study research in Germany. Four organisations were studied: the domestic appliance manufacturer Bosch Siemens Hausgeräte, the crop producer Hoechst Schering AgrEvo, the technical consultancy firm Gesellschaft für Technische Zusammenarbeit and the marketing and sales organisation for Sony Germany, an electronics producer.

The first four sections contain full case descriptions (based on data from 1998), including for each case:

- background information on the organisation, such as core businesses, number of employees, and current (learning-oriented) strategies;
- vision of the HRD professionals on their (new) roles in the learning (oriented) organisation;
- strategies they employ to realise these roles.

The next section describes factors that (negatively or positively) influence the achievement of these envisioned roles. General conclusions and a summary are provided in the final section.

Bosch Siemens Hausgeräte – domestic appliance manufacturer

The company

Facts and figures

Bosch Siemens Hausgeräte (BSH) is a multinational manufacturer of domestic household appliances such as dishwashers and freezers. These products are characterised by a high degree of standardisation as well as a high rate of innovation. Approximately 32,000 employees work for Bosch Siemens Hausgeräte world-wide. In Germany, the number of employees is about 14,500.

The HRD department of the German location is centralised function consisting of seven HRD professionals. The department supports and co-ordinates all kinds of HRD activities company-wide, develops innovative HRD concepts and focuses on executing company-wide HRD-related activities.

Business strategy and change processes

BSH has generated competitive advantages in the market of household equipment, particularly in the field of technological innovation. Thermal exchange technology, dishwashers with overhead rinsing and sensor-regulated hotplates in kitchen stoves are only a few examples. The company's activities are directed towards the needs of differentiated target groups and the exploitation of market volume or market development. To maintain BSH's current market position, the organisation constantly redefines its activities, processes and behaviours, and strives to improve and innovate its products. Individual, group and organisational learning are considered to be crucial to realise this continuous change, as illustrated by the following statement:

> Innovations are crucial for success in the quickly accelerating market. They are crucial in all thematic sections, not only in technology. Knowledge is decisive for the capability to innovate and change in the market. Readiness for change, subjectrelated knowledge and new ideas are considered to be crucial for developing products and services in world-wide markets and for generating competitive advantage.
>
> (Source: 'Personnel, Social and Training Issues', BSH internal document)

In order to promote its development toward a learning organisation, BSH is deploying a number of strategies to stimulate learning, e.g. business process reengineering projects (BPR) and the development of information technology (IT) networks which are aimed at facilitating and improving learning processes within the company. In order to improve the capability of employees for changing and learning, specific activities are designed, including for example a programme for motivation and mobilisation of employees and the so-called 'TOP'-initiative (time optimised processes) which aims to enhance productivity power for innovation and creativity.

HRD in Bosch Siemens Hausgeräte

People involved in HRD

Employee development and creating a learning culture are seen as a common responsibility of managers and employees within BSH. Human resource development activities are a central task for each line manager. They are expected to contribute to employee development by, among other things, formulating learning objectives, creating development plans and by coaching employees. Employees are expected to take an active role with regard to their personnel development by defining personal objectives and deciding on learning initiatives. But they are also expected to contribute directly to organisational development by giving management suggestions for improvements and innovations. As one HRD manager pointed out in this respect: 'a successful development is based upon initiatives from employees'.

The HRD department fulfils a supportive and consulting role towards both management and employees' learning activities. The department's main tasks include:

- co-ordinating 'self-directed' employee learning;
- co-ordinating and supporting HRD activities performed by line management;
- organising training activities, developing tools and learning methods (job-aids, questionnaires, computer based training etc.);
- supporting organisational processes and procedures like the EFQM model (quality management);
- initiating new HRD concepts.

The HRD department tries to support both single loop learning (improving existent processes and products) and double loop learning (changing basic assumptions, beliefs and objectives). However, they increasingly focus on initiating innovative HRD concepts, providing facilities and consulting services that are primarily aimed at double loop learning processes.

HRD objectives

Looking at the objectives of BSH's HRD department, it can be said that its overall aim is to 'contribute to the success of the company'. In order to realise this goal, the HRD department pursues a number of different objectives, such as:

- supporting and promoting the development towards a learning organisation;
- promoting entrepreneurial thinking and acting through a performance orientation;
- offering a demand-oriented training supply;
- promoting employee's personality and potential development;
- supporting the development of a learning culture.

HRD strategies

The HRD department undertakes a range of activities, aimed at realising these objectives. Of particular interest is a system they developed especially to support management learning (see Box 7.1). This is expected to help not only the development of line managers, but also to support the development of a learning culture in the long run.

Changes were made regarding HRD's policy to support the development towards a learning organisation. Although the HRD department is a centralised function, BSH has deliberately established its unique understanding of decentralised HRD: fulfilling HRD activities is considered a core issue for each line executive. The underlying vision refers to the idea that HRD is to be transferred to those decisionmakers who possess the necessary competencies and knowledge for undertaking such tasks. This also should enhance the link between HRD and organisational needs. The focus of the HRD department has changed. HRD is interpreted as a demanddriven function for all employees. The success of HRD depends on the needs and interests of both the company and individuals. This is the reason that activities performed by the HRD department now more closely follow organisational strategy.

Box 7.1 Feedback for line managers at Bosch Siemens Hausgeräte

BSH has implemented a system of feedback for managers, with two objectives. In the short term, the programme provides managers with a chance for self-reflection and, as a result, leads to improvements in co-operation and leadership. In the long term, BSH expects the practice to enhance an open-minded, constructive feedback culture, which the company regards as a prerequisite for continuous learning.

The technique resembles a 360° feedback system. First, executives evaluate themselves, and employees evaluate the manager. A facilitator analyses these results and provides feedback in a one-on-one meeting. The final activity is a group meeting in which the executive, employees and facilitator all participate. The meeting results in a written agreement of improvement objectives.

The HR department in co-operation with the 'TOP' centre promotes and supports this way of working. Furthermore, HR professionals offer support for any kind of consulting, coaching or facilitating any requests. The aim is to repeat the feedback cycle every year and to refine the concept in terms of (positive and negative) indications of participants.

The concept has been successfully implemented as a part of the organisation-wide focus on leadership competencies. BSH has ensured the participation of employees in evaluating leadership activities and providing feedback by integrating them both in the conceptualisation of the tool, and the later definition of executives training needs and development programmes. Thus, employee satisfaction has been increased, and the critical and constructive handling of leadership deficits enhanced by more open and efficient co-operation.

AgrEvo – chemicals manufacturer

The company

Facts and figures

AgrEvo is a crop producer that offers tailor-made products for agricultural companies. Its products and services are characterised by both a high knowledge intensity and a high rate of innovation. AgrEvo employs about 9,000 people world-wide.

The centralised HRD function, which employs six professionals, mainly focuses on world-wide management development activities. Development of other employees is considered as a company-specific responsibility for the decentralised personnel development departments. The HRD function, however, is not only working on the development of training topics and learning themes, and the development of tools and training courses. It also seeks to fulfil a co-ordinating role with regard to inter-personal processes within the company.

Business strategy and change processes

The main challenges facing AgrEvo include reorganisation of diverse market divisions, and innovation and growth potential in the biotechnological sector. The company's understanding of learning needs refers to the idea that only a highly flexible and dynamic business will be able to deal with a rapidly changing and competitive market. Employees are seen as the main competitive factor. The broadened awareness of managers and employees of these factors is based upon the common belief that a changing consciousness of all employees and a permanent increase of collective knowledge is the necessary condition for viability.

Just like Bosch Siemens Hausgeräte, AgrEvo is characterised by a strong customerand process orientation. Pursuing this strong customer focus and a desire for innovation, the company aims to continuously adapt organisational knowledge to changing environmental circumstances and to proactively develop new knowledge. This vision is reflected in the following vision statement:

> The corporate objective is to develop products to offer our customer advantageous solutions as well as to keep up with changes and consider them as an opportunity. In the future, we will perform strong and intensive research and development to guarantee a competitive portfolio of products. In order to keep being prepared for the future, we cannot stop learning.
>
> (Source: AgrEvo internal documents)

In the development process towards a learning organisation, AgrEvo is deploying a broad range of strategies to support and stimulate learning processes. Top management is demonstrating the commitment for continuous learning, for example by providing space, time and financial support. This support includes the development and implementation of innovative approaches such as strategic trainee programmes, the execution of a company wide strategic learning needs analysis and a restructuring process towards a global network organisation with world-wide information technology networking.

HRD in AgrEvo

People involved in HRD

As in BSH, employee development in AgrEvo is considered to be a line responsibility. The role of line management is to support employee development, for example by promoting employee awareness of organisational objectives, by making individual development plans, and by acting as a coach or mentor. The role of employees is to show commitment and to take initiatives to trigger their own development. The HRD department itself fulfils a mainly consulting and supportive role.

The HRD professionals advise management on issues like formulating training topics and identifying training needs. The department also develops training tools and methods, organises training courses, and co-ordinates the world-wide management development programme. Furthermore, the decentralised 'personnel development' functions are responsible for the development of line employees. Besides these training-related activities, HRD professionals are involved in all kinds of organisational change processes and innovations (planning, design, realisation and evaluation). Finally, by activities such as organising business process awareness workshops and management audits, they try to support double loop learning and to increase employees' readiness for active participation in organisational changes.

HRD objectives

The HRD department of AgrEvo has defined two major objectives on the basis of the company's vision of employees as the main competitive factor for the organisation. The first objective is to stimulate and support potential development and personality development. To reach this objective, the function is employing HRD instruments and activities facilitating employee learning and stimulating a learning culture. Examples of such tools are the development of knowledge exchange networks and the implementation of new customer-oriented incentive systems.

The second major objective is to foster systematic knowledge management. This encompasses providing knowledge by documenting and exchanging project experience, creating transparency with regard to competencies and career planning and supporting knowledge-related strategic initiatives such as world-wide networking and strategic alliances.

HRD strategies

Recently, a reorganisation of the HRD department was undertaken with the aim to improve customer satisfaction and process optimisation. One of the main changes was the separation of the HRD function into one part that is especially focused on management development and another that is especially aimed at the lower hierarchical levels and is organised on a corporate level.

Further changes have been made with regard to HRD policy. The function's focus has moved away from using a standard catalogue of traditional off-the-job training programmes towards improving organisational performance by enhancing linemanaged learning processes. For example, it established a competence management system and provides management audits or strategic training needs analysis.

Deutsche Gesellschaft für Technische Zusammenarbeit (GTZ) – consultancy firm for development co-operation

The company

Facts and figures

The Deutsche Gesellschaft für Technische Zusammenarbeit (GTZ) is a world-wide service company that offers a wide range of consulting services on technical co-operation in the field of development aid. Its activities are focused on the enhancement of social and economic stability in developing countries, for example by advising on the use of technology, and on technical capabilities and skills. The organisation's aim is to improve performance of organisations and their employees. The services provided by

GTZ are characterised by a high knowledge intensity and the activities of GTZ are highly customer-focused. Around 1,300 employees work in Germany. Additionally, there are around 1,600 employees working abroad.

Just as in the other German case organisations, the HRD department is a centralised function. The department defines itself as a consultant regarding employee development and organisational learning. A total of twenty-three staff are employed in the HRD department.

Business strategy and change processes

GTZ's main corporate objective is the enhancement of social and economic stability in developing countries. GTZ faces two important strategic challenges: reduction of financial funds of German government, and increasing requirements with respect to performance of GTZ. The need to discuss the concept of the learning organisation is mainly the result of the corporate objectives and the strong customer and process orientation.

GTZ does not have a formally defined organisation-wide concept of the 'learning organisation'; instead different departments of the company internalised the idea of organisational learning. The focus is on fostering a decentralised network organisation with highly committed and autonomous employees who constantly work on improving their knowledge repertoire. This focus on employees is clearly reflected by the following quote from the HRD manager:

> Because our business is performed by people, we have to enable them to adapt themselves to permanently changing requirements.

In the development towards a learning organisation, GTZ pursues a broad range of interdependent strategies. The common core of all strategies is the generation of conditions that promote learning, for example by developing flexible organisational structures, elaborating a learning-oriented culture, implementing new kinds of cooperation networks and the implementation of new information and communication systems.

HRD in GTZ

People involved in HRD

As in the two other German case studies discussed so far, the preferred role of the HRD department in GTZ is mainly that of a consultant and assistant to the line management. The HRD department defines itself as a consultant regarding employee development and organisational learning, and gives advice in a broad area: from restructuring processes to the realisation of training courses. The primary responsibility for employee development lies with line managers and employees. Middle management is responsible for creating opportunities for learning on the job, and top management plays an important role in creating conditions that promote learning (learning culture).

The HRD department provides support and advice for managers and employees regarding personal development plans, but also designs learning processes to develop social skills, communication skills, co-operative skills and consulting skills as well as management related and leadership skills. The department is responsible for providing technical support and designing new learning techniques. Furthermore, the HRD department actively tries to stimulate self-responsibility and promote open communication and a learning culture.

HRD objectives

The HRD department of GTZ defines HRD as 'a process of linking requirements of the company with the capabilities, skills and needs of employees'. Important objectives are increasing commitment and self-management of employees, enhancing national and international mobility, supporting the development of a corporate learning culture, promoting all employees' capability for learning, recruit qualified employees and retaining them within the organisation.

HRD strategies

In line with the changing competitive environment and objectives of the company, HRD policy is also changing. The department stresses the link between HRD and corporate strategy, and strives to contribute to the changing corporate culture. In order to realise this, the HRD department pays attention to increasing the knowledge and skills of its own professionals by working on the improvement of consulting skills, management skills, organisational development and conflict management skills. Thus, HRD actively ensures its own capability for performing an assisting and consulting role with regard to management and employee learning.

The activities deployed by the HRD department in order to realise new roles and changed policy are increasingly characterised by supporting committed and selfregulated learning such as the introduction of learning groups for managers (see Box 7.2). An increased use of modern learning methods such as computer based training and the development of on-the-job learning facilities are further examples of new HRD activities. With regard to the content of training, key issues include the promotion of consulting competence in an intercultural context, networking competence, and process competence. Other key factors are team building and changing the corporate culture.

Sony Germany – marketing, sales and service organisation

The company

Facts and figures

Sony is a world-wide manufacturer of electronic devices. Sony Germany, however, focuses not on production but on marketing, sales and services for Sony products in

Box 7.2 Executive development programme at GTZ

GTZ has implemented an executive development programme (EDP) to support the development toward a learning organisation. It aims to help managers develop their own role, self-image and personal identity by means of a process of systematic reflection on their own values, beliefs and attitudes in a strategic-oriented manner. By doing so, GTZ among other things hopes that its managers will actively contribute to the development and consolidation of a positive corporate culture (flexible, open, learning-oriented etc.). The training programme consists of a mixture of:

- training programme (12.5 days): mainly seminars and workshops;
- exercises (15 days): on- and off-the-job practice;
- process supporting action (3 days): learning groups and individual development talks at regular intervals during the entire programme, to support individual development by discussing individual questions and providing feedback.

The outcome is not only a set of new skills, insights and tools, but also individual training and learning plans for all managers.

While the initiative for the programme lies with top management, the HRD department manages the entire programme. Top management is responsible for agreeing on and implementing the learning plan, and for ensuring that the participant is available to attend the programme.

Executive development programs have been established as a successful tool for integrating organisational performance improvement and individual strategically focused learning. As the HRD director remarks:

These EDP teams have incredibly established themselves within the enterprise. Very often, if the top management urgently seeks somebody to deal with a specific issue, then they say: lets give the issue to an EDP team. That's happening nearly automatically. That means the EDP teams are accepted as a kind of internal consultants.

Germany. Activities in this sector are characterised by a high level of customer orientation and knowledge intensity. In Germany, Sony employs about 1,100 people.

The centralised 'Personnel Development Competence Centre' is part of the Human Resources Department. The HR department employs twenty people, four of whom work for the Competence Centre. The HR department focuses on both personnel and organisational development.

Business strategy and change processes

As with the other German organisations, Sony Germany is facing a strong competitive market. To respond to this challenge, the strategy of increasing the customer orientation is of critical importance. In addition, innovation of new technologies and products, diversification, strategic alliances and networking are of high significance for increasing the company's competitiveness.

Sony's concept of a learning organisation refers to an organisation that considers change as a continuous process and that is characterised by open communication channels, free availability of information and exchanging experiences. Employees are expected to recognise mistakes and problems and to continuously focus on improvements and innovations. Sony strives to ensure unhindered communication and to create a learning culture.

HRD in Sony Germany

People involved in HRD

The main objective of the Personnel Development Competence Centre is to provide impulses for change, to initiate processes and activities and to offer new concepts in order to support development of a learning culture. It defines itself as a:

> consulting institution, supporter of knowledge and identifier of problems. The new function of the HRD department is defined as a consultative service institution for organisational learning issues.
>
> (Source: Sony internal documents)

In this respect, new behaviour of HRD practitioners is required. The HRD department strives to operate as a partner for all organisational development processes. The Competence Centre tries to build a co-operative relationship with its internal customers. Line managers are considered to be primarily responsible for formulating training needs, specifying development goals, organising training activities on-thejob and coaching. Employees are responsible for defining their own training needs, and, in co-operation with their line manager and HRD professionals, individual training plans and training methods are developed.

HRD objectives

The creation of intensive internal customer relations, supporting a customer orientation of the entire company, supporting a learning-oriented corporate culture and open communication, as well as the development of knowledge exchange networks within the organisation, are important goals of the HRD department.

HRD strategies

The new HRD policy ensured that training activities are closely linked to corporate objectives and market developments. In line with the aim of creating strong customer relations, the department tries to segment HRD activities by referring to specific targets and differentiated target groups. As a result, the number of standardised training activities is declining in favour of more individual and target group-related training activities. Also the content of training activities is constantly changing. Besides direct training activities, the focus is also placed on coaching activities, the implementation

Box 7.3 Learning networks at Sony

Sony has introduced learning network teams in which executives and employees have the opportunity to learn in a self-organised way. The system is aimed at high-potential employees. An important aim is to improve the infrastructure for learning e.g. by supporting on-the-job and informal learning activities and by giving employees more responsibilities for their own development process.

In forming learning network teams, it is ensured that the members of each team have at least one common job element (e.g. common project, common tasks, similar professional requirements). There are no formal command chain links within the teams. In a first meeting, participants receive information about the elements of their promotion plan and the idea of building learning networks. In a further two and a half to three day 'kick-off' workshop, the group receives training in team-building activities and providing constructive feedback. After that, the team meets on a regular (mostly monthly) basis. Initially, trainers exert much control over these sessions, but they help the team to take over their function step-by-step, until at the end the team works in a self-responsible and self-organised fashion.

The team decides:

- when and how often they meet;
- which topics, problems and issues they want to discuss;
- for which topics they need external or internal specialists. It also invites specialists to explore certain topics if necessary. Voluntarily, the teams report to the HRD department on learning experiences, stages in the evolution and recognised problems. The method closely resembles action learning.

The main targets of learning network teams can be divided in three groups:

- 'operational targets', such as solving current and individual issues and conflicts, reports about important overlapping issues in the enterprise, improvement proposals etc.;
- 'learning targets', such as development of social and technical competence;
- 'team targets', such as mutual motivation of team members, coaching and supervision to exchange experience, trust and mutual completion.

The role of HRD professionals is process-initiating. HRD professionals developed the concept of learning networks and established it. Furthermore, HRD professionals conceptualise and organise the individual learning networks, especially in terms of selection of participants and the kick-off-meeting. Later on, HRD professionals are not involved in the self-organised learning process. Nevertheless, they offer supportive and consulting services which participants can request whenever the learning network is faced with any kind of problem.

There exists a high acceptance of the learning network amongst participants since they feel positively influenced by the group. However, the success of this initiative is particularly based on openness and trust within the group developed over time, the heterogeneity of various qualifications, functions and contacts, and the knowledge base shared between the participants who analyse organisational and/or personal problems.

of a corporate information system, the promotion of a learning-oriented culture and establishing learning networks (see Box 7.3).

Factors influencing HRD's role and how HRD deals with them

The preceding sections have described the visions and strategies of the four case study organisations with regard to becoming a learning organisation, as well as HRD's role in this process. This section describes factors which affect the achievement (or lack of achievement) of the envisioned role of the HRD department. Inhibiting factors, facilitating factors and strategies to overcome constraints are briefly discussed.

Inhibiting factors

All German case study organisations were found to be facing barriers in the change process towards a learning (oriented) organisation. Table 7.1 lists the most significant ones.

   The table shows that important negative forces mentioned by all four organisations are insufficient knowledge sharing and lack of time, since operational activities are given more importance than knowledge management and organisational learning activities. The first factor, in particular, reflects the notion that availability of new knowledge, experiences or external information is considered to be very important, but not self-evident, for becoming a learning organisation.

   Another inhibiting factor is a lack of motivation from employees as well as managers (Bosch Siemens, AgrEvo, GTZ). For employees, fear of newness and a lot of changing activities at the same time are important reasons for lacking motivation. Weak engagement and reorientation problems are inhibiting factors for managers. It is important to note that HRD departments in all case organisations expect an active role both of management and employees toward learning. HRD departments try to support them

Table 7.1 Inhibiting factors – German case study organisations

Inhibiting factors	BSH	AgrEvo	GTZ	Sony
Insufficient knowledge sharing	•	•	•	•
Other priorities (time pressure, lack of time)	•	•	•	•
Lack of motivation from employees (fear of newness, lack of reward in salary or promotion)	•	•	•	
Lack of motivation from management (don't promote or support employee learning)	•	•	•	
Lack of information on the need for learning	•	•		•
Lack of information on opportunities for learning		•	•	
Insufficient learning culture	•	•		•
Lack of evaluation of learning processes	•	•		•

in this respect. It is crucial that the motivation of both occupational groups grows to successfully achieve this division of tasks.

Other inhibiting factors are a lack of information for employees on the need for learning (Bosch Siemens, AgrEvo, Sony), a lack of information on learning opportunities (AgrEvo and GTZ), an insufficient learning culture (Bosch Siemens, AgrEvo and Sony) and a lack of evaluation activities of learning processes (Bosch Siemens, AgrEvo and Sony). These inhibiting factors may serve to explain the observed lack of motivation, and clarify the reason why promoting a learning culture (for example, by increasing employee awareness of organisational challenges) is one of the most important issues.

Conducive factors

On the other hand, a large number of factors that support the development towards a learning (oriented) organisation were pointed out. Table 7.2 gives an overview of the most important ones.

Most important positive factors seem to be informing employees on organisational developments and the need for learning in order to cope with competitive developments. This aligns with the demand for an active role of employees in making changes and in making learning plans. These factors are mentioned by all four organisations. A clear organisational strategy is also mentioned in some cases (Bosch Siemens and Sony). This is, of course, an important prerequisite for providing clear information on organisational developments to employees.

Factors associated with the organisational structure are a flexible organisation structure (Bosch Siemens, AgrEvo and GTZ) and new working methods that support informal learning on-the-job (AgrEvo, GTZ). Furthermore, managers who promote employee learning were considered to be a significant conducive factor (AgrEvo, GTZ).

Looking at the role of the HRD department, the existence of clear and concrete learning goals (Bosch Siemens and AgrEvo) and information on learning (Bosch Siemens, AgrEvo and GTZ) were pointed out as conducive factors.

Table 7.2 Conducive factors – German case study organisations

Conducive factors	BSH	AgrEvo	GTZ	Sony
Active participation of employees in own development process	•	•	•	•
Information on organisational developments and the need for employee learning	•	•	•	•
Clear corporate strategy and objectives	•			•
Flexible organisational structure	•	•	•	
Managers promoting employee learning		•	•	
New working methods (teamwork, learning networks)		•	•	
Information on learning in the organisation	•	•	•	
Transparency of learning goals	•	•		

Obviously, these positive factors have a clear relationship with the constraints. Whereas lack of motivation was an important inhibiting factor, creating motivation for learning by clarifying the organisational need for learning is a conducive factor. And lack of information on learning (due to lack of evaluation) and learning opportunities were also mentioned as inhibiting factors, while information and clear goals are mentioned as factors which support the development of the new HRD activities.

Summarising these observations, it can be concluded that general support for employees in taking an active role towards their own learning is very important. This support can be provided in different ways; providing information on learning opportunities, providing insight to the (organisational) need for learning, support by management and work methods which support informal learning (such as working in teams).

Coping strategies

To reduce inhibiting factors and to emphasise positive factors, the HRD departments follow different strategies. Many of these have already been discussed in the case descriptions (sections on HRD strategies). An important additional strategy to promote employee learning seems to be the application of new selection criteria such as 'readiness for change' for recruitment of employees. This can be seen as a way to improve workforce motivation for learning. Also, informing employees on learning needs and learning opportunities was named as an important strategy directed at the same objective.

Summary and conclusions

Organisational context

Four German case study organisations were discussed: Bosch Siemens Hausgeräte, AgrEvo, GTZ and Sony Germany. Table 7.3 provides a short overview of the selected organisations' main characteristics, including sector, number of employees, HRD function and the number of HRD practitioners.

All German case study organisations have to deal with highly competitive markets and quickly changing client needs. Individual and organisational learning are considered to be key competitive factors in order to maintain customer focus, improve flexibility and/or enhance innovations in the investigated organisations.

The four organisations stress different elements in their efforts to improve organisational learning capacity. BSH focuses on permanently improving and innovating processes and activities; AgrEvo on systematically identifying and generating new knowledge, especially networking and strategic alliances; GTZ on networking in a flexible organisational structure and Sony on establishing an open communication and learning culture.

In order to become a learning organisation, each of the organisations pursues different issues and strategies. The common core is that they all serve to activate and support learning processes of employees. Three of the four case organisations (Bosch

Table 7.3 Overview of German case study organisations

Company's name and sector	Number of employees	HRD
Bosch Siemens Hausgeräte, producer of domestic and household appliances	14,500	• Centralised department • 7 employees
AgrEvo, crop production company	9,000 worldwide	• Centralised department • 6 employees
GTZ, service enterprise for development cooperation with worldwide operations	Abroad: 1,600 Germany: 1,300	• Centralised department • 23 employees
Sony Germany, sales and marketing for Sony's electronic products in Germany	1,100	• Centralised human resources department including the Personnel Development Competence Centre • Department human resources: 20 employees • Competence centre: 4 employees

Siemens, AgrEvo and GTZ) explicitly mentioned the application of IT networks as an element in the change process. Sony pointed out that its communication systems are primarily IT based. So it seems that using technology to share information is an important tool for all case organisations.

Envisioned role of HRD

With regard to the distribution of HRD tasks, all four HRD departments consider line management to be responsible for traditional HRD activities. Management is expected to fulfil tasks such as the identification of training needs, making development plans, and coaching their personnel. Employees are expected to fulfil an active role towards their own development, and to co-operate with management in drawing up development plans. The role of the HRD department is changing towards a more supportive and consulting role.

The HRD departments deliberately aim to support the realisation corporate strategies – in general, such as Bosch Siemens, or with regard to a specific organisational strategy, such as Sony – and the development of a learning culture. Promoting employee development (Bosch Siemens, AgrEvo, GTZ) and supporting knowledge management (AgrEvo, Sony) are important objectives, as well. Both are to be considered as important elements in supporting organisations to become a learning organisation.

Strategies adopted to realise HRD's new role

In order to realise their new role and their primary objectives, the HRD departments stress the link between HRD strategies and corporate objectives and organisational practices. They strive to become competent partners that have to redefine and restructure their traditional self-conception as training administrators, by customer-segmentation (Sony) or by reorganisation of the HRD department (AgrEvo), for example. These measures also serve to integrate HRD activities with business processes.

A second important strategy is the use of new learning methods to support (informal) learning and knowledge exchange (most notably in GTZ and Sony). Delivering standardised training becomes less important, and this is outsourced to an increasing degree. Interestingly, only one organisation (GTZ) explicitly mentioned a need for professionalisation of its HRD practitioners in order to fulfil the role of consultant adequately. Nevertheless, it is to be expected that the HRD departments in the other cases experience similar needs.

An interesting observation to note is that none of the organisations has generated a systematic evaluation of HRD activities, that can serve to provide transparency concerning the value added of the HRD department in creating opportunities for learning. This is especially questionable with regard to the reputation HRD functions often have in their respective organisations. They are often seen as cost-intensive administrative departments, and as not providing a major contribution to organisational value-creation processes.

Influencing factors

Important factors hindering the HRD departments in realising their envisioned role are insufficient knowledge sharing and a lack of time, since operational activities are more important than knowledge management and organisational learning activities. Other inhibiting factors mentioned are a lack of motivation from employees as well as managers, a lack of information for employees on the need for learning and on learning opportunities in the organisation as well as an insufficient learning culture and a lack of evaluation activities of learning processes.

As expected, conducive factors have a clear relationship with the inhibiting factors. Whereas lack of motivation was an important inhibiting factor, creating motivation for learning by clarifying the organisational need for learning was pointed out to be a conducive factor. And lack of information on learning, evaluation, and learning opportunities was also mentioned as an inhibiting factor, while information and clear goals are mentioned as factors which support the development of organisational learning processes.

To reduce inhibiting factors and to emphasise conducive factors, the HRD departments follow different strategies. Interesting to note here are the application of new selection criteria such as 'readiness for change' for recruitment of employees and informing employees on learning needs and learning opportunities. Both strategies serve to enhance the motivation for learning of the workforce.

To summarise, HRD departments in the investigated German case study organisations are already established partners of top and line management and of employees for triggering organisational and personnel development processes. However, all respondents noted that they are just at the beginning of the change process shifting their traditional self-concept of delivering a rather standardised and demand-driven training catalogue towards facilitation, supporting and consulting learning and knowledge management initiatives throughout the entire organisation.

8   Cases from Italy

Massimo Tomassini and Andrea Cavrini

This chapter describes the results for the case study research in Italy. Four organisations were studied: the food producer Barilla, the chemical pharmaceuticals producer Bayer, the cosmetics manufacturer Lever and the barcode manufacturer Datalogic.

The first four sections contain full case descriptions (based on data from 1998), including for each case:

- background information on the organisation, such as core businesses, number of employees, and current (learning-oriented) strategies;
- vision of the HRD professionals on their (new) roles in the learning (oriented) organisation,;
- strategies they employ to realise these roles.

The next section describes factors that (negatively or positively) influence the achievement of these envisioned roles. General conclusions and a summary are provided in the final section.

Barilla – food producer

The company

Facts and figures

Barilla is a food product group, which manufactures, among other things, pasta and bakery products. The number of employees, including those in the subsidiaries, is about 7,500. The general organisational structure is very flat, organised into only five levels, from CEO to the lowest-level workers.

Five senior practitioners operate in the 'organisational and professional development' (OPD) unit: this unit and four other professionals deal with training, selection, organisational development and remuneration, each of them supported by small groups of assistants.

Business strategy

The Barilla Group is currently in a phase of intense globalisation, with two new plants to be opened in the US. The manufacturing of its traditional products is based on advanced technological processes and has to be continuously supported by significant investments in R&D, marketing and communication. Tradition and innovation are constantly in balance in Barilla, due both to its history and product range and to its dynamic evolution and performances. 'People come first' is Pietro Barilla's oftenquoted maxim. Barilla was an outstanding character of the post-war Italian capitalism who expanded the firm to its present size and whose heirs have led the company since 1993. This general orientation towards human resources creates a favourable background for new HRD policies, initiated to support a new phase of company expansion that is still developing at the time of writing.

In the present phase the company's main strategic objective is a constant growth of its competitive advantage based on its own excellent competence resources. At the same time Barilla wants to achieve continuous improvements in manufacturing in order to assure improvement in product quality while pursuing the highest efficiency in production processes.

Change processes

The company's learning orientation is linked to two specific types of HRD policies: competence development policies and the implementation of self directed work teams.

Competence development policies are assumed to be a fundamental part of the company strategy. Competencies are considered crucial resources insofar as they are, according to the definition of one of the interviewees:

> bodies of knowledge and skills, which are critical in the processes of value generation. They have to be constantly monitored and developed, understanding how tacit knowledge at different levels can be transformed in explicit and manageable knowledge, closely related to the company value chain.

Policies with regard to implementation of *self-designing working teams* in manufacturing areas are implemented by line managers with the assistance from the organisational development unit. These policies are carried out from the perspective of the diffusion of a process orientation. As another interviewee explained:

> Processes exist in the company also if we do not care about them. The problem is to pay attention to them and to develop them in order to increase overall competition capabilities of the company in parallel to the specific learning abilities of its members. The results can be of a very high level and bring about the apparent paradox of combining the continuous improvement of the factory activities and the breakthroughs in the overall position of the firm in the market.

HRD in Barilla

HRD objectives and people involved in HRD

The HRD department has a complex structure, in which different departments play specific roles. The most important role from the point of view of the learning orientation of the firm is played by a small unit called 'organisational and professional development' (OPD) which is in charge of both HRD strategy design and the creation of HRD tools and techniques. The role of OPD is perceived within the company as one of a unit which has to provide both overall visions of change objectives and effective operational tools to the staff and line areas.

The first main area of tasks and responsibilities of HRD professionals and managers is *competencies monitoring*. This is carried out within a conceptual framework aimed at describing the 'logical process' of competence contribution to the value chain (value as perceived by final consumers).

The second main area of tasks and responsibilities of HRD employees and managers is *training*. Training activities are aimed at bridging the gap between the company needs and the present employee's competence levels. 'Internal specialists', managers and professionals, develop most of these activities; the hypothesis is that 'nobody is better in understanding and explaining how processes and their components work than the people who are directly involved'.

New tasks and responsibilities have recently been undertaken in the field of *competencies assessment and evaluation* for remuneration purposes. This area of activities has been expanded from the perspective of linking together learning and tangible rewards for learning results. The latter are conceived independently from performance, that is from productivity results; this is a new aspect that should mobilise people's acceptance and support for new values which HRD wants to introduce in the company's organisational culture. For this purpose specific tasks and responsibilities have been given to line managers within their role of directly administering many of the tools set up by OPD. An interesting trend concerns the attribution of such responsibilities to the employees themselves; for instance, the same logical structure of tools implemented for self-assessment require several steps of individual reflection.

HRD policy linked to competence management is included in a specific company policy, which is approved and sponsored by top management. The policy system, including the diagnosis/evaluation steps as well as training interventions, is planned on a three-year scale. A new phase of competencies development has been planned based on evaluation criteria for competencies assumed as value assets. Specific proxies will be identified in relation to the contribution of individuals to the company value chain. The implementation and development of self designing work teams is also a main issue in HRD policy.

HRD strategies

Concerning specific HRD interventions it can be said that these interventions represent concrete translations of vision, strategies, policy and planning.

Competence monitoring interventions (in terms of diagnosis of the company needs and of the individual employees alignment) are divided into two main areas:

- technical competencies, related to abilities in specific product/process development segments;
- organisational behaviours, in their turn divided into general and role-specific behaviours.

Competencies and behaviours are taken into account in relation to four main areas representing the company distinctiveness/excellence; clients, brand, technological portfolio (in particular for product technologies), supply chain (from purchase to manufacturing and distribution).

Training is the second main area of HRD interventions. Internal training is the prevailing approach. Most of the training interventions are carried out by in-house specialists (technicians, line managers) in order to retain direct experience and to make explicit areas of knowledge which otherwise could remain only tacit. Therefore these kind of interventions, aimed at increasing direct learning, take place in working settings and not in classrooms.

The third main area of HRD interventions, concerning the competencies assessment and evaluation for remuneration purposes, represents a very sensitive issue in terms of adherence to organisational culture. In this area interventions are based on a mixed system allowing remuneration to both productive performance (compared to pre-defined objectives and rewarded also at a collective level, especially in manufacturing areas) and competencies and organisational behaviours (expressing individual's excellence and therefore rewarded only at the individual level).

The diffusion of self-designing work teams in manufacturing takes place by specific interventions aimed at reinforcing the already acquired results and by presenting them to different areas whose line managers decide to start their transformation. The interventions are of a step-by-step kind: OPD actively supports the specific needs managers have (e.g. a training programme). General guidelines have been established for interventions, based on key elements such as:

- team-working instead of individual positions;
- 'globalised jobs' (enlarged jobs inside a general re-definition of professional families);
- emphasis on work self-design;
- knowledge enlargement/integration;
- team autonomy and entrepreneurship;
- process continuous improvement.

With regard to HRD evaluation activities, it was also found that for competence development, criteria are of a medium-term kind, referring to the overall company trends. No specific evidence is available about on-going policies and activities, as they have been implemented only recently. A new phase of competence development has been planned based on evaluation criteria for competencies assumed as value assets.

Specific proxies will in the coming years be identified in relation to the contribution of individuals to the company value chain.

Bayer – chemicals manufacturer

The company

Facts and figures

Bayer is the Italian subsidiary of the German chemical-pharmaceutical group of the same name and operates in a variety of fields (health, polymer technology, special chemical products, information technologies, etc.). Bayer has been established in Italy since 1899, and its main mission is growth, based on the manufacturing of top-quality products, using methods compatible with environment protection.

Bayer employs 2,400 people, about one third of whom work in the headquarters in divisional staff and in central departments, about another third in the company's two factories and a last third are freelance (scientific and technical-commercial 'consultants'). The predominant organisation of work is typical of continuous-flow chemical processes. Given the high quality of the output, the staff working in the processes are very highly qualified (on average, all the workers hold an upper secondary school certificate).

The HRD department is lead by a general manager (who has one person on staff in charge of compensations). The department is divided into four different internal sections:

- administration activities (payroll, etc.): fourteen employees and a manager;
- industrial relations (directly supervise relations with trade unions and others): four professionals and a manager;
- recruitment and development : six professionals including the area manager;
- personnel counselling: seven professionals (including the area manager).

The last two sections carry out HRD activities.

Business strategy

Within its group, Bayer operates in a sector of increasing globalisation and stronger relationships both within the group and with clients (mass market and chemical user companies), representing more and more complex demands.

The learning-oriented organisation philosophy is prompted by the growing need to integrate functions and by the pressure towards greater communication and sharing between different areas within common company strategies and visions.

Learning is viewed in terms of greater circulation of cultural values and of knowledge and competencies inside a company with marked internal diversification. The diversification has several roots; organisational (because there are different lines of reporting between divisions and departments, mingling Bayer's internal relationships and those with the parent company in Germany) as well as technical and cultural (because different forms of specialisation and cultures coexist in the company as a result of the multitude of production lines). In this context, learning is considered a strategic factor for the development of a company that achieves excellent results but which intends to strengthen its internal integration, in order to improve its ability to respond to the needs of different clients.

Change processes

The learning-oriented organisation philosophy involves promoting inter-division learning along three basic lines: a profound sharing of the company mission, the preparation of plans and projects with a strong learning content, and the development of individual competencies related to the company as a whole and not just to single areas.

These competencies are defined by the company mission in terms of building efficient partnerships with external and internal clients based on shared objectives, opportunities and risks. Therefore competencies that need to be developed are technical and product-related skills in the company's success areas, and skills linked, on the one hand, to understanding the client's needs and the company's response potential and, on the other, to the effectiveness and flexibility in generating profitable responses.

These competencies are associated with managerial abilities related to *change management* (to keep pace with the market), *project management* (to carry out initiatives with the best value for time and money), *process management* (relating to the set of company processes), and *teamwork* (as a more general skill which supports the others).

HRD in Bayer

HRD objectives and people involved in HRD

The general approach is to standardise company interventions with regard to human resources. The vision of the role of the HRD department as a whole, is formulated in terms of promoting a *corporate* approach to development and learning. The department tends to develop this role not by disseminating solutions from above but by gathering opinions and practices spread throughout the various segments of the company. This bottom up approach is demonstrated by the process which, in recent years, has led to the shared definition of the mission.

The main vision basically leads to an integrated model of people development, which is capable of fulfilling two company needs:

- *management of cultural change*, which seeks to affect the values underlying the operation of the company;
- *development of distinct competencies*, linked to an identification of the key resources for the company and evaluation of roles and potential.

The HRD 'recruitment and development' section is in charge of personnel evaluation and drafting of corporate-level projects to be developed in collaboration with the divisions and central departments concerned. The section is, in practice, responsible for defining the vision of the HRD department, preparing interventions and checking them.

The people working in the 'personnel counselling' section are responsible for human resources at a decentralised level of production divisions. This involves a continuous relationship with line managers and with the HRD practitioners working in line with industrial relations roles. The main activities of this section are supporting management of the divisions and giving individualised counselling to their members.

Box 8.1 Networking at Bayer

With the use of networking Bayer aims to improve communication between employees and optimise the speed and quality of solutions to problems.

Networking means using communication between people to pool knowledge and information which helps to optimise the speed and quality of solutions to problems. To improve communication a database was installed, a tool which allows people to pool and catalogue experiences and send requests for help to other colleagues, receiving immediate replies.

A training day was planned on the subjects of communications and willingness to exchange, involving theoretical talks alternating with moments of experimentation. After the training a monitoring and collection phase started. With the use of a questionnaire some first impressions, suggestions and information on the use of the tool were collected. The results were very positive. The last step, partly to strengthen team spirit and give the correspondents another opportunity to meet, was to organise a cocktail party.

At the moment six network groups are present at Bayer:

1 'Commercial correspondents' (60 people) aims at creating models, methods and tools for learning distinctive competencies.
2 'Navigators of change' (31 people) aims at fostering dissemination, sharing and realisation of the company mission.
3 'The antennas' (20 people) aims at capturing what is happening in single situations and transmitting this news.
4 'Commercial experts' (25 people) aims at sharing important experiences in the use of technical products acquired with customers and to ask for contributions if there are technical problems to be solved.
5 'People satisfaction' (22 people) aims at analysing the climate and motivation of people in Bayer and launching improvement actions.
6 'Customer satisfaction' (22 people) aims at working on a infrastructure for the collection and analysis of data on customer satisfaction and launching action plans.

The role of the HRD department is both a practical and supportive one. The practical role refers to organising the training activities, the supportive role to the monitoring phase and the continuation of the network groups.

HRD policies are drawn up as a result of a decision-making process in which the HRD manager and the senior personnel advisors of the parent company are directly involved.

An annual budgeting plan is drawn up according to training periods, job rotation, people's development plans and other relevant factors. Also the development of a long-term planning is being carried out, indicating the strategic projects for the department.

HRD strategies

The main interventions recently undertaken or presently being carried out by the HRD areas 'recruitment and development' and 'personnel counselling' follow three main lines:

- First, training actions and broader interventions (including those carried out in collaboration with the 'communication and internal relations' department) concerning the competencies, abilities and values applied at overall corporate level. Examples of training interventions are the 'culture project', which focuses on developing a corporate culture, 'the navigators of change project' for management, which focus on managing the corporate culture change process, training courses focusing on client orientation and dissemination of best practices/ success stories (see Box 8.1).
- Second, interventions dedicated to single division-related businesses to develop the competencies needed to achieve their specific results. Examples are supporting job-rotation, specific skills training, counselling, coaching.
- Third, evaluation interventions: examples of evaluation interventions are methods for evaluation of potential and performance.

Lever – cosmetics manufacturer

The company

Facts and figures

The well-known international Unilever group, born in 1930 by the merger of Lever Brothers (UK) and Margarine Unie (The Netherlands), operates in more than ninety countries, employing around 300,000 people. Unilever Italia is the holding company that groups the Italian operating companies, belonging to different business groups. The case study focuses on Lever (home care products), which employs about 1200 employees and especially on its location in Casalpusterlengo (near Milan), a production site with about 700 employees. A range of important activities concerning human resource development are undertaken at the level of the national holding company and the case study will also take this into consideration.

The HRD department is split up in a centralised department within the national unit and a decentralised department within the operating companies. The centralised

104 *Massimo Tomassini and Andrea Cabrini* HRD department of Unilever Italia is part of the training department and employs two managers and three HRD professionals. The decentralised HRD department of Lever employs four managers and six HRD professionals.

Business strategy

A range of external factors – high competitive pressure, fast technological changes, short life-cycle of the products, progressive reduction in price/margin – can be pointed out as the reason for becoming a learning organisation. In mature markets, competition is a matter of resource allocation, market shares and control of costs. This requires a focusing process which implies a very clear development direction, which has to be defined by the top management and communicated to, and shared with, the employees. *Focusing* is the key word within Lever and, more generally, Unilever Italia.

Change processes

The main change which has occurred is the adoption in Lever of the well-known EFQM model as a reference for the assessment and the improvement of internal processes. More generally, activity and process based management has taken place, rather than the more conventional functional orientation.

HRD in Lever

HRD objectives and people involved in HRD

The main objective of the HRD department of Lever is to assist the company in developing its business. This broad definition shows a progressive 'close to the business' philosophy of the function. Objectives are not self-related and, in many cases, it is difficult to clearly separate the objectives of HRD from those of other departments.

Managers' responsibility with regard to HRD and HRD-related tasks has increased. For example, whereas the HRD department previously was called in on day-to-day problems concerning industrial relations, nowadays line and middle managers take care of such problems themselves.

The strategy related to HRD organisation is one of progressive decentralisation. This process led to a double structure: the HRD department is part of the national holding company, providing a range of services to the operating companies. What is interesting here is that HRD within the national holding company has the responsibility for organisational development. Individual learning is therefore more naturally linked to organisational change. However, decentralisation pushes the transfer of responsibility with respect to selection, compensation, training and organisational development to the HRD staff *within* the operating companies. The national holding company, thanks to the high level of competence of the central staff, now plays a consultative and orientation role.

HRD strategies

The main areas of activity of HRD are:

- *industrial relations* – day-by-day dialogue is more important now than once-in-a- year negotiation. Furthermore, daily industrial relations are more and more managed within the organisational units, also in order to improve their flexibility. HRD's role in this is a supportive one;
- *services* – recruitment, compensation, training, organisational development, which have increased their importance and represent the core. The policy here is to enhance the bottom-up approach and initiative, although some top-down initiatives are implemented. A wide range of resources is involved in the provision of these services; for example, a new open learning centre is now operational, with a wide range of facilities and tools. Professional skills are developed via open learning through tailor-made learning packages;
- *research and development* – an internal activity of the HRD department (both at national and company level), related to the review and improvement of the current practices, but even more to the free dialogue with the rest of the organisation in order to recognise new needs and collect/develop new ideas for action.

Datalogic – bar-code equipment manufacturer

The company

Facts and figures

Datalogic is a bar-code equipment manufacturing firm and at the moment the European leader in manufacturing of products and systems for the automatic identification data collection (AIDC) sector. It employs 480 people.

The HRD department is a relatively new department within Datalogic, it was established in 1993. The department is formed of a small group of professionals whose main tasks are compensation, recruitment, training and organisational development.

Business strategy

Datalogic is a rapidly-growing organisation in a very turbulent environment with a range of opportunities and threats. For example, Datalogic now faces a need to focus on its core business, to reach all the new potential markets, to create an integrated range of products, to assure all the subsequent organisational conditions, etc. After a period of natural and spontaneous development, which usually characterises the pioneering phase, the organisation has now more strictly defined its mission and positioning – *a bar-code equipment manufacturing firm* – and is currently engaged in reshaping its boundaries. This implies outsourcing part of the sales force and a worldwide acquisition policy of small manufacturers in the same sector.

Change processes

Datalogic – a well-organised, well-structured, well-managed organisation – needs to develop a systematic approach to its organising and managing processes, together with all the related competencies and skills. Datalogic wants to change from a spontaneous learning-oriented organisation to an explicit and intentional learning-oriented organisation. Learning is a new key word, primarily for main decision makers and, then, for the other managers and employees. With respect to HRD, the challenge is to reshape the business, but maintaining the conditions that along the years led the organisation becoming a knowledge creating company, with a strong technological leadership.

HRD in Datalogic

HRD objectives and people involved in HRD

The main objective of the HRD function is:

> to guarantee the appropriate manpower, both in quantitative and qualitative terms, according to the organisational needs related to the business.
>
> (Source: Datalogic internal documents)

HRD's objectives (and their daily deployment) are strictly business-related. This is seen as a necessary condition to ensure effectiveness and recognition of HRD.

Evaluation criteria, needed in order to examine whether goals are reached by the HRD department have moved from quantitative activity-related indicators (training days per employee) to qualitative objective-related indicators. As the HRD department has progressively achieved an active role, by recognising needs and proposing initiatives, internal clients' satisfaction has increased in importance.

It is difficult to identify a clear development strategy/policy for HRD. The level of functional specialisation is not very high, signifying a strong evolutionary trend in the role of the HRD department. This is also confirmed by non-bureaucratic and informal working mechanisms. However, a progressive specialisation can be recognised with respect to the three main activity areas: training, selection and compensations. Organisational development is not explicitly recognised but many 'training' initiatives could in fact be better described as 'organisational development' and 'learning' activities.

In more general terms, an essential development strategy for the HRD Department is to increase line managers' sensitivity to HRD issues, in order to enable them to assess their needs in this respect. This approach creates the most favourable conditions to facilitate the internal partnership. Therefore, in the management performance assessment programme specific attention is dedicated to managers' attitude and ability to recognise learning needs of the workforce and to support them in acquiring/developing their knowledge and skills.

A clear HRD intervention is the facilitation of training opportunities. Facilitation of all kinds of learning, implicitly linked to organisational development is considered as of strategic importance to the development of Datalogic. As a consequence, courses and other learning opportunities, particularly addressed to the top and middle management, are designed and implemented in-house, with the contribution of few external experts and consultants. The strategic relevance also supports the establishment of long-term co-operation with these experts and consultants, stimulating an in-depth reciprocal exchange of information and experience.

Other important HRD interventions are, for example, supporting knowledge management and competence management. It was found that the HRD Department plays a major role in 'distributing' or 'spreading' knowledge, paying particular attention to the management level. More widely, however, HRD is an internal observer of the organisational way of functioning, recognising organisational development and learning needs.

It can be said about competence management that the market globalisation which is currently affecting the bar-code industry implies that competition occurs at every level and function of the enterprise. The HRD department is working on a integration of the technological competence leadership with a significant competence development system.

Factors influencing HRD's role and how HRD deals with them

The preceding sections described the visions and strategies of the four case study organisations with regard to becoming a learning organisation, as well as HRD's role in this process. This section describes factors which affect the achievement (or lack of achievement) of the envisioned role of the HRD department. Inhibiting factors, facilitating factors and strategies to overcome constraints are briefly discussed.

Inhibiting factors

All the Italian case study organisations were found to be facing some inhibiting factors in the change process towards a learning (oriented) organisation. Table 8.1 lists the most significant ones.

For most cases it can be said that lack of a learning culture is the most important inhibiting factor (Barilla, Bayer and Datalogic). For Datalogic the situation is a bit complicated. Datalogic is a spontaneous learning-oriented organisation with a very

Table 8.1 Inhibiting factors – Italian case study organisations

Inhibiting factors	Barilla	Bayer	Lever	Datalogic
Insufficient learning culture	•	•		•
Lack of motivation and support from management	•	•	•	
Lack of motivation and responsibility for learning from employees	•	•		
Lack of time and money			•	•

strong learning attitude and culture with regard to its professional domain. What is new for them is facing learning issues explicitly. Datalogic's learning culture is rather good but implicit. This has a double effect: on the one hand, it facilitates the initiatives of HRD since there is no bureaucratic, resistance-to-change culture. On the other hand it may create some difficulties since some people, particularly at the employee level in R&D or application design departments, can resist explicit and external initiatives, assuming a 'learning self-sufficiency' of the departments they belong to.

For two cases, Barilla and Bayer, it was found that a lack of motivation from employees played a role. This factor is strongly related to a lack of a learning culture. For example, it was found that one of the implicitly shared values at Barilla was 'being good at work and keeping personal knowledge as a private asset'. This can be considered as a typical theory-in-use not to be openly communicated but that everybody understands as the basis of several organisational practices concerning co-operation at work and career advances. This seem to be rooted in traditional ways of behaving especially among senior managers. On the bright side, organisational culture at Barilla is changing fast. The awareness of competitive conditions facilitates increasing acceptance of the competencies approach and related policies; more and more people at different levels understand that traditional values must be evolved through a collective effort, facilitating the establishment of new ways of working, getting satisfaction from work, clarifying career paths and assessment criteria, etc.

A lack of motivation from management to engage in HRD tasks, as experienced by Barilla, Bayer and Lever also is related to a lack of learning culture. To provide an example: for the HRD department of Bayer the lack of motivation from managers came mainly from a traditional autonomy of the divisions, not only in organisational terms but cultural as well. Division managers put up resistance when they must give up their best resources for other types of experience within the context of job-rotation programmes.

A more practical constraint, reported by Lever and Datalogic, is a lack of time and money.

Conducive factors

A large number of factors that support the development towards a learning (oriented) organisation were found. Table 8.2 gives an overview of the most important ones.

Positive first results of HRD initiatives in Lever and Datalogic, and clear communication on HRD's purposes and intentions in Barilla, Bayer and Lever is found to positively influence the change process. In general it helps if HRD has a positive image. For Lever, for example, it was found that HRD's high reputation, both internal and external, helped the HRD department realise its new role. This reputation has been developed over many years and has to be recognised as the HRD capital, together with the high level of competence of the staff. The adopted 'close-to-the-business' policy has contributed to that reputation.

Whereas lack of motivation of management was an inhibiting factor for three organisations, active involvement of this group (also) serves as a conducive factor in Barilla and Datalogic. To give an example, Barilla's top management unambiguously

Table 8.2 Conducive factors – Italian case study organisations

Conducive factors	Barilla	Bayer	Lever	Datalogic
Active involvement of management	•			•
Positive first results of new HRD initiatives			•	•
Clear HRD communication	•	•	•	
Innovation-oriented culture		•		•

supports new HRD policies that have been included in the long-term corporate strategy. This reinforces HRD's position inside the organisation and adds credibility to its policies, and it is also assumed that professional capabilities of the new generation of HRD practitioners are widely recognised from the top of the company to the bottom.

The last facilitating factor is a cultural one. A positive attitude towards innovation and change which is embedded in the organisational culture and climate will help the change process, as HRD professionals in Bayer and Datalogic have experienced (just as resistance to change may stifle it).

Coping strategies

Communication and a flexible attitude seem to be key strategies for the Italian case study organisations to deal with inhibiting factors and capitalise upon conducive ones. For Barilla it can be said that overall communication strategies and closer links with line managers were key elements in coping with new exigencies. HRD's vision is continuously adjusted in relation to emerging realities. Inhibiting factors have to be assumed as challenges for improving the HRD practitioners performance. For instance, the adoption of more direct inquiry methods about competencies facilitated the relationships with managers, and indirectly with employees.

Bayer' s HRD department tackles inhibiting factors with a continuously updated supply of initiatives. The main lever is the involvement of middle management in activities, who have their own valence in terms of training, communication, individual and group development.

The coping strategy of Lever's HRD department is somehow embedded in its very flexible, non-bureaucratic profile and, especially, in its focus on dialogue with the organisation.

Direct horizontal communication with line management is also the main coping strategy of Datalogic's HRD department. As is normal for middle-sized companies, new emergencies and exigencies are rather frequent; part of the success of the HRD department is due to its flexible approach and listening attitude, which lead to team-work between managers and HRD practitioners. In practical terms, the traditional distinction between line and staff is overcome.

Summary and conclusions

Organisational context

Four Italian organisations were discussed: Barilla, Bayer, Lever, and Datalogic.

Table 8.3 provides a brief overview of the charactierstics of the organisations such as sector, number of employees, HRD function and the number of HRD practitioners.

All four Italian organisations were found to be facing strong(er) competitive markets and/or fast(er) changing technologies. As a result improving and renewing their products, processes and services, and becoming more client-centered are important strategic issues. For Bayer and Datalogic it can also be said that they also have reasons internal to the company to want to pursue the concept of the learning organisation. Bayer wants to improve its internal communication and knowledge sharing, while Datalogic wants a more systematic approach for all organisational processes. It is interesting to note that Datalogic can already be considered as a spontaneous, implicit, learning organisation. It wants to make its learning more explicit. Focusing is the key word for Lever, which implies a clear development direction defined by top management and communicated to the employees.

Employee learning is considered an important means to realise these objectives, therefore creating possibilities for learning is of strategic relevance for these companies. In this respect, Barilla uses the statement: 'people come first'.

Strategies used to increase the learning orientation of these companies differ for all organisations. Barilla and Bayer use competence management, and Barilla and Lever have a process orientation in common.

Table 8.3 Overview of Italian case study organisations

Company and sector	Number of employees	HRD
Barilla, food industry	7,500	• Centralised organisational and professional development unit • 5 employees
Bayer, chemical-pharmaceutical industry	2,400	• A central HRD department divided into four internal sections: 1 Administration 2 Industrial relations 3 Recruitment and development 4 Personnel counselling • 33 employees
Lever, personal care products	1,200	• Central HRD department for Unilever Italia • Decentralised HRD department Lever • Unilever Italia: 5 employees • Lever: 10 employees
Datalogic, bar-code equipment and identification systems	480	• Small group of professionals • 2 employees

HRD's envisioned role

For all four Italian case study organisations it can be said that the HRD departments' tasks are broader than just providing training. They also fulfil tasks such as monitoring competencies, supporting teams, employees and managers and assessment and compensation of employees. Managers appear to have an active role in defining learning needs and other HRD tasks, but this was made explicit only at Barilla.

The main objective of the HRD departments in all four case study organisations is to support organisation's policy and development. For Barilla this is not very clear from the objectives stated, but it is clear when looking at the way the HRD department works; HRD professionals and managers work very closely together and it appears that HRD practices and policies are sometimes hard to distinguish from 'normal' working practices and policies. Supporting managers and employees in learning is an important objective for three of the four cases (Barilla, Bayer, Datalogic).

Strategies adopted to realise HRD's new role

Strategies often used by the Italian cases are competence monitoring (Barilla, Bayer, Datalogic), facilitating training courses and broader learning projects (all cases), supporting informal learning e.g. by coaching or job rotation, by focusing on learning at the workplace, by creating an open learning centre or by supporting management in stimulating learning at work. Particularly noteworthy is the practice at Datalogic, where managers are, among other things, assessed on their ability and attitude to support employees in learning. This seems a very systematic way of anchoring management's responsibility for HRD.

A very interesting approach is taken by the HRD department in Lever, which takes a very bottom-up approach. They have their own research and development activity which on the one hand stimulates the organisation to use new approaches, but on the other hand looks at existing practices, and spreads these across the organisation. All in all, it seems to be a very 'hands-off ' approach: the department does not only focus on 'offering' HRD practices, but whenever the company takes responsibility for HRD practices, this is supported by the department with specific expertise. This seems a very good way to ensure that responsibility for learning is not 'taken over' from line management and employees.

Influencing factors

For most cases it can be said that lack of a learning culture is the most important inhibiting factor for realising HRD's vision. Also lack of motivation and support from management, lack of motivation and responsibility for learning from employees and lack of time and money were mentioned as constraints.

Whereas lack of motivation of managers sometimes forms an inhibiting factor, active involvement of this group serves as an conducive factor. Positive results of new HRD initiatives, clear communication of the HRD departments and the existence of an innovation oriented culture were all also mentioned as positive forces.

Clear communication and a flexible attitude seem to be the key coping strategies for the Italian case organisations in order to deal with constraints and capitalise upon positive factors.

9 Cases from The Netherlands

Hilde ter Horst and Saskia Tjepkema

This chapter describes the results of the case study research in The Netherlands. Four organisations were studied: the chemicals producer Akzo Nobel Chemicals (BU Salt), the telecommunications company Ericsson, the IC-T service organisation BAC (the IT centre of the Dutch Internal Revenue Service) and the construction company KIBC.

The first four sections contain full case study descriptions (based on data from 1998), including for each case:

- background information on the organisation, such as core businesses, number of employees, and current (learning-oriented) strategies;
- vision of the HRD professionals on their (new) roles in the learning (oriented) organisation;
- strategies they employ to realise these roles.

The next section describes factors that (negatively or positively) influence the achievement of these envisioned roles. General conclusions and a summary are provided in the final section.

Akzo Nobel Chemicals – chemicals manufacturer (salt)

The company

Facts and figures

Akzo Nobel Chemicals BV (Akzo) is a multinational concern with operations in over 50 countries. Its core business is chemical production. The location in Hengelo is a production facility with four business units: Salt, Base Chemicals, Functional Chemicals, and Energy. The case study focuses on Business Unit Salt, which employs 240 people. Its primary process is salt and brine production and processing.

The HRD function is a shared function of the central HR department and the local HR department (one HR manager, one HRD practitioner) from BU Salt, together with line management.

Business strategy

Akzo Nobel was faced with drastic changes in its markets that made it necessary to improve the organisation's learning capacity. Akzo Nobel held a monopoly position for a long time, but saw this position disappear. Moreover, prices lowered and client demands changed. As a result, quality management and cost reductions became the main business targets. Continuous improvement is a prerequisite. In order to realise this, the company wanted to change its culture.

The concept of the learning organisation is seen as one in which employees have more responsibilities and which has a work environment and an organisational culture in which employees accept broader responsibilities. Training is an important element of this type of organisation, according to Akzo Nobel. As its location director stated:

> The concept of the learning organisation as such isn't used at Akzo Nobel. But it's all about giving employees more responsibility within the organisation. But if employees get more responsibility, they have to be able or willing to take this responsibility. They need to become flexible and able and this requires training.

The plant manager from BU Salt made a similar statement:

> Training and development is an important step: it gives confidence, it's a way of telling employees what you, as an organisation, are doing.

Change processes

In order to realise the strategic objectives and the desired culture change, several activities were undertaken. First, the structure of Akzo Nobel was changed, the organisation was split up into four business units (BUs) under the leadership of a plant manager.

Second, Akzo Nobel started a process of on-going change, in order to adapt to new situations but also to show employees that making changes is very important for organisational development and that employee development is crucial. For instance, the company implemented a new system of setting mission and targets. The company formulates a mission and at different levels, managers and employees have to derive department or team targets. Improving the communication within the company also received attention; much information is made available for everyone. Next to this, attention was paid to 'managing total quality' and the introduction of quality improvement teams. In quality improvement teams, for example, employees with diverse functions are working together on problems Akzo Nobel is facing or improvements that need to be made. In this way people can learn from each other and the organisation benefits from the outcomes of projects performed by the teams.

A third activity, seen as crucial in increasing employee responsibility, was the introduction of self-directed work teams. Training activities were part of the implementation. Employees received training for multi-skilling, as well as social and communication skills. Managers were also trained in their new role as coaches.

An initiative to stimulate employee development and responsibility for their own careers is the 'job path' plan: for several jobs, development paths have been defined. For each stage, knowledge and skill requirements are formulated and learning modules developed. Managers and employees decide together how employees function and if they want to grow to new jobs. Together they also formulate individual training plans. The system of 'star tasks' is similar, but more simple. It is essentially a job enrichment scheme; employees can enrich their jobs with extra tasks, normally performed by staff departments, for which they have to follow training (provided by staff departments themselves). The objective is to increase motivation for learning new tasks and to show people they have more possibilities for growth.

HRD within Akzo Nobel Chemicals

People involved in HRD

HRD is regarded as one aspect of the managerial process, and line managers fulfil an active role in assessment of training needs and formulation of training plans. Employees are also expected to fulfil an active role with regard to their own development. HRD professionals support them and support the organisation as a whole by providing advice and HRD products (training, training plans etc.). HRD policy is formulated by the HR manager and management of the business unit.

HRD objectives

HRD's current policy is focused on supporting both organisational and personal development. The first happens through longer-lasting training processes on topics derived from organisational strategy. As mentioned before, Akzo Nobel currently pays a lot of attention to increasing employees' participation in organisational development. Among the activities used to reach this goal are implementing self-directed work teams and quality improvement teams, and improving communication and information flows. The HRD function supports these activities by organising training and work sessions and by supporting teams and management. Second, individual training programs are developed in strong co-ordination between management and employees, mainly based on function stretch rather than organisational needs. Though training is seen as a means to reach organisational objectives and create a flexible, profitable organisation, some managers are of the opinion that the current HRD policy is still too focused on individual employees' needs instead of organisational needs.

HRD strategies

In what ways does the HRD function try to realise its envisioned role? It was found that HRD practitioners from Akzo Nobel consider HRD policy as a tool of management, but at the same time they are of the opinion that this hasn't been realised yet. To change this, the function of training co-ordinator was suspended, because this was just a control function, which was not felt to offer added value to the HRD department. The tasks of the training co-ordinator have been taken over by line managers and the HR practitioners. Boundaries of tasks and responsibilities aren't clear yet, but managers have an important responsibility. The removal of the function of training co-ordinator and the decentralisation of HRD tasks to the diverse business units should improve the match between HRD policy and company policy. Current HRD policy is mainly focused on job enrichment. Employees are supported in reaching a higher operator level (job path programme). Moreover, every employee can learn extra tasks; the so called 'star tasks' (see previous section).

With regard to the collective HRD interventions at Akzo Nobel, it can be said that the focus is on training courses (with a special focus on social and team skills) to support the implementation of self-directed work teams and quality improvement teams (e.g. by training courses on team development and problem solving skills).

Ericsson – telecommunications company

The company

Facts and figures

Ericsson Group is a world wide organisation with operations in 130 countries and 90,000 employees. The Dutch location which served as a case study is Ericsson Telecommunication (ETM). Its main activities include improving telecommunication infrastructures and companies' communication networks. The case focuses mainly on the research and development department, which employs about 450 people. The R&D department not only works on product development, but also participates in sales, delivery and maintenance of products.

The HRD function of R&D is a shared function of the central HR department of Ericsson, the Training Support Centre and the fifteen competence managers working for the R&D department.

Business strategy

Just like Akzo Nobel, Ericsson was faced with drastic changes in its market because of liberalisation of the telecommunications market, changing clients and client demands, and growing competition. Moreover, technology in telecommunications is evolving very fast. A strong client orientation (instead of the old product orientation), efficiency and a focus on knowledge and competencies of employees as the central resource are important strategies in order to adapt to these external challenges.

At Ericsson, the concept of the learning organisation is never mentioned in organisational statements or documents. In addition, the word 'learning' seems to have a negative focus; it seems to be associated with time-consuming, passive activities that take place outside the workplace. But even though they don't always recognise it as such, the opposite is true. In fact, employees at Ericsson are continually learning in an informal way, during work. One of the respondents, a senior manager, stated that there seems to be an 'enormous drive for learning' at Ericsson. This is considered to be very important by the company, pro-activeness is an important element of the organisational culture. The HR department's head stated that:

> it is important that an organisation is being created, which is ahead of future situations concerning organisational culture and strategy. This invites employees to new behaviours. It's of great importance that employees want to be successful. This is the greatest source for learning and development. The ability of an organisation to learn and develop depends on the degree in which employees want to be successful.

Change processes

In 1993, a new Ericsson management team introduced the ETM Better Best programme, which was characterised by striving for business excellence through continuous changes and client service. An important element was a change in the organisation structure, which was again changed in 1995, from an organisation with departments to a process-oriented organisation around so called 'client axes'. In a client axis all processes for a particular type of client are linked up and a multi-disciplinary team, composed of employees from all departments, is responsible for product development, sales, delivery and maintenance of products delivered to these clients, but also for internal processes such as process management, product management and competence management. In other words: for all activities necessary to provide a good product for a client.

Other important activities to change the existing culture and practices include the introduction of an annual management cycle (strategic plan, self-evaluation, action plans) together with a new integrated management information system which makes available relevant strategic information (which is, of course, necessary to conduct self-evaluations and make action plans). In order to reach the desired business excellence, a total quality management system was implemented. And, finally, to prepare employees for future challenges, a system for competence management was introduced. With this system, Ericsson hopes to keep its source of competencies up-to-date through on-going evaluations of competency gaps (see Box 9.1).

HRD within Ericsson

People involved in HRD

With the introduction of competence management, Ericsson has separated process management and people management. There are now three types of managers: operational managers, process owners (who are responsible for process management) and competence managers (responsible for people management). The latter function as a kind of internal job agency: at the start of each new project, they see to it that each project team incorporates the necessary competencies (i.c. the necessary employees) to fulfil its objectives. Competence managers are not part of the HRD

Box 9.1 Competence profiles at BAC and Ericsson

Both BAC and ETM introduced a competence management system and competence profiles with the aim to support employee development and prepare the organisation and the employees for future needed competencies.

Competence profiles at BAC are composed for three competence areas: (1) behaviour skills, (2) IT expertise and (3) subject matter, organisation and client expertise. For each area four development stages are specified: the learning stage, the practising stage, the expertise stage and the design stage. For each function or role a set of the most relevant competencies is composed. For each competence a development stage is determined, based on the role or function.

For Ericsson a competence profile is also composed of three competence areas: technical and professional competencies, social competencies and business competencies. And just as BAC, Ericsson also uses four levels (A,B,C and D). Employees who have yet to reach level A have at Ericsson the T-status, which means that he/she is in training.

Most HRD activities are fulfilled by competence managers who play an important role in this management system. Competence managers are responsible for employee development and to do this they have a broad range of activities from supporting employees in their work to making training plans for employees.

It was found that competence management is used for several reasons. The first one is that a competence profile is seen as a tool for employees to play an active role in their own development and career planning. The second function is that competence management is used for strategic resource planning (forecasting). On the basis of strategies competence profiles can be changed for the future. The last function is that competence management is a tool for determining if the right person is working in the right place.

---

function, they report to line management. Besides supporting employees with producing personal development plans and career development plans, they are also responsible for analysing required competencies in the organisation now and in the future (see Box 9.2).

An active role is expected from employees in their own development. They have to address their own development needs and career wishes, and work on a personal development plan. The competence managers formulate HR policies, which includes competence management policy. The Training Support Centre provides advice on fulfilling individual training needs, provides training and acts as a broker for external training agencies.

HRD objectives

HRD's main objective is to support the company policy, and more concretely, its strategic plan (which is formulated every year). The main tool is the competence management process, which is used to make sure the competencies resources are sufficient to fulfil strategic objectives. The pro-active orientation is important: the HRD function not only wants to support current objectives, but also the future ones.

Box 9.2 Competence/resource managers at Ericsson and BAC

BAC and Ericsson both employ competence managers (called 'resource managers' at BAC). Their task is to keep the 'total competence base' up to date, with the aim to prepare the organisation for future challenges (strategic role).

These are regular managers with mainly HRD tasks. Besides supporting employees in formulating personal development plans and career development plans (practical role), they are also responsible for analysing required competencies in the organisation now and in the future. The HRD department is, in both organisations, not the major partner in competence management. Their role is a supportive one. In strong coordination with competence managers and the employees, training activities are offered and HRD policy is linked to competence management.

On the basis of competence management, and in co-ordination with the employees and HRD professionals, personal development plans are made, which form the basis for the planning of training activities. It seems that for competence managers as well as HRD professionals it is not always clear who is responsible for what tasks. Yet, it is important that clarity is achieved.

A related objective is to support and stimulate the 'drive for learning' within the company, although this is mainly a managerial responsibility. By providing information on corporate challenges and involving employees in strategic planning, the company hopes to increase employees' awareness of the need for learning.

Another important area for HRD is supporting knowledge management, for instance by using job rotation as a means to absorb new knowledge and share existing knowledge.

HRD strategies

To a large degree, one could say that the HRD function has already implemented its desired role. In order to realise a competence-based organisation (a corporate objective), competence managers were installed. Together with employees, these managers produce competence analyses and personal development plans. The Training Support Centre provides the training to realise these plans (either internally or externally). Of course, in practice, realisation is sometimes difficult. Operational managers are not yet used to asking for '*competencies*' for a certain project, they ask for specific *people*. Problems arise for the competence manager when several managers ask for the same people. A second difficulty is that competence managers have to fulfil the current need for competencies but also need to safeguard individual development of employees, and sometimes these two tasks don't match. A third problem is the fact that each competence managers works for some 150 employees. This is a large group and it is difficult to find the time to talk regularly with everyone. Competence managers have to be careful not to let their role be limited to a mentoring role, losing the strategic (planning) aspect.

BAC – IT Centre of the Dutch Inland Revenue Service

The company

Facts and figures

BAC is the IT Centre of the Dutch Internal Revenue Service (IRS). Its most important task is supporting the primary processes of the IRS (levying and collecting taxes) with IT tools and techniques. Core activities are designing and building information systems and technical infrastructures, and exploiting and maintaining these structures on the diverse locations of the IRS. BAC employs 2,500 people in total. The case study focused on the Systems Development division, which employs 1,100 people. This division's main task is to develop information systems and provide advice.

The HRD function is a shared function of the central HR department of BAC (two HR practitioners, one HRD professional), the Open Learning Centre and ten local resource managers who allocate employees over the different projects (and who are responsible for facilitating employee development and career counselling).

Business strategy

BAC is a special organisation, in the sense that it offers services to just one client, the Internal Revenue Service. Changes in this organisation, such as striving for a faster collection process, have had a great impact on BAC's work because these changes have technological consequences. The fast changes in IT technology and social trends (such as a lack of IT staff on the labour market and the introduction of the Euro) also requried BAC to change. The organisation wants to become more flexible and improve its client centeredness by changing from a activity-oriented structure to a process chain structure and by decentralisation.

Just like Ericsson, BAC hasn't officially stated that it wants to become a learning organisation. Still the concept is of great importance for the HRD function of BAC. Learning from mistakes, learning from each other and sharing knowledge are important issues for the HRD department. They believe each of these should be integrated in the methods and procedures at BAC. According to the HRD professional at BAC:

> our organisation hasn't explicitly stated that it aims to becoming a learning organisation. BAC is working on improving knowledge management: 'How can we share information in our organisation and how can we learn from each other?'

The managing director stated:

> we are trying to integrate the concept of the learning organisation in our processes and procedures. This appears from the way we are dealing with mistakes. We are continually examining if mistakes could have been prevented. We make a case study of it and in this way every employee can learn from it.

Change processes

In order to respond adequately to changes in technology, in the IRS and society as a whole, and to improve knowledge management, several organisational changes have been made. Several supporting units (including HR) were decentralised to the separate units, and a chain-oriented horizontal structure was implemented in which BAC, suppliers and clients all take part in the chain of activities necessary to provide a service or product. BAC tries to become more flexible in responding to external developments through this management orientation. BAC has also introduced the Dutch Quality Management model (NKP-model) as a management tool. This model functions as a framework for organisational development and quality management at BAC.

In addition, BAC has started some activities to involve employees more actively in their own careers and to increase awareness of the importance of employee learning for BAC's development. The most important ones are: introduction of competence management and personal development plans, and the installation of an Open Learning Centre, where employees can study at times that suit them. The intranet is used as a means to provide information on possible training and learning possibilities, linked to competence profiles. A coaching scheme was implemented for management (result oriented management). This entails a process in which managers and employees together decide on development areas and desired performance, and assess the realisation of these objectives. Managers support employees in reaching the targets (see Box 9.3).

Box 9.3 Coaching scheme at BAC

BAC has implemented a system of coaching, with the aim of supporting employee development in a systematic way and on a continuing basis. Coaching forms the basis for the process between manager and employees. In regular coaching meetings between manager and employee questions like 'how is the work going' and 'what can I as manager do to help you' are discussed.

Assessment takes place once a year and on the basis of contribution criteria. Results are laid down in an assessment form.

On the basis of both activities, a personal development plan is produced for each employee. At the end of the year a new assessment takes place in which development activities are included.

The role of the HRD department is to support managers in their new role as a coach and to provide training and courses to employees on the basis of the personal development plans.

HRD within BAC

People involved in HRD

Until 1996, the HRD function was performed by the HR department. This was mainly a brokers' role and an administrative function. Now, most operational HRD tasks are decentralised, and every division has its own HRD practitioners. The HRD consultant at the central HR department now has more of a 'directors' function and a consulting role towards management. He also formulates HRD policy for BAC as a whole. The division has its own training coordinator who fulfils the role of broker. Just like Ericsson, BAC has introduced resource managers who just like competence managers, are responsible for supporting employee development and for looking at future needed competencies (see Box 9.2). The Open Learning Centre, managed by the HR department, is an important part of the HRD function.

HRD objectives

The HRD department made the first moves towards implementing competence management (see Box 9.1) with the aim to monitor employee development and match employee development and organisational development. The department wants employees to have an active role towards their own development. As a concrete objective, BAC wants seventy five per cent of its employees to have a personal development plan.

A second important objective is to improve knowledge management, especially sharing of knowledge by improving communication among employees (part of creating a learning culture).

Improving employees' mobility and multi-skilling is also an important target. BAC wants to have versatile employees, who are prepared for changes.

Recently, the training network was founded: local training coordinators from different divisions communicate together with the aim to improve the HRD function and create conditions for lifelong learning.

HRD strategies

Decentralisation of HRD was a very important strategy to improve the integration of HRD within the company and to link HRD policy to company policy. It enabled the central HRD professional to fulfil more of a director's and strategy-making role. HRD policy is now closely linked to organisational issues such as competence management, knowledge management and quality management. The policy is oriented towards supporting organisational objectives. Strategies concerning HRD interventions are quite diverse. On-the-job learning (informally), coaching and using intranet and theme meetings are important methods to increase employee flexibility (multi-skilling, readiness for change). Theme meetings and the intranet are also important to achieve knowledge sharing. To improve knowledge management, a special project group was installed (see Box 9.4). Other activities to increase employee learning (and employee

Box 9.4 Knowledge management project at BAC

At BAC, a knowledge management project took place with the objective to find out how dissemination of knowledge takes place within the company. A special workgroup composed by members who are interested in knowledge management executed a pilot study.

The workgroup interviewed for example members of a multidisciplinary improvement team working on solving an existing problem. The interviews took place every two weeks. Questions they asked included:

• What is the central problem?
• Where are you searching for knowledge to solve the problem?
• Who are you discussing this information with?

The role of the HRD department was a more supporting role. The HRD function was a partner in this project. For BAC it was found that the most important problem they were facing is that most employees find it very difficult to admit that they have a problem and to ask colleagues or managers for information to solve the problem. Knowing these results, BAC introduced these problems in a culture change process which is now ongoing.

responsibility for learning) were already mentioned in the previous section: Personal Development Plans, competence management, the Open Learning Centre etc.

KIBC – construction company

The company

Facts and figures

KIBC is a large group of Dutch and Belgian construction companies that realise projects in housing, commercial and industrial building (thirty per cent by own property development). KIBC plays an important role in stimulating innovation within the building industry, which is on the whole a quite traditional and hierarchical sector. The case focuses on Utility Construction, a division which employs 650 employees (in total, KIBC employs 1,900 people).

The HRD function is shared between KIBC's central HR department and the local HR department (two HR practitioners, one HRD professional) from the Commercial Building Division.

Business strategy

At the moment KIBC is facing some influential external developments, mainly stemming from new client demands. Building companies are expected to play an increasingly broader role in the entire process of realising a new building. They are not only involved in the actual construction, but also in tasks such as making plans (together with architects) and financing projects. Moreover, the building industry in the Netherlands is a very unstable sector (with many mergers) with few possibilities for growth, which increases competition. A related problem is the difficulties of finding well-qualified staff.

In order to face competition adequately, KIBC aims to become a market- and client-oriented organisation that is able to respond in a timely way to new questions and other market developments. Instead of the current strategy that is highly inwardly oriented, it wants to develop an externally-oriented strategy. KIBC describes itself as wanting to become a learning organisation. In its mission statement the firm states that it 'wants to be a client-oriented, learning organisation, which timely and adequately adapts to the expectations from clients and to the changes in the market' (source: KIBC internal documents).

In KIBC's view, a learning organisation is, in the words of the HR manager:

> an organisation that (…) communicates with clients, investigates market develop-
> ments and knows what its clients want; derives a clear strategy from these market
> developments and client's wishes, implements this through projects, evaluates
> its projects and presents the results to employees; has a clear view on where it
> wants to go, translates this into necessary activities and competencies; expects an
> active role of employees who communicate on their own careers.

Central to KIBC's first steps towards becoming a learning organisation are two points: (1) making available or directly providing all information needed to employees and (2) making sure this information is used in the organisation, especially for improvements and innovations. The managing director HR formulated this as follows:

> we use the concept of the learning organisation because in this organisation a lot
> of knowledge is available and created at different places. We have to organise or
> direct the organisation in such a way that knowledge is available for every employee
> who needs this information, that constantly new knowledge is created for example
> because of contacts with clients or by embedding problems.

Change processes

In common with the other case study organisations, KIBC has implemented structural changes to support the development process. The old organisational structure, a collection of building companies, was replaced by a new structure based on different sectors for basic activities. Business plans are now made jointly, on the basis of mutual strategy formulation.

Other important activities include new methods for strategy formulation (strategy sessions, joint strategy formulation processes) and the development of a clear organisational profile for the market.

Activities related to stimulating employee learning include a new performance assessment system in which managers and employees set individual performance targets, managers coach employees in realising these targets and at the end of the year the employee's performance is assessed. This approach enables a systematic discussion on development needs, and provides a means to link business development with personal development.

A second important (and related) activity is the implementation of a competence management system. This is in a very early stage of development.

Managers also receive attention, through an internal management development course. Managers are provided with workshops on coaching and on the new performance assessment system.

HRD within KIBC

People involved in HRD

HRD tasks are at the moment predominantly a responsibility of the central HR department and the local HR practitioners in the different sectors. The centralised HR department is mainly focused on HRD policy, the decentralised HRD practitioners are working on the more traditional HRD tasks. From employees and managers a more active role is expected. The HRD manager thinks HRD tasks should be their responsibility and not so much of the HR department. The younger managers are picking up on these new tasks quite readily. In the ideal situation HRD will become more of a shared responsibility of HR professionals, managers and employees. The HR department should fulfil a director's role as a 'manager of learning and change' and a 'learning and training consultant'. Management should take the initiative by recognising training needs and supporting employee learning.

HRD objectives

At the moment, the HR department is making a shift from a more traditional control orientation on human resources towards an approach centred around development. The HR department is focusing more and more on organisational development and linking HRD policy in order to support organisation's policy, and less on operational control tasks with regard to personnel. New activities are for instance translating the business plan into functions and matching competence profiles and leading a strategic discussion on KIBC's future. Important issues for the HRD department are for example a new vision on leadership, innovation of assessment policy and implementation of competence management.

Key objectives are the implementation of coaching and result-oriented assessment (new management style), and stimulating employees to take initiatives with regard to their own training and career.

HRD strategies

The new manager of the HR department has had a great impact on the HRD function. He is the initiator for the new development-oriented policy. Decentralisation of HRD tasks towards local HR departments and (line) managers is also an important strategy to realise the new HRD role.

The decentralised HR departments are still very control-oriented while the central HR department is working on making a move towards a more development-oriented HRD policy. Initiatives like the use of competence management are still 'under construction'.

To support current organisational issues the HR department organises training courses on topics such as coaching and result-oriented leadership and client orientation. But other activities to support employee learning in general are also undertaken. For instance, the HR department pays much attention to organising training courses on management development and innovating the assessment procedures. Both should lead to a realisation of the objectives of coaching, result-oriented leadership and active employees.

Factors influencing HRD's role and how HRD deals with them

The preceding sections described the visions and strategies of the four case study organisations with regard to becoming a learning organisation, as well as HRD's role in this process. This section describes factors which affect the achievement (or lack of achievement) of the envisioned role of the HRD department. Inhibiting factors, facilitating factors and strategies to overcome constraints are briefly discussed.

Inhibiting factors

All Dutch case study organisations were found to be facing some inhibiting factors in the change process towards a learning (oriented) organisation. Table 9.1 lists the most significant ones.

For all organisations it can be said that work pressure is the most inhibiting factor for achieving the envisioned HRD role. Other important projects are so time demanding that HRD activities are decreasing in importance.

A second important factor is lack of motivation and support from management. Sometimes this is related to the time factor: managers are so busy already, that they are not eager to take on new tasks, even though the HRD professionals try to support them in doing so.

Table 9.1 Inhibiting factors – Dutch case study organisations

Inhibiting factors	Akzo Nobel	ETM	BAC	KIBC
Lack of time	•	•	•	•
Lack of motivation and support from management	•	•	•	•
Lack of motivation and responsibility for learning from employees	•		•	•
Lack of understanding of HRD policy			•	•
Difficult position competence/resource managers		•	•	
Insufficient learning culture			•	•

A lack of motivation on the part of employees, as experienced in Akzo, BAC and KIBC, can probably also be traced back to the same reason. An extra problem is that employees sometimes don't see the need for learning, so they don't feel responsible. This goes for uninformed employees, but also for older employees who have worked for the same company for a long time.

Lack of understanding of the HRD policy compounds the motivational problem. Employees and managers will only be motivated once they understand the reasons and methods of the new policy, but this is not yet the case in all organisations (BAC, KIBC).

An interesting problem is the difficult position of the competence managers and resource managers (BAC and Ericsson). This presents a serious problem because these managers play a key role in the implementation of competence management in BAC and Ericsson. For Ericsson especially, the constant work pressure for competence managers is seen as an important inhibiting factor. Because of a lack of time competence managers are continually working on the daily support of employees. They have no time to focus on future needed competencies, which is also a very important task. The company is now working on extra administrative support for competence managers in order to decrease their work pressure.

A similar situation can be encountered for the resource managers from BAC, who have a similar role and face similar problems. Employees expect them to pay attention for employee development, project managers want them to provide good employees who are able to work on all kinds of tasks and who are quickly available and top managers want the resource manager to continually look for long term developments and consequences for employees. It is not easy to resolve these tensions.

Finally, an insufficient learning culture is an inhibiting factor for BAC and KIBC, as a result of a long-term focus on formal training only.

Conducive factors

A large number of factors that support the development towards a learning (oriented) organisation were found. Table 9.2 gives an overview of the most important ones.

Whereas a lack of a clear HRD policy and communication on HRD's new role is an inhibiting factor, a clear policy and good communication are conducive to the change process, because this positively influences motivation for change. For Akzo, for example, improvements in the general information and communication flows on HRD as well as other policies turned out to be a successful strategy to improve

Table 9.2 Conducive factors – Dutch case study organisations

Conducive factors	Akzo Nobel	ETM	BAC	KIBC
Clear HRD policy	•	•	•	•
Clear (HRD) communication	•	•	•	•
Increasing learning opportunities and facilities	•		•	•
Supporting teams	•	•		
Support of management				•

participation of employees. As they knew more about the company, their involvement and willingness to learn, grew. A similar story can be told for the other companies, who experience a positive influence on employee motivation for learning from new organisational structures and strategy-formulation processes (as a result of which employees know more of the company and its objectives).

Increasing learning possibilities and facilities for learning also help the change process (mentioned by Akzo, BAC, KIBC). For instance, at Akzo Nobel, the new possibilities for job enrichment and social skills had a very positive influence on employees willingness to learn and learning skills.

Likewise, supporting teams can also help the change process (Akzo, Ericsson). For instance, BAC mentioned improvement teams as a positive factor. Employees from all functions work together on problems, and learn to solve problems in a systematic way. They learn to work with other people and to look at problems from different points of view. The supportive role of the HRD department proved to be of great importance for these teams.

Lastly, HRD professionals from KIBC considered the new board of directors, especially for HRD, as an important conducive factor. The new board of directors and the new head of the department HRD both disseminate that they totally agree with the new direction in which KIBC is developing. This is an important stimulus for employees to play an active role and to take initiatives.

Coping strategies

Strategies to cope with the inhibiting factors differed for the four case organisations. For Ericsson, a major problem is the difficulties competence managers experience in their new role. Therefore, the company is now working on providing extra administrative support in order to decrease their work pressure (so they have more time to work on strategic personnel issues). For BAC, lack of time (other projects demand more attention) and lack of a learning culture are important constraints. In order to improve the link between HRD policy and company policy the HRD department wants to implement director groups in which HRD professionals, top managers, line managers and resource managers participate to improve this link (see Box 9.5). To stimulate a learning culture the HRD function works to increase possibilities for informal learning and knowledge sharing. Finally, KIBC found that improving HRD policy and improving communication and information flows are both very useful in decreasing resistance and increasing motivation for learning.

Summary and conclusions

Organisational context

Four Dutch organisations were discussed: Akzo Nobel Chemicals, Ericsson Tele-communication, BAC (IT Centre of the Dutch Internal Revenue Service) and KIBC. An overview of the characteristics of the case study organisations, such as sector, number of employees, HRD function, number of HRD practitioners and HRD investments is provided in Table 9.3.

Box 9.5 Director groups at BAC

A director group's task is to match organisational developments with learning processes. In order to reach this aim, the group is focusing on the organisation of learning processes.

Plans have been made to introduce director groups for developing training plans. Group members are employees directly involved in the development of employees: managers, resource managers, HRM advisors and employees, but also IT experts or product/process managers. The main tasks for the director groups include outlining organisational developments and linking training plans to these developments, linking training plans to competence management, responding to inhibiting and conducive factors, involving managers and employees in development processes, informing on how training processes are carried out and evaluation of training processes, not only by asking employees their opinion on the training, but also by evaluating if employees really use what they have learned in their workplace. What is important here is that the group tries to match organisational developments with learning processes. In order to do so the group needs to focus on organisation of learning processes, and also important is that the group has empathy with employees and their learning needs.

HRD professionals are partners in the director groups. They have a consulting role. Tasks for HRD professionals are, for example, thinking about stimulating (informal) learning, supporting competence management and promoting employee development. But next to these activities are also more traditional tasks like providing training.

Table 9.3 Overview of Dutch case study organisations

Company and sector	Number of employees	HRD
Akzo Nobel Chemicals, Business Unit Salt, chemical industry	Total: 700 BU Salt: 240	• Central HR department/local HR practitioner • 1 HR manager central • 1 HR practitioner BU Salt
Ericsson Telecommunications, research & development (R&D) telecommunications	Total: 1,500 R&D: 450	• HR department • Training Support Centre • competence managers (15 in R&D)
BAC (IT Centre Internal Revenue Service), Systems Development Division, information technology services	Total: 2,500 SO: 1,100	• Central HR department (2) • Open Learning Centre (1) • local resource managers (10)
KIBC, Utility Building Business Unit, building sector	Total: 1900 UB: 650	Central HR department (2 HR practitioners) Local HR department (1 HRD practitioner)

For all Dutch case study organisations it was found that the main driving force for change was the need to deal with strong competitive markets (for all but BAC) and/ or fast technological changes. In order to respond to these developments the case organisations want to improve their client-centeredness (Ericsson, BAC, KIBC). Related strategic objectives are: increasing flexibility (BAC), increasing cost effectiveness

(Akzo Nobel, Ericsson) and realising quality improvements (Akzo Nobel, KIBC). Very important in all cases is the creation of a new organisational culture, which reflects the market orientation but which also stresses the importance of employee learning to achieve client service (because employee learning and knowledge sharing are essential tools in achieving issues such as flexibility, client service, improvements and innovation).

In order to improve client-centredness, all cases engaged in a reorganisation. Ericsson and BAC adopted a process oriented structure, in which they try to manage their work processes as a long chain from suppliers to customers. Three case organisations (Akzo Nobel, BAC, KIBC) adopted a new method for strategy formulation and planning, in which a central strategy is translated in different operational policies and targets on the lower management levels. Two case study organisations also improved their communication systems and the way information is shared among employees (Akzo Nobel, Ericsson). Both strategies can be regarded as ways to increase employee commitment to and knowledge on the organisation and the challenges it faces. This may positively influence the motivation for learning.

Total quality management is also an important strategy (Akzo Nobel, Ericsson, BAC), which can be seen as a means to realise on-going improvements, using employees knowledge of the work processes.

Several efforts to increase possibilities for employee learning are also visible in these case organisations. Most common are the use of a competence management system (Ericsson, BAC and KIBC) and a new role for managers who set performance targets with employees and at the same time derive learning needs (sometimes written down in a PDP) (Akzo Nobel, BAC, KIBC). It is interesting to note that three companies provide training for managers in order to fulfil their new role as coaches (Akzo Nobel, BAC, KIBC).

HRD's envisioned role

It seems that HRD departments from all four case organisations share the opinion that the more traditional HR and HRD tasks should become the responsibility of line management while the HRD department is changing towards a more supportive and directing role. Not every department has realised this task division yet. Linked to this notion is the active role that is expected from employees in their own development, especially within BAC and Ericsson (highly-educated professionals) but also within Akzo Nobel and KIBC (less educated manual workers). The emphasis of new HRD tasks is on matching HRD policy with organisational policy and on a consulting role towards line management.

Likewise, HRD departments of all four case study organisations hold the view that HRD policy is a 'tool of management' to be used to realise the attainment of organisational objectives. Next to this, all HRD functions aim to support employee development, as a tool for organisation development. Competence management and the use of personal development plans are the tools used to achieve the link between these two. Sometimes employee development and organisation development are difficult to combine. Akzo Nobel for instance, still experiences that the accent in the personal training plans is on personal development; the link with company strategy is more obscure.

Strategies adopted to realise HRD's new role

When looking at strategies with regard to HRD organisation it can be said that all HRD departments have changed the organisation of their department to a greater or lesser extent. Decentralisation of HRD tasks is an important means to realise HRD's envisioned role of policy-maker and consultant. Managers have become important new participants in the HRD function, especially at BAC and Ericsson where resource managers/competence managers have been implemented. They are responsible for employee development focused on present but also on future needed competencies for the organisation and for individual employees.

Facilitating courses remains the most important means to fulfil identified learning needs, but some organisations are experimenting with other, more informal ways of learning. For instance BAC, where knowledge sharing through the intranet and theme meetings is stimulated, Akzo Nobel, where employees can learn through participating in quality improvement teams, and KIBC, where managers are supported in their new role as coaches. Ericsson does underline the importance of informal learning on the job, but does not deliberately try to stimulate or support it. It does, however try to motivate people for learning and changing (stimulate the 'drive for learning').

Influencing factors

For all four HRD departments it can be said that work pressure is the most inhibiting factor for attaining the envisioned HRD role. Other important projects are so time demanding that HRD activities are decreasing in importance. A second important factor is lack of motivation and support from management and a lack of motivation on the part of employees. Lack of understanding of the HRD policy may compound the motivational problem. A particular problem is the difficult position of the competence managers and resource managers in BAC and Ericsson.

Whereas a lack of a clear HRD policy and communication on HRD's new role is an inhibiting factor, a clear policy and good communication are conducive to the change process, because it positively influences motivation for change.

Increasing learning possibilities and facilities for learning also help the change process.

Strategies to cope with constraints differed for the four case organisations. Ericsson is now working on providing extra administrative support in order to decrease competence manager's work load. BAC wants to implement 'director groups' in order to improve the link between HRD policy and company policy. To stimulate a learning culture the HRD function works to increase possibilities for informal learning and knowledge sharing. KIBC, finally, found that improving HRD policy and improving communication and information flows are both very useful in decreasing resistance and increasing motivation for learning.

10 Cases from the United Kingdom

Sally Sambrook and Jim Stewart

This chapter describes the results of the case study research in the United Kingdom. Four organisations were studied: the postal service Royal Mail, the aero engines manufacturer Rolls-Royce Aerospace, the insurance company Royal Scottish Assurance and the beer producer Wolverhampton & Dudley Breweries.

The first four sections contain full case descriptions (based on data from 1998), including for each case:

- background information on the organisation, such as core businesses, number of employees, and current (learning-oriented) strategies;
- vision of the HRD professionals on their (new) roles in the learning (oriented) organisation;
- strategies they employ to realise these roles.

The next section describes factors that (negatively or positively) influence the achievement of these envisioned roles. General conclusions and a summary are provided in the final section.

Royal Mail – postal services

The company

Facts and figures

Royal Mail is Britain's national postal service, with the British government as sole shareholder. The company, with 160,000 employees, is divided into nine divisions plus the Strategic Head Quarters in London, with divisional units according to geographic location. In this case study, we focus on the Midlands Division (18,000 employees) and, in particular, the Nottinghamshire operational unit (1,800 staff).

HRD within Royal Mail is practised/located at three levels: Strategic Head Quarters (eight HRD staff), divisions (70 T&D staff) and the Training and Development (T&D) Group (Coton House) at Post Office Services Group (120 T&D staff).

Business strategy

The purpose of Royal Mail is to:

> develop and sell quality, affordable and trusted mail services throughout the UK
> and the rest of the world.
>
> (Source: Royal Mail internal documents)

Royal Mail currently experiences a need to be 'fit to compete in a more commercial environment' and to be 'fit for the future'. A large part of the business is currently protected by monopoly, but this will cease with deregulation of postal services in the UK in 2003. EU legislation has already liberalised cross-border mail. Royal Mail's commercial freedom is under review by the British government. To compete more efficiently and effectively, Royal Mail is investing in technology and trying to incorporate electronic advances. This results in new working practices, where employees need new skills to operate new machinery and need to learn new ways of delivering the service.

Quality focus and customer focus seem to be key elements in organisational strategies in order to respond to a strong competitive market and quickly changing technology. The vision of becoming a learning organisation is clearly linked with this focus on quality and customers. Although Royal Mail is striving to become a learning organisation, this is not explicitly stated. The metaphor for the learning organisation is the 'Training Partnership' with the aim of 'creating a thirst for learning'. The Training Partnership was set up several years ago. Its vision is:

> By doing the right things we shall create a thirst for learning that helps each individual grow and create a step change increase in capability to meet Royal Mail's objectives.
>
> (Source: Royal Mail internal documents)

Change processes

The Training Partnership, now part of the T&D Team at SHQ, is a virtual organisation, comprising four people and three roles, which has as its objectives to prioritise the annual plan, monitor progress, and to encourage new initiatives. The Partnership has been very successful in designing and delivering HRD innovations, in line with a learning approach. The Training Partnership works closely with training and development staff in the divisions to capture, design and develop innovations in HRD, which are then rolled out throughout Royal Mail as a part of corporate strategy. Examples of such innovations include:

- Development dialogue: every employee has a one to one discussion about their learning needs with their managers, which results in a personal development plan.

- Pathfinders: teams where employees work on solving real business problems, and at the same time get the opportunity to develop their working and learning skills (see Box 10.1).
- WorkTime Learning: an initiative to create more time in work for learning: employees work in groups on real problems and report back every week (see Box 10.2).

Learning is deemed an act of leadership, where managers act as role models, sharing self-assessment with their teams. This promotes learning as individuals (setting personal targets) and as a team (how the team can perform better). However, this innovative approach 'frightens some people in the business', which is still rather bureaucratic.

'Development' historically focused on management development, provided at the Coton House. There is now a new strategy which focuses on leadership, but also

---

Box 10.1 Pathfinders at Royal Mail

At Royal Mail, the Training Partnership has establised 'Pathfinders', an annual activity with a twofold objective. First 'Pathfinders' aims at solving business problems. Second, by working together in teams it also includes involving individuals in their own learning, helping them improve their own job activities, developing skills associated with working with others and hopefully seeing the bigger picture.

Pathfinders is a team-based project in which teams, sponsored by a business manager; work on a real business problem. The team members are given training in basic skills such as problem solving skills, presentation skills, report writing, personal effectiveness etc. The team members also receive time away from their own job to work on the problem.

An example of a Pathfinders activity is a 'seeing is believing' benchmarking and problem-solving exercise for front-line employees that was recently conducted. Eight employees were selected from each division, on an open and competitive basis, to form a team to examine a 'real' business problem and suggest improvements against a chosen business approach.

The business problem was sponsored or championed by an operational manager, who was involved in helping the team. The team was also supported by a divisional training co-ordinator who facilitated team development, and provided basic project planning and presentation skills. The Pathfinders were released from their own jobs for a total of fifteen working days to resolve the business problem.

Solving the problem could be achieved through benchmarking with other parts of the organisation, and with other organisations. Once completed, they presented their findings to their Pathfinder colleagues from other divisions at an annual event, and also to their divisional managers and the senior management team.

Business problems that have been tackled by Pathfinders include activity based costing, harassment at work, and developing appropriate behaviours for Royal Mail employees. Over the first three years, the scheme lost only three out of 350 employees.

Most Pathfinders have then moved on, for example, into studentships or management roles. A significant benefit for employees is that Pathfinders has 'given me back my self respect', as one of them puts it.

Box 10.2 Worktime learning at Royal Mail

A weekly activity entitled 'WorkTime Learning' is being introduced at Royal Mail as an attempt to create time in work for team learning. Front-line employees meet in groups of 10–15 with their manager. They meet each other each week, at the same time and same place (not on the shop floor, but in a designated room) and the event is lead by the same manager. For the manager there is a four-week rolling calendar, where he/she receives information about a forthcoming session (week 1), then has to conduct research (week 2), prepares the session (week 3) and then leads the learning event (week 4). The manager leads a thirty-minute 'learning event', which must be business plan focused, and make inputs relevant to the relevant work unit. The weekly sessions are structured to cover:

*   Organisational issues (corporate messages, such as the launch of a new product);
*   Operational or performance issues at the local level (such as the introduction of new technology or refresher training on existing machinery).

At each session, there is also an opportunity for employees to raise issues and make suggestions. WorkTime Learning is a 'product' of the Training Partnership. Developers in each of the divisions support WorkTime Learning at the local level, for example, helping managers to develop skills to lead the learning events. It is envisaged that it will take a few years to fully implement the scheme and incorporate it into schedules, where there are difficulties due to work shifts and work loads.

Although in its early stages of development, managers remark that even getting employees to attend is seen a major improvement in involving them in thinking about their work and group learning.

encompasses the front-line staff, 'the forgotten many', who are 'the core of the business'. Therefore, the aim is to develop a culture of inclusivity and innovation to re-engage employees, to develop a learning culture.

An important strategy used by the Royal Mail in order to develop towards a learning organisation is the Agenda for Leadership (A4L) programme. This management programme includes a framework for leadership behaviours and standards within a clear structure, and a range of management roles and capabilities to increase the leadership of the 8,000 operational managers. The development of quality standards – Total Quality and Business Excellence – and aiming for the Investors in People award, for the whole business are important elements of the change strategy.

HRD in Royal Mail

People involved in HRD

HRD professionals are located at different levels in the organisation. The HRD practitioners at the strategic headquarters resource and coordinate all types of formal and informal learning, to support the business and divisions. At the division level, there is a professional trainer manager (divisional development manager) whose tasks is to ensure appropriate learning takes place at the local level, and help develop learning products. In the T&D group (part of Post Office Services Group) some 120 employees act as the preferred 'in-house' supplier of all types of T&D products and services (particularly management development courses). Though their role is changing towards a more customer-focused approach (not 'telling' managers what to do), they have always been more than 'chalk and talk'.

An important aspect of developing a learning culture is the role of line managers in encouraging and supporting learning. Also a key feature of the vision of becoming a learning organisation is the emphasis upon employees, who must develop self responsibility for their own learning. They must be prepared to admit they have development needs, review and challenge what they are doing, ask 'are there better ways,' and act within the philosophy of continuous improvement in line with Royal Mail's Total Quality (TQ) initiative to improve work practices and secure future employability.

HRD objectives

For the HRD department of Royal Mail it can be said that their vision towards their new role is to plan, supply and evaluate all forms of learning, to support the business and engage all employees. As an HRD practitioner spoke about the vision:

> our role is to kick start initiatives and bed them in as part of the business plan, help people understand the T&D implications, define a sponsor, the process, provide guidelines, and keep an eye on the process.

The overall vision is one of greater access for all employees and consistent messages. For example, if Royal Mail is saying that customer satisfaction and quality are important, are employees being given the tools to improve and evaluate their own skills and performance? To help achieve the vision, as an organisation, Royal Mail believes in 'Investors in People' (IiP). IiP is about how the organisation can harness human resources and align learning with business objectives.

Royal Mail's strategy is to get employees *involved and engaged*. The task of the HRD department is how can they support this strategy by helping/encouraging employees to engage in learning – beyond formal courses and including learning in work – and get them involved in the business, linking this with developing individuals to increase their job satisfaction, motivation and commitment.

HRD strategies

The department strives to change the common view of learning as 'academic learning' and to stimulate awareness of the workplace as a place for learning. This vision has been translated into a range of 'products'. Formal interventions include management development and Training Partnership products, which have been developed in collaboration with divisional development managers. These interventions occur in divisional training centres, away from work and on-the-job.

Examples of strategic initiatives are Customer First, a TQ approach, based on series of small steps to make thousands of improvements and Agenda for Leadership (A4L). A4L requires that all managers have been assessed against Royal Mail's key capabilities, supported with a two-day development workshop where managers talk about their learning needs, form action learning sets and devise a personal development programme (PDP) to enable them to meet the leadership capabilities. The PDP can be resourced from formal courses, secondments and projects.

An example of a Training Partnership product is Pathfinders, a project where employees work to find solutions for real business problems, and at the same time get the opportunity to develop their learning skills (see Box 10.1). Other examples include the implementation of open learning centres and career counselling (all employees have access to expert counsellors, which aims to help people make choices about how to fill their potential, and to make links with their PDPs). The modular induction programme for front-line employees, Starting Post, which is a combination of formal and non-formal learning is also of interest. The programme uses the concept of 'discovery learning' and includes an element of open learning where new entrants are given a workbook to work through at their own pace, in addition to taught core modules. These include business awareness, health and safety and options relevant to variuos roles. This is classroom based, but the open learning part is supported by using other front-line employees to coach new entrants.

Rolls-Royce Aerospace Group – aero engine manufacturing

The company

Facts and figures

Rolls-Royce is involved in precision engineering within the manufacturing sector, and is split into the Aerospace Group and the Industrial Power Group. The Aerospace Group is divided into a number of business units, of which Airline Business is responsible for the design, development, assembly, sale and product support of all Rolls-Royce commercial aero engines. Within this structure, Airline Business Operations is responsible for the assembly and testing of all Rolls-Royce civil engines. Airline Business Operations employs almost 2,000 people.

HRD is practised centrally, as part of the recently re-named human resources function (eight employees and a department head), and devolved to business areas, through line managers and training co-ordinators. In addition, there are in-house training providers. The HR function provides resources and co-ordinates formal and informal learning to support the business.

Business strategy

The strategic intent of Rolls-Royce Airline Business Operations is:

to provide an affordable build and test service that achieves the customer's agreed need.

(Source: Rolls-Royce Airline Business Operations internal documents)

Airline Business Operations seeks to become a learning organisation because of increasingly competitive markets and changes in technology. In order to respond, the company feels a need to get its products to the market more quickly. This means reducing lead times for building and testing engines. Changing technology and technological advancements within precision engineering enable shorter lead times, and the ability to respond to customer requirements much faster, ahead of competitors. Initiatives to address this include 'Better Performance Faster' and 'Quality Renaissance'. A strategy has been set to be more customer focused and people oriented, emphasising quality and business excellence. People are considered important because to achieve the strategic intent, the organisation and its employees need to keep learning: everybody's input is required. Rolls-Royce Aerospace has not explicitly stated the desire to become a learning organisation. However, similar principles are articulated in the company's values and behaviours.

Some specific behaviours which Rolls-Royce associates with being a learning organisation are:

- receive and encourage new ideas;
- implement identified change fast;
- share information and make it work;
- develop, attract and retain high quality employees.

Change processes

An important strategy to achieve development towards a learning organisation has been the introduction of a *new cellular structure*, where teams work together in semi-autonomous groups (cells), with cell leaders. This approach supports the organisation's aim to build a 'high involvement workforce', through high involvement leaders and an empowered workforce. This restructuring has involved what one manager called 'workplace learning' – where specific areas of the business designed their own induction programmes for everyone 'when we went cellular'. In addition to the new cellular structure, there is also a quality improvement structure and a business improvement plan, aimed at achieving the strategic intent. The business improvement plan is a three-year rolling programme, known as the 'Success through our Team' or STOT Initiative. Performance against the initiative is monitored regularly through business meetings and results are displayed on STOT notice boards across the organisation.

Another important strategy is Investors in People (IiP). IiP is about valuing people. It is a national standard, awarded to organisations, or parts of organisations, that demonstrate their commitment to training and development, by articulating business objectives to all employees so they understand their roles, by having PDPs for all employees, and by evaluating interventions against business performance. In 1997, Airline Business Operations achieved the IiP standard. To attain this, Airline Business

Operations had to identify and communicate its strategy and objectives, and business *Cases from the United Kingdom* 139 and development plans. This was achieved by a group-wide cultural change programme entitled 'one small step'. A key element is the weekly debrief to all employees, on a cascade basis, where all information relating to the business is shared, and two-way communication encouraged. Strategic objectives include meeting targets and improvement plans. The overall improvement plan identifies any training needs. During the last recession, training and development took a back seat. As one manager explained:

We were appointing supervisors and managers, and omitting to provide them with the skills to carry out their role. Therefore, now we are investing major money to bring supervisors and managers up to spec.

Achieving the IiP standard has resulted in an increase in *management development activity* to support the emphasis on team work, communication and improved people management. As an HR Officer commented, 'we have a responsibility to ensure they have skills to manage people, that is the line manager'. The Investors in People standard has been the tool to take the company forward, in an age where the business is changing faster than ever.

HRD in Rolls-Royce Airline Business Operations

People involved in HRD

The HR function provides resources and co-ordinates formal and informal learning in order to support the business. One of the tasks of the HRD department is to organise and resource interventions identified from individual training plans and business plans, collated to form an overall training plan. The HRD function also has an obligation to support managers with their time and expertise, to help to form and meet both individual and departmental objectives.

The role of the manager seems to be to encourage people to develop, to give them learning opportunities (time, money), to inform them of learning opportunities and to support them and give feedback. From the employees more involvement is expected in their own development as well as organisational development. When looking at employee development, an active role is expected from employees in defining training needs and making development plans.

HRD objectives

HRD policy is aimed at achieving the strategic intent and maintaining the IiP standard by encouraging and supporting learning in all forms. The overall policy is to ensure employees are trained to meet the needs of the business, and to be able to do the tasks expected of them.

The vision of HRD staff regarding their role in creating a learning organisation is to support employee learning in its broadest sense, and is not limited to providing courses. This includes, for example, developing an open learning centre and encouraging individual responsibility for learning through personal development plans/diaries and learning contracts. Attention is paid to informal learning. An HRD manager commented:

> There is an immense amount of on-the-job learning. Many employees would not have been conscious of this form of learning. If you asked them to list what learning they had been involved in, they would think 'what course did I go on, what hotel did I stay in, what exam did I take?' Learning means doing the job, learning from colleagues, training others, doing a first aid certificate, having an enlarged job. Coaching is important – often the coach learns more than the coachee. Every new experience is an opportunity to learn. Personal development diaries have been introduced, where employees jot down every learning opportunity.

The HRD department believes they have created a 'fertile land' which needs to be nurtured and guarded to capture and implement learning. A suggestion scheme captures improvement ideas. Employees are rewarded if their ideas are implemented, according to the impact of the improvement. They are increasingly involved in terms of their own input and responsibility for continuous learning and development. This requires clarifying roles and responsibilities, defining what employees can expect and how they can be supported.

HRD strategies

Training and development is an integral part of the quality manual and included in the Airline Business Operations planning process. The training and development policy is published to show how the training and development of employees will contribute to this.

Recently there has been an increase in apprentices, and the organisation is more supportive of adult further education. There are more opportunities for progression, through secondments and internal promotion. Rolls-Royce has 'restarted education' and is committed to continuing education. As a manager commented:

> There is personal and business benefit, not necessarily in their current job but there is future benefit, it's a more long-term view. We support personal development.

The learning activities can come from a variety of sources: from (external) courses, to coaching and on-the-job learning. The Learning Resource Centre (LRC) is worthy of note as it is open to the general public. Computer-based learning (CBL) is used greatly. The LRC has been open several years, it is on-site, handy and friendly, and a valuable tool. Individuals use it to develop themselves to meet business needs as well as personal aspirations. Informal activities include peer coaching and secondments.

Royal Scottish Assurance – financial services

The company

Facts and figures

Royal Scottish Assurance (RSA) is a strategic joint venture owned and operated by the Royal Bank of Scotland (RBS) and Scottish Widows. RSA operates in the financial services market, and offers three types of products: protection, pensions and investments. The company can be described as a 'virtual organisation'; RSA directly employs only a staff of fifteen, but 'controls' a further 392 staff and an additional 150 staff contribute directly to its operations. This means that in total over 550 staff work for RSA in the sense of devoting their time to dedicated tasks of RSA.

The HRD department in RSA is named Bancassurance Training and Development (seventeen HRD professionals). The primary function of the department is to support, facilitate and co-ordinate learning and development activities and processes undertaken by themselves, by operational departments and managers and by individual members of staff. The department and its staff are also involved in recruitment and selection of some categories of staff and in management development and succession planning.

Business strategy

RSA's mission is:

> to be the 'first choice' of Royal Bank customers for life assurance, pensions and investments by providing exceptional service, excellent value and advice they can trust.
>
> (Source: RSA internal documents)

Current plans for future development of the company include expanding the customer base. Excellent customer service based on relationships built on trust is at the heart of Royal Scottish Assurance's (RSA) intended strategy. To facilitate and support this strategy, the company recently launched an initiative, headed by a member of the management board, to establish and implement a 'Vision and Values System' within RSA. This initiative follows from the belief that 'culture' and 'people' form the competitive edge and that ways of behaving and relating throughout the company need to both reflect and reinforce the vision and primary value of 'trust'.

Royal Scottish Assurance has a strong and articulated belief in the value of learning and development. It has achieved the UK Investors in People standard. Senior managers demonstrate and reinforce this belief by their own actions. A number of directors, including the chief executive, have recently completed or are currently studying for masters level degrees. The management board collectively engage in individual and team development through board 'away days' and strategic planning events. The philosophy is also demonstrated and reinforced through the mechanism of a 'Critical Success Factor' relating to 'People'.

This is one of four critical success factors derived from the mission and positioning statement and it is described as follows.

- People: quality staff, well trained and motivated who are passionate about service quality and who effectively communicate with each other and their customers (internal or external).
- Guiding principle: managers and their staff will work together year on year to improve skills and abilities to ensure success for the business and improved employability for staff.

Reasons for adopting a learning-oriented philosophy include a belief that 'staff' and 'service quality' provide an achievable competitive difference which will ensure success in the market. As one manager argued, organisations in financial services need to be flexible and responsive to fast changing market demands, and learning and development is essential in achieving those organisational features. This analysis and argument was supported by a senior manager who stated that 'if you look after staff they will look after customers'.

Change processes

As well as keeping up the IiP standard and changing the corporate culture, a key focus of learning and development in RSA is enhancing the CVs of staff and their 'employability'. Providing continuous opportunities for personal development, especially of the kind that results in accreditation or qualifications, is an important part of the psychological contract operating in RSA. The intention of this element of the philosophy according to some senior managers is staff retention. It does of course have potential career benefits to individuals both within RBS and with alternative employers. The main purpose though is developing and retaining high quality staff within RSA. As one middle manager stated 'The business requires top quality staff', and, as the chief executive put it, the learning-oriented philosophy of the organisation reflects a 'continuous drive for quality, a continuous drive for learning and a continuous drive for their CVs'.

One further factor requires mention. Financial services in the UK is now regulated in a way which requires sales staff to be trained, developed and qualified. Staff working in this area are therefore statutorily required to hold the Financial Planning Certificate. However, for RSA, this represents an absolute minimum. Their philosophy results in individuals from the chief executive downwards constructing and regularly reviewing personal development plans (PDPs) which themselves result in individuals going beyond statutory qualifications. The PDP process has a wider focus than meeting work requirements alone.

HRD in Royal Scottish Assurance

People involved in HRD

Managers in RSA have a clear responsibility for the performance of their staff and, as part of this, to support the learning and development of individuals. This is achieved through for example the conduct of monthly 'one-to-one' performance review (see Box 10.3) and development planning meetings, and the use of regular team meetings. They also have a responsibility for supporting the efforts to create a learning climate and culture.

Individuals working in RSA have ultimate responsibility for their own learning and development (e.g. they have to construct their own personal development plan). They also have a responsibility for supporting team and organisational learning through contributing information, ideas and experience in for example team meetings.

The primary task of the HRD department was described as to *create the right environment*. This means to encourage and enable learning and development, rather than to directly provide training and development courses. However, because a primary responsibility of the department is to ensure compliance with regulatory requirements in terms of staff qualifications, formal training is also provided to support staff working towards achievement of those qualifications.

A second responsibility is *to support the intended business strategy*. This translates into tasks such as provision of induction and contributing to regional and national sales meetings to reinforce cultural values. The responsibility is also associated with the direct, personal support given to managers by HRD professionals to support Personal Development Planning, and in their task of 'developing, training and coaching the salesforce'. HRD professionals also advise employees. RSA staff have access to a wide range of learning materials and resources in a variety of formats (e.g. paper based distance learning, textbooks, videos, CBT packages and CD Rom) through RBS. Training and development staff of RSA can and do provide advice, support and guidance on the use of these resources.

Concerning the future, some of the HRD staff suggested a continuing changing role for them away from provision of courses towards a more coaching and facilitative role.

HRD objectives

The primary responsibility of the HRD function in RSA is to support and facilitate individual, team and organisational learning and development with the aim to realise business goals. The HRD department has formulated several objectives. First, the HRD department takes the lead in ensuring policies, procedures and processes reflect and meet the requirements of the UK Investors in People award. Second, HRD staff work very closely with operational managers to ensure learning and development is focused on and supports achievement of business goals and objectives. Third, the HRD department engages in the design and accessing of learning materials in a wide variety of formats which can be and are utilised by managers and individual employees

Box 10.3 Monthly one-to-ones at Royal Scottish Assurance

The 'monthly one-to-ones', as introduced in Royal Scottish Assurance, are a 'whole person' focused development process where individual employees at all levels plan and monitor their personal development plans through monthly meetings with their line manager.

The process is named 'Route to Success'. This represents a pun on the meaning of 'route', as in a journey, and 'root' as in plants. The latter is represented by the use of a tree metaphor where the branches and leaves stand for the future. The roots of the tree are labelled 'family', 'health', 'education', 'career', 'service' and 'financial'. Employees are encouraged to identify how one, or a combination of the roots, needs to be worked on in order to contribute the 'nutrients' required to bring about their desired future. This metaphor is depicted on the inside front cover of a colour printed, A4-sized document holder which holds the self-carbonated pad of pro-formas completed during each monthly meeting. The pro-forma is headed by a space for the month, and has three pages:

- Page one has two headings, 'How Am I Doing?' and 'Previous Months Action Points'.
- Page two has three headings; 'KPI', 'CPD' and 'HR'. These are key performance indicators, continuing professional development, and human resources. Activities and issues relevant to each of these are noted.
- The final page has one heading only, 'This Month's Action Points' and designated space at the bottom for signature and dating by the employee and manager.

The manager retains the top copy of each sheet and the bottom copy remains in the pad attached to the document holder issued to every employee. HRD staff have designed and implemented the monthly one-to-one intervention, an open-ended and flexible process between individuals and their manager. The role of HRD is to provide documentation to support and to focus the meetings. Materials provided by the HRD Department support the personal development process. Action points from the meeting may involve not only the individual but also the manager and other training staff. HRD's role is to support and facilitate agreed learning.

These performance review meetings are a recent innovation. An interesting and significant feature is that work and job performance is not the sole or exclusive focus. The process and supporting documentation encourage individuals to examine, analyse and reflect on the whole of their current life experience, and to identify goals and aspirations in all aspects of their life. While the process has the support of senior managers, it is in its early stages and is not yet consistent throughout the organisation.

to support achievement of their own development objectives (see Box 10.4). Finally, the department aims to directly facilitate organisational learning. For example, learning that may emerge from the experiences of an individual worker will be shared with his or her colleagues through regional sales meetings. This will be passed on by an HRD practitioner to other training staff, who in turn will disseminate in their regions.

Box 10.4 Competency development guide at Royal Scottish Assurance

The competency development guide, as used in Royal Scottish Assurance is a document that employees can use for their own development. It aims at increasing and supporting an active role for the employees in their own development process.

The guide is a printed document which links learning material available for loan by employees to the Royal Bank of Scotland (RBS) competency framework. As the majority of staff within RSA are directly employed by RBS, the competency framework is relevant and staff have access to the learning materials. The document is seventy-eight pages in length. It is organised into sections covering each of the seven competencies, which are communication, decision making, knowledge/skill, leadership/influence, performance management, personal qualities, and planning and organisation.

Each of these has a number of sub-headings, leading to a total of 40 competency statements. The learning materials are categorised as book, video, CBT, multi-media, text distance learning course, or Anderson Soft Teach. Each of these has a pictorial icon which is used against the title of each item to identify its form or format. Relevant learning materials are listed under each of the seven main competency statements under the headings of 'general' and 'advanced'.

The guide also contains instructions on its use and how to order materials, as well as an alphabetical listing of all materials. It is professionally and attractively presented and is likely to encourage and support use of the learning materials in self-managed development.

Staff in the HRD department can utilise the guide in advising individual employees and managers on resources and development opportunities available. They also provide additional guidance on the contents of the guide.

The guide and associated resources are well established in the overall training strategy and they are much valued by employees.

HRD strategies

HRD policy in RSA is formulated and agreed by the management board, with support from the head of training and development and his staff. It appears to be less formal than in some other organisations in the sense of not relying on an abundance of written documents, though the process and outcomes do meet the standards of the UK IiP award. The policy seems to have a number of elements. First, to exceed regulatory requirements in terms of staff qualification levels. Second, to develop the whole person, and not just focus on the technical requirements of particular roles or jobs. Third, to provide the necessary infrastructure and resources. Finally, to identify and support development of individual potential as a means of achieving staff retention.

Royal Scottish Assurance employs a range of interventions. As already indicated, these include provision of standard courses. The topics include technical knowledge related to RSA products, technical skills such as selling or giving presentations and 'personal development' subjects such as time or stress management. But there is also much attention for developing and introducing less formal methods of training and development. Two methods which seem to be of significance currently are coaching and mentoring.

Another significant HRD intervention has been the design and implementation of the monthly one-to-one performance review (see Box 10.3) and development planning process. Together with the provision of learning materials and open learning resources, this constitutes an important contribution to supporting and facilitating individual learning. As mentioned earlier, facilitating organisational learning constitutes a further type of intervention. Participation in the design and conduct of national and regional sales meetings enables HRD staff to facilitate and influence team and organisational learning. In addition, some HRD staff act as advisers to managers, coach managers who act as coaches, and provide one-to-one coaching for employees themselves.

Wolverhampton & Dudley Breweries – beer production

The company

Facts and figures

The Wolverhampton & Dudley Breweries (WDB) is the largest 'regional' brewer in the UK and is listed on the London Stock Exchange. The company began in 1875 and currently employs a total of 10,500 staff. Approximately seventy-five per cent of staff are employed part-time, and the majority of these are employed in retail operations.

There are twelve staff employed within HRD at WDB, including two administrative support staff. A structural distinction is drawn between head office/corporate HRD and retail training and development. The primary functions of HRD staff relate to co-ordinating learning and development across the company, and monitoring the construction and implementation of training and development plans for individuals, departments and the organisation as a whole.

Business strategy

Wolverhampton & Dudley Breweries' published vision/mission statement, is:

> Dazzling pubs, irresistible beers, stunning service and our people's creativity are the catalyst for customer appeal and both Employee and Shareholder reward.
> (Source: WDB internal documents)

The company's main goal is to remain an independent regional brewer. But the organisation is facing a strong competitive market. In order to stay independent the organisation considers it important to focus on optimisation of employee contribution, performance improvements and customer satisfaction.

In this respect it was found that the WDB group takes learning and development seriously. This is, among other things, evidenced by attaining the UK IiP award, and by the company winning numerous national and industry awards for their HRD policies and practice. As well as direct achievement of corporate and business objectives and strategies, the company appears to value learning and development as a means of attracting and retaining high quality staff, especially in what are referred to as 'core operations'. The promotion of a learning philosophy is also seen as a means of gaining the highest level of contribution from such staff through developing an organisation culture which encourages individual responsibility and a willingness to take risks through a higher tolerance of failure. HRD policy and practice, especially through the use of non-course based methods such as mentoring, coaching, technology-based programmes and open learning, appear to be intended to encourage and support these characteristics.

The learning-orientated philosophy within WDB seems to be about creating continuous improvement in the quality of products to gain a competitive advantage in fast moving and changing markets. Policy and practice, including specific initiatives, appear to be intended to bring about cultural change in order to continue to improve business results. They focus on maximising individual, team and organisational learning as an attempt to ensure long term survival as an independent brewer.

Change processes

Learning and development is closely aligned to, and indeed forms part of, the corporate and business strategies. These rest on increasing sales and profit performance to increase returns to shareholders. The key to achievement is seen by the company to be quality of products and service which, in turn, rely on the qualities of employees and the organisation culture as expressed by managerial and employee behaviour. Initiatives to bring about the desired change in culture are designed and lead by HRD staff. Examples of these include 'Customer First' workshops (see Box 10.5) and 'Challenge 2000+'. The former engages diagonal 'slices' of staff in examining the meaning and operationalisation of customer service. They are followed up by HRD staff working with teams and sections/departments to produce 'Customer Charters', which specify achievable but 'stretching' standards.

Charters have been agreed and adopted for retail and trade customers, and for some internal customers by support/corporate functions. Additional workshops are held to monitor and review progress, and plan/decide areas and means of improvement. Challenge 2000+ is a team-building programme which again utilises diagonal slices of staff. The focus is inter- and intra-team working, and the purpose is to improve cross-functional communications and relationships to support a corporate focus on quality of products and services. It is perhaps significant that members of the Board of Directors have and do engage as participants in these initiatives. The importance attached to learning is reinforced by additional aspects of the HRD policy and practice. Each individual employee has an annual appraisal meeting, which is reviewed quarterly. This produces an individual training and development plan and a departmental plan. Implementation of these is co-ordinated by the HRD Manager. However, responsibility for learning and development rests with line and operational managers. The company adopts and promotes a philosophy of 'My manager is my trainer'. As one senior manager put it, 'We absolutely rely on managers to take on training and development'. The philosophy is reinforced by employee training and development being a

---

Box 10.5 Customer First at Wolverhampton & Dudley Breweries

'Customer First', as implemented at Wolverhampton & Dudley Breweries, is a culture change programme that encourages connections between work and learning. All staff attend an initial Customer First workshop. Participant groups are drawn from a cross section of departments and organisational levels. The workshops focus on identifying the general principles of customer service and their application in design and operation of work methods and procedures.

Actual work teams, facilitated by HRD staff, then work on producing a 'Customer Charter' during team meetings back at work. These charters define and specify the standards of service that employees, individually and collectively, will commit themselves to in their work. Charters have been and are being developed for both external and internal customers. The HRD department has produced its own Charter.

Follow-up Customer First workshops are held regularly to monitor progress, share learning ideas and experience, build relationships across department/sections and to reinforce enthusiasm and commitment.

The Customer First workshop was designed and is lead by the HRD department. HRD staff work with existing teams and sections/ departments to produce achievable but 'stretching' standards. Members of the board of directors have also been involved and continue to engage in these activities.

This programme has been running for two years and is cited as a factor which enhances learning. Charters have been agreed and adopted for retail and trade customers, and for some internal customers by support/corporate functions. Additional workshops are held to monitor and review progress and plan/decide areas and means of improvement.

---

performance indicator in managerial appraisals. However, some staff in WDB are considered responsible for their own training and development.

HRD in Wolverhampton & Dudley Breweries

People involved in HRD

Managers and employees appear to share responsibility for identifying and meeting learning and development needs. Managers conduct annual appraisals and review them quarterly. They are also responsible for devising and implementing departmental training plans. They contribute directly through for example coaching, mentoring and, in some cases, delivery of formal courses. Individuals manage implementation, with support from their managers, of their individual training plans.

HRD practitioners provide support and advice to ensure learning and development contributes to achieving business priorities and objectives. The primary functions of HRD staff relate to provision of learning opportunities through a wide range of methods, co-ordinating learning and development across the company, and supporting the construction and implementation of training and development plans for individuals, departments and the organisation as a whole. In this sense, their function is to support the identification and meeting of learning and development needs, rather than to perform those functions themselves.

HRD objectives

The HRD department see their role as being the 'champions' of learning and development as a means of achieving organisation success. They aim to facilitate, encourage, and support learning and development for individuals, within work teams, between teams and across/throughout the company. Fulfilling this role also involves taking an overview of the organisation and its business performance, and attempting to focus learning and development on business objectives and strategies.

Looking at future organisational developments, it can be said that HRD will play a leading role, as they have done in the recent past. They currently have a significant role in bringing about desired changes in corporate and organisational culture. As well as continuing to improve business awareness among all employees through HRD interventions, there are plans to introduce and implement a new system of teambased performance appraisal. This is intended to reinforce the desired team ethos and to support team and organisational learning. The initiative will be lead by HRD, including the design and introduction of the system. In terms of technology, HRD will have an important role in ensuring the necessary skills and abilities are developed and available.

HRD strategies

The HRD policy operated at WDB emphasises the strategic objectives of the business. This means for example that support for further or higher education courses is available, but a business case must be made. Further elements of policy are to maximise income from government funded programmes and initiatives and maintaining the IiP award.

In addition to the formal courses (e.g. to support the acquisition of national vocational qualifications) the HRD department is keen to utilise a wide range of noncourse based methods such as coaching, mentoring, visits and secondments to encourage managers and employees to change their perception of training and development from associating it with 'courses' to being willing and able to link work and learning. An example of this is what is called in the company 'three in a car'. Here, a trainer will coach managers to improve their coaching skills by observing and providing feedback to a manager coaching one of their staff. A further example of this approach is the HRD department preparing and providing 'learning manuals' for use by managers and staff in induction and initial training and development.

The two initiatives already mentioned, 'Customer First' and 'Challenge 2000+', are also important elements of the HRD strategy.

Factors influencing HRD's role and how HRD deals with them

In the preceding sections, visions and strategies of the four case study organisations with regard to becoming a learning organisation were described, as well as HRD's role in this process. This section describes factors which affect the attainment (or lack of attainment) of the envisioned role of the HRD department. Inhibiting factors, conducive factors and strategies to overcome constraints are briefly discussed.

Inhibiting factors

All British case study organisations were found to be facing some inhibiting factors in the change process towards a learning (oriented) organisation. Table 10.1 lists the most significant ones.

It seems that lack of time for learning due to work pressure and insufficient HRD resources are the most common inhibiting factors (all cases). An insufficient learning culture, or lack of commitment for learning and development was also mentioned by Royal Mail, Rolls-Royce and RSA. It is, apparently, difficult to develop a learning culture. Perhaps the third factor, resistance to or fear of change, contributes to this (mentioned by Royal Mail, Rolls-Royce and WDB).

Resistance may come from employees, but also from management, who fear the empowerment of their employees or taking on new roles themselves. Lack of support or skills from management was also mentioned separately by Royal Mail and Rolls-Royce. If top management does not support the changes, or if managers do not possess the necessary skills to support employees in learning, the new way of working will be difficult to implement. That is also the reason why Royal Mail for instance pays so much attention to the changing role of managers (through their leadership programme A4L), who they see as key players in the change process, and why other organisations provide coach-the-coach interventions.

Finally, a lack of written HRD policy was mentioned by RSA. This could lead to reduced clarity about HRD's vision and create ambiguity about the new role.

Conducive factors

A large number of factors were found that support the development towards a learning (oriented) organisation. Table 10.2 gives an overview of the most important ones.

Whereas managers sometimes form an inhibiting factor, they can also be a positive influence, as becomes clear from this table. Managers possessing people skills or a people orientation were mentioned as a conducive factor by Royal Mail, RSA and WDB. Support and commitment were also mentioned by all four cases. Paying attention to the new role of managers (by providing clarity or by helping them achieve new skills) also helps the change process (Royal Mail and Rolls-Royce). These conducive factors are interesting, because they are a mirror of some of the inhibiting factors (such as lack of skills, lack of commitment by management).

Communication throughout the change process also helps. Communication from the HRD department on its new role, but also communication between management and employees, and communication to share best practices, and were all mentioned as positive influences on the process by all cases.

All organisations were found to be investing in new HRD methods, and all organisations also find a wide range of HRD activities to be a conducive factor.

Table 10.1 Inhibiting factors – UK case study organisations

Inhibiting factors	Royal Mail	Rolls-Royce	Royal Scottish Assurance	Wolverhampton & Dudley Breweries
Lack of time for learning/ work load demands	•	•	•	•
Insufficient HRD resources	•	•	•	•
Insufficient learning culture/ commitment to learning	•	•	•	
Resistance to / fear of change	•	•		•
Lack of support/ skills from management	•	•		
Lack of written HRD policy			•	

Table 10.2 Conducive factors – UK case study organisations

Conducive factors	Royal Mail	Rolls-Royce	Royal Scottish Assurance	Wolverhampton & Dudley Breweries
People skills /orientation of managers	•		•	•
Support and commitment of management	•	•	•	•
Clarity of new role for managers and management development	•	•		
Communication	•	•	•	•
Wide range of HRD resources /facilities	•	•	•	•
Early successes (start of culture change, achievement of IiP)	•	•		
Constant reinforcement, active role of HRD departmen	•		•	

The final two conducive factors are closely related. Early successes (in changing the culture for instance) help the change process (Royal Mail and Rolls-Royce). If these successes are not yet there, constant reinforcement of the message is important (Royal Mail and RSA).

Coping strategies

A great diversity of strategies for dealing with the experienced constraints was found. For instance,

- the HRD department of Royal Mail is putting a new emphasis on learning as part of the job;
- the HRD department from Rolls-Royce Aerospace Group is improving communication towards employees on changes, changes in organisation of work; (in the

form of wider job structures with larger development possibilities for employees) and a focus on eliminating the fear employees have for changes;
* careful planning of HRD department activities and policy is one of the coping strategies used by Royal Scottish Assurance;
* the HRD department from Wolverhampton & Dudley Breweries is working on an internal and external network, redeployment of some employees and critically evaluating effects of HRD in order to cope with negative forces and capitalize upon positive ones.

Summary and conclusions

Organisational context

Four case study organisations have been discussed: Royal Mail, Rolls-Royce Aerospace Group, Royal Scottish Assurance and Wolverhampton & Dudley Breweries. Table 10.3 provides an overview of the characteristics of the organisations such as sector, number of employees, HRD function, number of HRD practitioners and the HRD department.

It was found that all four case study organisations in the UK are dealing with increasingly competitive markets. In order to respond adequately to this competition, each wants to increase its customer focus. As well as attention to product and service quality (as in WDB) and using technology to decrease lead times (as in Rolls-Royce), employees play a key role in creating desired customer satisfaction. This was the case

Table 10.3 Overview of UK case organisations

Company name and sector	Number of employees	HRD
Royal Mail, national postal service	Total: 160,000 district: 1,800	Training departments at three Nottinghamshire organisational levels: • Strategic level: 8 HRD • Division level 70 employees, in T&D department • T&D group with 120 employees
Rolls-Royce Aerospace, manufacturing aero engines	Airline Business Operations: 2,000	• Central department as part of the human resource function • Training college • HR director • Staff of 8 HRD employees
Royal Scottish Assurance , financial services	550	• Training and development department • 12 HRD professionals
Wolverhampton & Dudley Breweries, beer brewing and retail catering and hospitality (pub and restaurant operations)	Total: 10,500 Retail operations: 9,500 Brewery: 1,000	• HRD department • 10 HRD professionals • 2 administrative staff

not only in Royal Scottish Assurance, which is unsurprising (financial services is primarily a 'people business'), but also in the other three case study organisations.

With regard to the change processes, it is interesting to note that all four cases have a culture change programme, to transform the organisational culture to a learning culture and/or a client oriented culture. Also noteworthy is:

- the specific attention paid to development of management (which plays a key role in supporting and stimulating employee learning) in Royal Mail and Rolls-Royce;
- the fact that all cases either have the Investors in People standard, or are seeking to achieve it. This can be considered typical for the British situation, since it is a national initiative.

A final point, worth mentioning is the fact that in one case, WDB, the HRD department plays a leading role in achieving the business strategy.

HRD's envisioned role

The role of HRD practitioners seems to be one of facilitation, co-ordination and support rather than merely providing training and development. This is an educational role, informing and encouraging managers and other employees to consider the wider range of opportunities for, and methods of, learning and development. The role is one of being a champion of, and role model for, learning, where learning is not restricted to attending formal courses. The HRD practitioner's role is one of a working partnership with managers, to support the achievement of business objectives. Managers and employees both also carry much of the responsibility for learning.

HRD practitioners fulfil a supportive and consulting role, for example, by providing resources for learning and giving advice on personal development plans. All four HRD departments are characterised by an explicit customer focus.

The objectives of the HRD departments have in common that they all wish to support business success, by stimulating and supporting learning on different levels, and in different ways. Achieving and /or maintaining the IiP standard is also an important issue for all four cases. This seems to provide a good way for organisations to manage the process of linking learning to business requirements. The HRD departments of Rolls-Royce and Royal Scottish Assurance deliberately mention the development of a 'learning environment' in the workplace as a means to support individual and organisational learning. This concept probably has much in common with the idea of creating a learning culture, but seems to go further in the sense that it incorporates learning resources and an 'infrastructure' for learning.

Strategies adopted to realise HRD's new role

Strategies adopted by the HRD departments emphasise employee development in all cases. The departments pay more attention than before to providing career counselling and personal development plans, for example. The companies do not always expect an immediate pay-off from these individual learning activities, but they do expect benefits such as a better-motivated workforce, which will be more committed to realise organisational objectives and remain working for the company.

A second interesting feature of the strategies is a broadening of the array of learning interventions to more activities which support work-based and informal learning. This can be seen as an effort to create the 'learning environment' discussed above. A second objective is to broaden employees view of learning. Many people unconsciously equate learning to a classroom activity ('academic' view of learning), which may block them from using learning opportunities in the workplace. The case study organisations (most notably Royal Mail, Rolls-Royce and WDB) want to change this view. They would like employees to see and appreciate the possibilities for learning in the workplace (as a first step in using these possibilities). In the end this should lead to an integration of learning in daily work activities, which is something all case organisations strive for.

Finally, specific attention for developing coaching skills in managers is apparent in Royal Mail, Royal Scottish Assurance and WDB. Managers are expected to fulfil a new role in supporting employees in learning, but they need new skills in order to perform this role. That is why these organisations have developed leadership programmes or coach-the-coach activities.

Influencing factors

It seems that lack of time for learning due to work pressure and insufficient HRD resources are the most common inhibiting factors. An insufficient learning culture, or lack of commitment for learning and development were also mentioned. It is difficult to develop a learning culture. Perhaps the third factor, resistance to or fear of change contributes to this.

Managers possessing people skills or a people orientation were mentioned as an important conducive factor. Support and commitment were also mentioned by all four cases. Paying attention to the new role of managers (by providing clarity or by helping them achieve new skills) also helps the change process. These conducive factors mirror some of the inhibiting factors (such as lack of skills, lack of commitment management).

Communication throughout the change process also helps. Communication from the HRD department on its new role, but also communication between management and employees, and communication to share best practices are all important.

A great diversity of approaches to deal with the inhibiting factors was found. Communication is one of the common elements, for instance in strategies such as putting a new emphasis on learning as part of the job, improving communication towards employees on changes and working on an internal and external network. Working carefully as an HRD department is also helpful, for instance by critically evaluating effects of HRD and careful planning of HRD activities and policies.

11 Conclusions from case studies and survey

Saskia Tjepkema

The case studies, reported in Chapters 4 to 10, were followed by a survey of a 165 companies in the seven participating countries. The purpose of the survey was to investigate whether findings from the case studies could be considered representative for a larger number of learning-oriented organisations throughout Europe. Since the survey results tended to corroborate the case study outcomes, in this chapter, the main conclusions from both are discussed jointly. The chapter provides a general account of the results, focusing on 'content' outcomes, rather than on numerical results. Readers interested in the specifics of the case and survey results, are referred to the original project reports (Tjepkema, *et al.*, 1999; Tjepkema *et al.*, 2000).

The study set out to answer three main research questions:

1 How do HRD departments in learning-oriented organisations throughout Europe envision their own role in stimulating and supporting employees to learn continuously as a part of everyday work (with the intention of contributing to organisational learning, and thus enhancing organisational competitiveness)?
2 What strategies do European HRD departments adopt to realise their envisioned role?
3 What factors inhibit the realisation of this new role? How do HRD practitioners cope with these factors?
4 What factors facilitate the realisation of HRD's new role?

The main results from the case studies and the survey are provided for each of these questions. First, it is important to point out that from these data, it is not possible to make judgements concerning the situation in any specific country, because the project only incorporated some 'good examples' of learning-oriented organisations from each participating EU nation. The researchers did not select a representative group of companies, since this is not possible in either case studies, or small-scale survey research. It is impossible to make a judgement on the situation in a specific country based on only a few cases, but the data were checked for national differences nonetheless. In general no significant differences were found between the situation in the seven participating countries.

Organisational context

Before describing results for the actual research questions it is important to briefly address the organisational context. This section therefore examines issues such as: the firms' main strategic business issues, reasons for wanting to increase their potential for organisational learning, and main change strategies employed in pursuing this goal.

Business strategy

It was found that all twenty-eight cases, as well as almost all of the 165 organisations participating in the survey, are currently facing strong(er) competitive markets (caused for instance by globalisation) and/or fast(er) changing technologies. As a result, *improving and innovating* products, processes and/or services and *increasing client centredness* were found to be key elements in most business strategies. These strategies have in common that they require great *flexibility,* since this enables the organisation to respond quickly to, for instance, technological innovations or shifting client needs. Some organisations even explicitly adopted strategies directly related to increasing flexibility, for example reducing delivery times.

Human resources were mentioned by almost all of the case organisations as well as the survey participants as an important means to realise these business objectives. People are regarded as a key asset in meeting the main strategic challenges, such as increasing client focus, innovation, improvement and flexibility. While business is inevitably becoming more technological, paradoxically it is people that are becoming the key to competitiveness (see also: Lifelong learning for European Business, 1993). Employee learning and related issues, such as knowledge management/knowledge sharing and creating a learning culture were found to be key issues for most organisations in this study.

By the way, not all case organisations officially stated that they intend to become a learning organisation. Nevertheless, most firms appear to be developing towards a learning organisation (by means of, for instance, improving employee learning and working on a learning culture) without explicitly stating this as a major organisational goal. Becoming a learning (oriented) organisation is not so much a strategic business objective itself, but rather a way to realise such strategic business objectives, and as such a response to an increasingly turbulent business environment (increased competition, technological advances, etc).

Though a strategic intent to become more client-centred, among other things by realising on-going improvement and innovation, and greater flexibility, seems to be a main motivator for wanting to become a learning organisation, more people-oriented reasons appear to play a role as well. Such reasons include, for instance:

- a lack of vocational training which forces the company to create learning opportunities for staff (in two of the French cases, see Chapter 6);
- the intention to retain employees and/or reduce employee turnover (which is the case for instance in the Belgian cleaning company ISS, see Chapter 4);
- increasing quality of working life.

Change processes

The organisations in this study were found to adopt a large variety of change strategies, in order to realise their (new) strategic goals. Change processes most commonly addressed topics such as:

- creating a client-oriented culture;
- changing the management style;
- improving the strategy development process (e.g. creating a shared mission statement);
- changing the structure (e.g. implementing team working);
- optimising (IT) systems;
- creating a learning culture;
- supporting employee development.

Given the outlook of this study, those change strategies focusing on creating a *learning culture* and on *employee development* are of greatest interest. Creating more learning opportunities, improving worker motivation for learning and supporting a continuous development process for employees constitute examples of change initiatives directed at development of a learning culture. Examples of activities targeted at employee development include the implementation of competence management and personal development plans. It is interesting to note that organisations appear to focus on the role of *human resources* in the organisation, in general. They don't seem to limit themselves to employee development but also use other HR initiatives and instruments, such as selection and recruitment, and job rotation.

In general, companies employ a rich array of change initiatives, in which no one type of change is particularly dominant. Which types of changes are initiated in any given firm is probably determined by a mix of factors, such as strategic business objectives, employee characteristics, current organisational problems, organisational structure and management style. Untangling these relationships falls beyond the scope of this project, which focuses mainly on HRD, not on the companies as a whole.

One final observation is worth mentioning here. Though a common theme throughout the research has been the motivation for becoming more learning-oriented, in order to realise improvements in business performance and competitive advantage, this seemingly causal relationship does not seem to be extensively evaluated in any of the organisations. In other words, no one has looked for 'proof' that increasing the organisational capacity for learning will indeed increase organisational effectiveness. Their trust in the concept of the learning organisation can therefore probably be explained as an act of faith, or as one of faithfully copying what apparently successful organisations seem to be doing.

HRD's envisioned role

The first research question was: how do HRD departments in learning-oriented organisations throughout Europe envision their own role in stimulating and supporting employees to learn continuously, as a part of everyday work? In order to come up with an answer, HRD objectives were investigated, as well as the 'HRD partnership': who are involved in HRD, and what roles do these different people assume? This section summarises the results.

HRD objectives

Survey results regarding important HRD objectives are highly similar to the case study outcomes. In general, objectives in four areas could be distinguished:

- supporting the business;
- supporting (informal) learning and/or supporting knowledge sharing;
- providing training;
- changing HRD practices.

Supporting the business

A first category of objectives is related to the strategic goal of 'supporting the business', either in a general sense, or by supporting specific current strategic company objectives. Examples of such business-oriented objectives are: 'helping the company to meet current and future challenges', 'making sure training contributes to corporate strategy' and 'keeping the organisational skill base up-to-date'. Or in other words, making sure the workforce possesses the necessary knowledge and skills to fulfil those tasks required to realise company objectives. This task encompasses activities such as analysing the existing skill base, analysing current and future competence requirements and recruiting and training employees to make sure these requirements are met. Related objectives are, therefore, 'defining key competence areas or organisational learning needs', 'helping to retain employees' and 'stimulating employee versatility'.

As well as objectives regarding support for the business in a general sense, some HRD functions mention *specific organisational objectives which they seek to support*. For instance: 'enhancing organisational flexibility', 'supporting managers in their new role', or 'supporting the customer orientation of the company'.

Supporting (informal) learning and knowledge sharing

A second set of objectives exists of goals regarding support for (informal) learning of employees and/or teams and the organisation as a whole. Within this category, three types of objectives can be distinguished.

First, objectives with regard to *supporting employee learning in general*, such as 'promoting employee development', 'contributing to learning', 'contributing to competence development', or 'creating conditions for lifelong learning'.

It is interesting to note the inherent tension between the desire to support the business that was mentioned earlier, and the objective to support individual learning. Linking these two is not always a straightforward task, as some case organisations also experience. For instance the Finnish paper machine manufacturer Valmet strives for a strong connection between training activities and business activities (see

Chapter 5). In order to strengthen this link, once a year, development discussions are organised. In these meetings, employees' needs and possibilities for development are evaluated. But, according to managers, a connection to the organisational strategy is not always created. In using personal development plans, the focus is very much on personal learning issues. This is probably quite a widespread phenomenon.

A second group of objectives can be distinguished which express explicit support for *informal learning*, such as: 'implementing a learning culture', 'stimulating and supporting new knowledge creation', 'engaging and motivating employees in learning and working' and 'stimulating appreciation and use of informal learning opportunities on-the-job'. Of note here is the variation in terminology; whereas some companies use terms such as 'learning culture' and 'informal learning', others speak of 'knowledge creation'. This is probably largely a matter of terminology, but it might, however, also reflect a somewhat different outlook on the types of learning processes these firms concentrate their attention on. The term knowledge management appears to reflect a greater emphasis on *sharing* knowledge or making sure knowledge becomes available to more people in the organisation, whereas in the concept of the learning organisation, the focus seems to be more on creating opportunities for learning and development for individuals (and also for teams and the organisation as a whole).

Supporting learning does not seem to be simply a matter of providing opportunities for learning. Stimulating *motivation* for learning is a recurring issue in some of the objectives mentioned above (e.g. 'engage and motivate employees'). Also, attention to creating a *broad perspective* on learning can be detected. In general, most employees and managers (and even HRD professionals) hold a somewhat limited view on 'learning'. They usually (implicitly) equate it to classroom training. In some case organisations, the HRD professionals were found to actively try to establish a broader vision of learning. For instance, the British aero-engine manufacturer Rolls-Royce Airline Business, mentions it as an explicit objective (see Chapter 10). One of its HRD managers explained the relevance of creating a broader view on learning:

There is an immense amount of on-the-job learning. Many employees would not have been conscious of this form of learning. If you asked them to list what learning they had been involved in, they would think 'what course did I go on, what hotel did I stay in, what exam did I take?' Learning means doing the job, learning from colleagues, training others, doing a first aid certificate, having an enlarged job. Coaching is important – often the coach learns more than the coachee. Every new experience is an opportunity to learn.

Finally, both case study and survey evidence suggest that most companies do not focus exclusively on individual learning, but also aim to support *team and even organisational learning*. The emphasis, however, is on the individual level.

Providing training

Whereas informal learning does receive explicit attention, objectives with regard to providing training, such as 'development and co-ordination of training' and 'offering a supply of training activities' also form an important group.

The objective of the French semi-conductor plant Motorola, which mentions that it seeks to centralise its training efforts in order to get a more global and accurate view and a better strategic control of the training investments (see Chapter 6) is worthy of note here. It seems that this is a necessary prerequisite for ensuring that training contributes effectively to the corporate strategy, which is HRD's main aim.

Changing HRD practices/organisation of HRD

In order to provide (informal) learning opportunities, and to provide a strategic contribution to the firm, some organisations have formulated objectives with regard to changing HRD practices or structures. Of course, this is an intermediary objective, it is not a purpose in itself, but something HRD functions pursue in order to better fulfil their main responsibilities. The most important objectives in this field are related to integrating HRD more strongly in the work organisation, for instance by sharing HRD tasks with line managers. Examples of these objectives include: 'providing services to/supporting management', 'working on a demand-oriented basis', 'stimulating management to become more sensitive to HRD issues' and 'integrate HRD in business functions'.

Other objectives, reflecting changing HRD practices are:

- adopting a more pro-active role as HRD department, for instance: 'changing from a reactive to a proactive role' and 'playing a leading role in the development of a new management system';
- adopting new work methods, for instance: 'realising/improving competence management';
- adopting a new approach to HRD, for instance: 'increase self-management in learning' and 'change from human resource control to human resource development'

Most important objectives?

Though it was attempted to establish one in the survey, differences in importance between these sets of objectives are too small to reflect a real rank order. Whichever objective is stressed most depends on the specific situation of each organisation. It is interesting to note though, that the expectation of survey respondents was that objectives in the field of supporting informal learning and promoting knowledge sharing are expected to increase most in importance in the future. It is also relevant to point out that supporting the business (objectives) is one of the most important HRD objectives, but survey results suggest that this involvement is usually not very great. So, the question as to how far HRD fulfils a strategic role remains open.

People involved in HRD

'Who does what in HRD?' With regard to the sharing of HRD tasks, it is clear that HRD professionals still carry the biggest share of responsibility for HRD (at least in their own estimation of the situation). Managers and employees are important active partners, and are expected to become more so in the future.

HRD professionals

In general, HRD professionals' work in the learning-oriented organisations in this study still largely consists of what we might call 'traditional' HRD tasks, such as developing, providing and/or co-ordinating training. This finding supports the assumption made in the previous section that training is still a significant part of the work field of HRD professionals in the learning-oriented organisations. Other 'basic' HR tasks such as giving advice to employees, for instance on career paths, and selection and recruitment were also mentioned.

Perhaps more interesting than the regular HRD tasks are the *'new' tasks*, which were also found. In the vast majority of both the case and survey organisations, HRD professionals mentioned such non-traditional tasks as part of their work portfolio. The most important ones are: consulting to line management and providing tools and (practical) support with regard to learning issues to line managers (and employees).

Both tasks reflect a shift in the responsibility for learning towards managers – who are expected to assume a more active role in supporting their employees in learning – as well as towards employees themselves. We will look more closely into both their roles below. As for the HRD professionals, if managers and employees take over some of the more practical HRD tasks, this means HRD professionals will have to support them in doing so, in order to ensure quality of HRD interventions. An effective way in which to give this support is to provide them with methods and tools (e.g. personal development plans) that stimulate self-management in learning. A good example is provided by British insurance agency Royal Scottish Assurance, where the HRD department has developed a competency development guide for employees, listing all the available resources for learning (see Chapter 10). This supportive role is in essence a rather *practical* one.

Having managers fulfil an active role in HRD also gives HRD practitioners room to give advice and to consult on HRD issues, which can be considered to be a more *strategic* role. Advice might be directed towards helping managers to link training to corporate needs, to increase and use opportunities for informal learning at work (for instance by coaching or working on a learning climate) and to monitor competencies in a team or department.

Line managers

As mentioned above, the supportive and consulting role of HRD professionals is consistent with the way in which HRD views the role of managers and employees. In HRD's envisioned role, management fulfils an active role in supporting employee learning.

Sometimes management is *already held responsible* for employee learning. Sometimes HRD practitioners indicate that management will carry that responsibility *in the future*. In practice this means that managers are, or will become, responsible for some of the *practical* HRD tasks, such as making individual development plans, monitoring competencies, defining learning needs, competence assessment, evaluation of training or even more *strategic* tasks, such as implementing HRD policy, implementing the learning organisation concept or fulfilling a steering role with regard to HRD.

An interesting exception to the rule is encountered in the Belgian cleaning company ISS (see Chapter 4). This company employs two HRD practitioners, who are responsible for the administration and logistic support of training programmes. Their role is very restricted and reactive, and consists primarily of providing employees with adequate and sufficient training possibilities. Responsibility for defining and implementing the concept of the learning organisation lies with top management, who define HRD policies. Finally, line management is responsible for HRD in the daily work environment. This situation is interesting because it clearly differs from that in most organisations in this study. In most cases, HRD professionals fulfil a more active or even strategic role in the development of their companies, though the degree of pro-activity differs from company to company. In some firms, HRD even serves as real change agents and a driving force in the development towards a learning organisation.

Employees

Employees are also expected to fulfil an active role in their own development. They either already have a responsibility for their own learning or will share that responsibility with management in the future. Though rarely mentioned, employees sometimes are even involved in providing training or fulfilling HRD tasks in general. The French retail organisation Auchan provides an interesting example of the latter (Chapter 6). Experienced and well-performing employees are selected and trained to become trainers for the new staff. An important aim of the employee/trainer system is to motivate newcomers to learn and develop, by setting the right example.

Two points are worth considering, given these results. The first is that there does not appear to be a difference between companies with a high degree of manual labour, and companies with a highly-educated workforce. Employees are being held responsible for their own learning both in companies from manufacturing industry, such as the Finnish metal factory Outokumpu Zinc, the Dutch chemicals plant Akzo Nobel and the British brewery Wolverhampton & Dudley on the one hand, and in professional organisations such as the Finnish Okobank, the German consulting firm GTZ and the Dutch IT centre BAC on the other. Case study and survey results did not produce clear indications, but it would not be surprising if employee responsibility for learning is more difficult to achieve in production companies resembling Mintzberg's machine bureaucracy archetype (either currently or in the past), than in service industry companies that resemble professional bureaucracies. In the latter, employees traditionally already carry a large amount of responsibility for their own professional development (Mintzberg, 1979; van der Krogt, 1991).

A second point to be made is that the specific type of responsibilities to be taken on by employees seems to be less clear than for managers. For managers, responsibility for HRD means to fulfil several practical, or even strategic HRD tasks. For employees, the picture is not so clear. It appears that they are mainly expected to engage in active discussions with managers in analysing their learning needs or drawing up their personal development plans, and show an active and motivated attitude towards their own learning and development in general. In some organisations, they are also expected to act as trainer or mentor, or to engage in business improvement teams (where learning and working go hand in hand).

External HRD professionals

The survey revealed a fourth active partner in HRD, namely external institutions. Survey results indicate that these are also regularly involved in executing HRD tasks, though not on a large scale. Their most important task is (as could be expected) providing training. A large proportion of survey respondents lists them as being involved in this HRD task. Other relatively important tasks appear to be consulting on employee development and identification of employees with potential. External institutions are involved only very rarely in tasks such as making personal development plans, implementing HRD policy, promoting a learning culture, monitoring competencies and training needs analysis. These are all HRD tasks with a potentially strategic impact, which could be the reason why companies don't easily choose to outsource them.

HRD as an integrated business function?

When considering this description of the HRD professionals' new role, it is important to recognise that a gap may exist between HRD's self-image and vision and the expectations from the company. To give one example, according to HRD professionals from the Finnish Okobank, their role has changed already (see Chapter 5). Previously, they worked mostly as trainers, but now their main work consists of organising and co-ordinating personnel development functions. They try to clarify what the customers of the competence development unit need, maintain the flow of available training programmes, motivate and stimulate employees for learning, and create a learning culture. But according to line managers, there is still too much distance between the HRD unit and the business functions. Due to this, co-ordination between management and HRD is not yet clear and sufficient. Managers express an interest in more interaction, co-operation and new HRD initiatives. They hope for a more consultative role from HRD professionals and claim they want support in their responsibility for learning and development. Thus, it appears that the role of HRD professionals is changing, but still needs attention in this company. This probably also holds true for many more of the organisations in this study.

Though most HRD functions have not yet reached that point, it seems justified to conclude that the organisation of the HRD function is becoming more and more diffuse, and increasingly hard to identify and describe as a separate unit, as HRD is becoming ever more integrated within the business. This integration process appears to take place both with regard to policy-making (HRD policy linked more closely to, and eventually integrated in general strategy) and with regard to the execution of

HRD activities (from being performed by HRD department, to a shared responsibility of HRD professionals, managers and employees). The competence managers, active in the research and development division of the Dutch branch of telecommunication company Ericsson (Chapter 9) form an example of a high degree of integration. There are now three types of managers in this company: operational managers, process owners (who are responsible for process management) and competence managers (responsible for people management). The latter operate as a sort of internal job agencies: at the start of each new project, they see ensure that each project has the necessary competencies (i.e. the necessary employees) to fulfil its objectives. Competence managers are part of the HRD function. Besides supporting employees with developing personal development plans and career development plans, they are also responsible for analysing required competencies in the organisation now and in the future.

Barham and Rassam (1989) describe this transition towards HRD integration as a 'shift from a fragmented or formalised approach to a focused approach on HRD', which they predicted to emerge in ever more companies. In the *fragmented* approach, training is a peripheral activity for the organisation. Training is seen as a very separate functional activity, managed exclusively by training professionals. The organisation is 'offered' training packages, in a manner which is usually described as the cafeteria approach: the HRD department lists the available training supply in a training catalogue, from which managers and employees then pick their courses.

Companies whose training efforts were fragmented in the past may decide to put more resources into training and make the whole process more systematic. This approach is described by Barham and Rassam as the *formalised* approach, because the training system is often linked into organisational systems (e.g. the appraisal system) to ensure that training takes place on a regular basis, and is linked to business needs.

Under the *focused* approach, training and development are still much more closely integrated in the organisation. As Barham and Rassam describe it:

> It is [an approach] in which training is part of the lifeblood of the company, rather than being seen as a luxury or a dubious accessory. These firms are beginning to centre their training on three requirements: strategic business objectives, specific departmental needs and individual aspirations. Moreover, a recurring message is that the line managers themselves are taking a lead in directing training, rather than, as in the past, having to accept schemes devised by isolated training specialists. These companies are making a conscious attempt to root their training in what the organisation and its people actually need.
>
> (Barham and Rassam, 1989: 122)

According to these authors, the roles of trainers in this approach broaden to include those of advisers, consultants, providers of resources and facilitators of learning (as opposed to 'directive interventionists'). They go on to explain that companies who use training and development in this way see continuous learning by individuals as a necessity, as part of their competitive strength. They see both off-the-job training and work itself as opportunities to learn. As Barham and Rassam (1989) explain: 'they don't fall for the artificial distinction between work and learning', but instead recognise that most people are learning all the time. Support is needed for all learning activities, from formal off-the-job training to informal learning on-the-job. Based on the results described in this section, it can be concluded that most companies from this study are all making progress towards this focused approach to HRD.

HRD strategies

In the preceding section, a picture was sketched of the envisioned role of the HRD professionals. The image that emerged was one of an HRD function that aims to actively support the business by providing training and other opportunities for (informal) learning and knowledge sharing, so that the organisational knowledge and skill base is up-to-date and appropriate for realising the strategic objectives. HRD professionals, managers and employees are all active partners in this HRD function, it is not limited to an HRD department.

This section takes a closer look at the strategies adopted by the HRD professionals to support learning in their businesses, and more specifically, to achieve their objectives. In other words, this section provides an answer to the second research question: what strategies do European HRD departments adopt to realise their envisioned role?

Those HRD strategies encountered in both the case studies and the survey, can be categorised according to the main HRD objectives, described in the section on HRD's envisioned role. So, four sets of strategies could be discerned, with regard to:

• supporting the business in general, or supporting current strategic business objectives;
• supporting (informal) learning and knowledge sharing;
• providing training;
• changing HRD practices/structures.

Support business in general/support current strategic objectives

A first category of strategies was directed towards ensuring that HRD activities support the business (either in general, or with regard to a specific current strategic objective). An interesting example of such a strategy is having a *strategic approach to training*. The French semiconductor plant Motorola for instance, is moving from a catalogue approach to training, towards an approach in which contact with management is sought to ensure a solid link between training and company needs (see Chapter 6). Likewise, German chemicals manufacturer AgrEvo has also moved away from using a standard catalogue of traditional off-the-job training programmes towards an orientation on corporate objectives. To this end, it has established a competence management system and executes a strategic training needs analysis (see Chapter 7).

The second type of strategies is aimed not at supporting the business as a whole, but directed at *specific strategic business objectives*, such as implementing teamwork or changing the organisational culture. For instance, the Italian food producer Barilla supports the implementation and diffusion of self-designing work teams in manufacturing by specific interventions aimed at reinforcing the already acquired results and by presenting them to different areas, where line managers decide to start implementation. The interventions are of a step-by-step kind, steered by the specific needs managers have at any given time. Training programmes are being used, but so are other learning interventions (see Chapter 8).

A third type of strategies is formed by the *use of HR instruments* to ensure an adequate mix of competencies on the level of the organisation, thereby contributing to the organisation's competence level. In particular, competence management and applying new criteria in recruitment were mentioned. Both can be used as instruments to ensure the organisational skill base meets requirements. For instance, the Finnish steel producer Outokumpu Zinc has included a willingness to learn as a criterion in recruiting new staff. They use this as a means to create a staff that is motivated for learning (see Chapter 5).

Support (informal) learning and knowledge sharing

As well as formal training, which remains an important strategy, other methods to support (informal) learning were also found. The first cluster of strategies that can be distinguished consists of those employed to support (informal) *learning from each other and knowledge sharing*. Examples of such strategies include coaching, mentoring, learning groups, working on a variety of projects/secondments, and benchmarking. With regard to the latter, an interesting initiative was found at the British postal services, Royal Mail. This firm has installed a programme called 'Pathfinders', a benchmarking and problem-solving exercise for front-line employees. Eight employees are selected from each division, on an open and competitive basis, to form a team to examine a 'real' business problem and suggest improvements against a chosen business approach. The business problem is sponsored or championed by an operational manager, who is involved in helping the team. This is an illustration of a project that integrates learning and working, and stimulates employees to learn from each other (see Chapter 10).

An example of a learning group can be found in Sony Germany, where 'learning networks' are established. These operate in a way that resembles 'Action Learning'. Employees, who have at least one job element in common (e.g the same project, similar functions in different parts of the company) meet regularly to identify learning needs, and to develop competencies jointly, usually while working on a real business issue (see Chapter 7).

Strategies inspired by the theme of *knowledge management* were also found: for instance creating a knowledge database or building knowledge exchange networks. One organisation, the Dutch IT service provider BAC, has specifically investigated the possibilities for implementing knowledge management in its company (see Chapter 9). Technology is sometimes used explicitly to support knowledge sharing. For instance, the German manufacturer of household equipment, Bosch Siemens, and technical consulting firm GTZ have both developed information technology (IT) networks, aimed at facilitating and improving learning processes within the company. It is important to note, however, that these constitute *corporate projects*, and not HRD initiatives.

Another cluster of strategies to be discerned focuses on *fostering employee responsibility for learning*. Instruments and work methods such as personal development plans, self-directed learning, Open Learning Centres and learner-oriented learning methods all serve to increase employee self-management with regard to learning. An interesting example was found at the Finnish paper machine manufacturer Valmet (see Chapter 5). As an alternative to a traditional language course, Finnish participants who normally do not work as a team, were sent off to visit German clients. During this trip, speaking in Finnish was banned. In this way, participants developed international relationships, while at the same time improving their German language skills. This way of working is illustrative of a learning initiative where employees have a great influence on the actual programme and in which informal learning opportunities are deliberately created.

It needs to be recognised that HRD professionals sometimes also deliberately use informal learning methods as a way to change current notions on 'learning'. For instance, the HRD department at the British brewery Wolverhampton & Dudley is keen to utilise a wide range of non-course-based methods such as coaching, mentoring, visits and secondments next to the more formal courses, to encourage managers and employees to change their perceptions of training and development from associating it with 'courses' to being willing and able to link work and learning (see Chapter 10). An example of this is an approach called 'three in a car'. Here, a trainer coaches managers to improve their coaching skills by observing and providing feedback to a manager coaching one of their staff.

Though the strategies mentioned above often also stimulate group learning, a third type of strategy could be found, aimed specifically at supporting *team or even organisational learning* (mentioned six times). For instance, at the British insurance company Royal Scottish Assurance (RSA), HRD professionals participate in the design and conduct of national and regional sales meetings, in order to facilitate and influence team and organisational learning. Learning that may emerge from the experiences of an individual worker will be shared with his or her colleagues through regional sales meetings. This will be passed on by an HRD practitioner to other training staff, who in turn will disseminate it in their regions (see Chapter 10).

Providing training

A substantial amount of HRD professionals' work of course consists of developing and providing formal training. Both the survey and the cases provide too little specific information on the nature of training efforts, to permit a conclusion more detailed than the general observation that 'traditional' training does have an important place in the strategies employed by the HRD professionals to achieve their objectives.

Of particular interest here are the initiatives to use training in such a way that it prepares workers for other forms of (informal) learning. The Belgian cleaning company ISS, for instance, provides certificates for employees who have received a certain amount of training, as a means to support the development of a learning culture, and more specifically to stimulate motivation for learning (see Chapter 4). This might seem contradictory to the objective of stimulating informal learning, but in fact it can be seen as a measure which gives employees who hold negative ideas on learning a positive feeling and more self-confidence. Both are prerequisites for using learning opportunities and sharing knowledge. So this measure can be seen as a stepping stone towards creating a learning culture and self-management in learning, even though it is associated with traditional training. Similarly, Alcatel Bell, a telecommunications company from Belgium, has introduced a minimum amount of training hours. More specifically, every employee is obliged to follow twenty hours of formal training, twenty hours of on-the-job training, and ten hours of Bell Permanent Training. This educational project should increase the employability of employees. Though at first glance it seems at odds with the general striving for increasing the use of informal learning opportunities, it can actually support such forms of learning. For example, it enables employees to rotate in different jobs, or because it increases their learning skills and self confidence in learning (see Chapter 4).

Changing HRD practices

A very interesting category of strategies is that of the interventions used to change HRD practices or HRD organisation.

These include initiatives to *decentralise* HRD activities or at least achieve a less centralised organisation of the HRD function. This can be seen as a means to distribute HRD tasks and responsibilities to managers and even employees, and to ensure that HRD professionals are in close contact with the organisation (which is considered essential for ensuring a link between HRD and the business). For instance, the German household equipment factory Bosch Siemens deliberately adopted a decentralised HRD strategy, despite the fact that the HRD department is a centralised function. Responsibility concerning many HRD activities is now transferred to local decision-makers, who posses the necessary competencies and knowledge to judge which are necessary. This should serve to enhance the link between HRD and organisational needs (see Chapter 7).

Supporting management in HRD tasks and providing tools for HRD tasks, and *increasing employee responsibility* can be considered to be directed at the same purpose. In particular, providing models and methods for Personal Development Plans is an effective way for HRD professionals to transfer some HRD tasks to line managers and employees. In the British insurance firm Royal Scottish Assurance, HRD staff have designed and implemented monthly 'one-to-one interventions', which are development-oriented meetings between individuals and their manager. HRD provides documentation to support and to focus the meetings, and materials provided by the HRD department (such as a handbook where learning questions can be written down) support the personal development process (see Chapter 10). Such interventions are probably not always so much explicitly intended as strategies to implement HRD's new role, but can be considered as the actual manifestation of a new 'partnership in learning', shared between HRD practitioners, line management and workers.

It is interesting to note that a small number of companies explicitly pay attention to *developing skills of managers* with regard to HRD. For instance, the Italian software company Datalogic has evaluated its managers to measure their ability and motivation to support employees in learning (see Chapter 8). Such measures clearly go beyond providing practical support for HRD tasks. An equally interesting point to note is that, in general, there appears little attention to the *professional development of HRD practitioners* themselves. The German consulting firm GTZ was found to actively develop new skills in its HRD professionals in order to fulfil the new role of consultant and provider of support for line management (see Chapter 7). Since this new role is so radically different from the traditional roles of HRD professionals, such as developing and providing training, it might seem logical to expect that such a training would be beneficial for HRD professionals throughout more of the organisations. There is no evidence that the HRD professionals in the 27 other cases didn't work on their own professional development, it might be that more than one case engaged in such activities in this respect. However, it can be concluded that this is certainly not common. The survey results also did not indicate that professional development of HRD practitioners was a widely-used change strategy.

Leading HRD strategies?

Overall, it can be concluded that training is still an important HRD strategy, but it is complemented by strategies to support other types of learning (such as coaching, using information and communications technology (IC-T) to promote knowledge sharing etc.), and by activities meant to ensure a close link between HRD and business strategy.

HRD professionals not only invest in creating opportunities for informal learning, but also deliberately try to change attitudes towards learning, to ensure that these opportunities are actually used. For instance, methods to support informal learning are also sometimes used to change views of learning as a classroom activity. And sometimes even training-related measures are used to increase motivation for learning and boost learner self-confidence.

Though the case studies yielded a wide range of strategies employed by HRD professionals to realise their envisioned role, there was no clear indication of the relative weight of each of these strategies. The survey attempted to establish somewhat of a ranking order; which strategies are considered most important? This proved difficult, since nearly all strategies were rated 'relevant' or 'important' by respondents.Survey results did not indicate that great differences exist, but it does seem that some strategies are used more often than others. Most noticeable is the importance (still) attached to formal training programmes. In addition to newer methods for supporting learning (e.g. learning networks), formal training remains a learning mode of significant importance. Among the least often used strategies are instruments and initiatives to increase employee responsibility for learning. In general, however, differences are not very striking. Just as with general change strategies on the organisational level, HRD change strategies form a rich array in which not one strategy dominates.

A related question asked in the survey was: do respondents expect the nature of HRD strategies, techniques and instruments to change in the near future? Which HRD strategies will become more important, and which will decline in use? Strikingly, respondents estimate that *all* strategies will become more important in the future. There is no immediate contrast between strategies in the field of training and in other areas (such as supporting informal learning or changing the HRD function). Though differences are relatively small, it is interesting to note that the limited number of strategies for which the difference between present use and expected use is relatively high, are using competence management and stimulating knowledge management. Both are currently not used very often, but it is expected that they will be implemented more often in the future. Nevertheless, differences are too small to attach much weight to these observations.

These results do not paint a picture of very innovative HRD practices, dominated by new initiatives such as knowledge management networks or stimulating a learning climate in the workplace. Of course, this is partly caused by the fact that HRD objectives are not that far-stretched (in other words: the envisioned role is not that ambitious). Providing training is still an important task (see the section on HRD's envisioned role in this chapter). On the other hand, these outcomes might indicate that HRD practices to some extent fall behind HRD visions. HRD professionals *do* want to broaden their horizon by also supporting more informal modes of learning, and by forming partnerships with managers and employees, but in practice, their work is still dominated by the more traditional, training related tasks. Of course, this is to be expected; new insights as a rule precede changing behaviours. Moreover, HRD professionals also have to deal with expectations from employees and managers regarding their own role, and the products they deliver. It is not possible to change overnight. But perhaps there are other factors influencing the change process? The next section examines this question.

One thing needs mentioning here. Just as there was little indication that companies looked for proof that working to become a learning organisation paid off, in terms of helping to achieve business objectives (see the section on organisational context, above), there were no signs that HRD professionals on a large scale sought to evaluate their contribution to the development, or lack thereof, of their company towards a learning organisation. Many HRD professionals do evaluate their training courses, but in only a few companies have they outlined a plan for evaluating their contribution on a more strategic level. There are exceptions, of course. Belgian telecommunications firm Alcatel Bell, for instance, collects statistics on job rotation (a means for informal learning) and on training hours. And Belgian insurance company DVV is using evaluation instruments on different levels in the organisation, such as organisational business plans, balanced score cards and competence management. By using these instruments, DVV also wants to measure whether HRD's role has changed successfully. But they realise that measuring the success of being a learning-oriented organisation is difficult and takes a long time (see Chapter 4).

Influencing factors

So, though HRD *objectives* indicate that HRD professionals are not only interested in providing training, but also seek to support other forms of learning, HRD *practices* reveal that traditional training is still very dominant. As a result, training related tasks are still very important in their total task load, next to newer tasks, such as consulting to line management on creating learning opportunities. And though HRD professionals feel it is important to share responsibility for HRD with line management and employees, they still carry most of the responsibility themselves (according to their own estimation).

It is worthwhile investigating whether there are specific reasons for this situation. Are certain specific influences keeping HRD professionals from changing their practices? Or is the current prevalence of training activities a desired result? This section presents the study's results concerning the practical change process, addressed by the third research question: what obstacles do European HRD departments encounter when trying to realise their new role, how do they overcome these constraints and which factors are conducive to the realisation of HRD's new role?

Both case study and survey results revealed a wealth of factors influencing the change process. For instance, rather fundamental issues such as employee motivation for learning, management's readiness to take on learning tasks, clarity of HRD's role, learning culture (or lack thereof) and more pragmatic issues such as time and money were all identified. Of particular interest is the finding that whereas in some organisations a highly motivated workforce was found to be a positive influence, other companies had to deal with the opposite; a lack of motivation for learning stifled change. In general, each conducive factor had an obstacle as its counterpart. Moreover, in many instances, firms mentioned one factor, e.g. management involvement, as both a conducive and an inhibiting force at the same time, because in some parts of the company managers were highly motivated and supported changes, whereas in other parts, managers were not so motivated and thereby held back changes. The survey was used as a means to investigate the general direction (positive, negative or neutral) of some of the most common factors affecting the change process. But it proved impossible to make any generalisations in this respect. It depends on the individual organisation what factors play a role, and what effect they have on the change process (positive or negative). Below, we will take a closer look at the obstacles and driving forces for changing HRD.

Roadblocks to change

Of the factors that sometimes hinder the realisation of HRD's new role, a very important one is a *lack of motivation* on the part of managers and/or employees to take on new learning tasks or to engage actively in learning processes. It is not clear from this research what might cause such a lack of motivation. Perhaps managers and employees are still used to a different way of working and don't want to give it up yet. Another possible explanation is a lack of faith in the concept of the learning organisation or in training in general. Barham and Rassam (1989) found that managers in companies that used to have a fragmented approach to training, sometimes do not view traditional courses as valuable learning experiences, or come to see training as a cost, rather than an investment for the future. Of course, it takes time to change such a pattern of expectations once it exists, especially when managers and employees still implicitly equate 'learning' to 'training'. Employees and managers may be waiting to see positive results of this new approach. But other factors, such as a shortage of time on the part of managers, lack of rewards for employees or little self-confidence when it comes to learning, could equally well play a role. Though the cause of low motivation or low sense of responsibility is unknown (and might be different for different organisations or even different managers and employees), it is clear that, if it occurs, it can hinder the realisation of a shared responsibility for HRD between management, employees and HRD professionals.

Low motivation for participating actively in learning might in some cases be linked to another possible constraint, namely a *lack of clarity on HRD's role or lack of clarity on the need for learning.* Either they find it difficult to establish their own role very distinctly, or (and?) they find it difficult to communicate this role in a clear and convincing manner to managers and employees. Whatever the case, it appears important to pay attention to this issue. How can HRD practitioners tempt managers and employees to become active partners in creating learning organisations? It is not unlikely that managers and employees are sometimes unmotivated to perform their new roles because it is not clear to them what is expected, why learning is relevant and what support HRD professionals will provide.

The third type of inhibiting factors might seem like 'stating the obvious'. Nevertheless, *a lack of a learning culture* was experienced as an inhibiting factor to realising HRD's intended role. Apparently, it is very difficult to create a learning culture, if such a culture doesn't already exist, at least partially. Most organisations in which this point was raised point to an insufficient learning culture in general, others narrow it down to insufficient knowledge sharing. This result indicates that it is very difficult to motivate employees to share knowledge or engage in learning processes if they are not used to this, or perhaps even show a reluctance to do so (this might indicate a relationship with the first category of objectives: lack of motivation for learning on the part of employees).

As well as these rather fundamental issues, pragmatic factors such as a lack of time for learning, and insufficient time or money to develop new HRD initiatives sometimes also influences the change process negatively.

One factor encountered quite often is a *lack of time for learning on the part of employees.* Work pressure is so high that it is hard to find time for learning. Of course, this compounds to the problem of lack of motivation and lack of a learning culture. The problem is that it creates a closed cycle; when people are continuously working very hard to keep up with new developments and changes (reactively), but are too busy to learn and reflect on existing practices, this makes it very hard to find solutions which might decrease the work load (pro-actively).

Some of the other more practical problems HRD professionals face concern *their own role:* scarce resources, too little time to develop new HRD initiatives, insufficient time to update materials or, in general, not enough HRD professionals. Of course the lack of time is associated with a scarcity of resources; if more money was available, extra human resources could be hired. Interestingly enough, there is no apparent relationship between the organisations that mention a lack of HRD professionals or lack of time, and the size of the HRD departments. Some of the organisations that mention this problem employ only two HRD professionals, but it is also reported by HRD departments with a staff of 70. So it seems that the cause for this problem lies more in the fact that realising the new role is very time-consuming, because at the outset it means more tasks for the HRD professionals (the new tasks as well as the traditional tasks, see the section on HRD's envisioned role, above). Perhaps more room will be created only when managers and employees have actually taken over some of the HRD tasks.

Regarding these pragmatic factors, it is interesting to consider a possible relationship with the outsourcing policy many companies adopted during the beginning of the 1990s. It is not certain whether this applies to many of this study's organisations, but during the last few years, many companies have cut back on their training budgets, and have chosen to hire or buy training rather than develop it in-house. It might be that some of the companies who are currently experiencing a lack of specialist practitioners have been through such an outsourcing process.

Positive forces

In addition to factors which obstruct innovation of the HRD function, all organisations could also point out positive influences on the change efforts. In many cases these are just the opposite of the constraints that sometimes hold back change.

Probably the most important conducive factor is *active involvement, particularly from (top) managers* (whereas low motivation for learning related tasks from this group was an important inhibiting factor). Sometimes HRD professionals find themselves dealing with both active and motivated managers and with those that are not motivated simultaneously. *Employees with a high learning motivation* were also mentioned as a conducive factor (whereas a lack of motivation for learning was experienced as a constraint). This leads to the impression that if a lack of motivation can be turned around into a strong involvement, this will strongly influence the change process in a positive way.

Clarity on HRD's new role can also be an important conducive factor, as can positive results of *new HRD initiatives*. These increase the organisation's motivation to change.

Another possible positive force is the existence of a *learning culture*, or a strong orientation towards innovation. If a company already has a corporate culture which is open to learning, this makes it easier to change HRD practices.

New organisational structures can provide employees with more possibilities for learning during work, which gives HRD professionals a good starting point to support work-related learning. This was also sometimes mentioned as a positive factor. For instance, the French transport company GT group mentions that its employees have more possibilities for learning due to increased contact with customers (Chapter 6). And the German chemicals producer AgrEvo and consulting firm GTZ identify that the introduction of teamwork and learning networks creates new learning opportunities (Chapter 7). So, whereas old organisational structures can hinder the adoption of a new HRD approach, the re-design of such structures can actually support them.

Finally, *pragmatic* factors can also play a positive role. Some organisations experienced such factors to be helping the change process. The most important of these are ample opportunities for training and development and/or sufficient HRD resources. Sufficient resources, or sufficient time for learning or for developing HRD materials, were *not* explicitly mentioned as conducive factors (though a lack of them was mentioned as an inhibiting factor). Thus, it seems that time and professional resources are frequently abundant

Dealing with constraints and capitalising upon positive influences

Some of the conducive factors might very well be *necessary but insufficient conditions* for firms to become learning-oriented organisations. Take 'time for learning' for instance. In situations where there is a fundamental lack of time for learning, which undermines change initiatives regarding, for instance, creating a learning culture, it is essential to find a solution for this problem. Even if other conditions are met, for instance HRD resources are plenty and senior management is highly committed to the concept of the learning organisation, until workload pressures are addressed, and time is made for learning, employees will continue to see learning as 'extra' to their daily work practices (which negatively influences their motivation for learning). It is not possible to provide advice that is valid in all situations, each organisation has to find out what are the necessary conditions that are lacking in their specific situation.

As the existence of conducive factors will usually prove to be not enough in itself to boost change, conversely, inhibiting factors do not necessarily preclude the achievement of becoming learning-oriented. If we take the same example, time for learning, in some firms, for instance Royal Mail, despite shift work and daily targets, time is being found to enable learning events to be scheduled in work time and in the work environment (see Chapter 10). These organisations have found effective strategies to cope with constraints.

The last question that was addressed in this research is how HRD functions cope with the roadblocks to charge (and/or fully use or stimulate the conducive forces). It was found that for many HRD departments, the general strategies employed to realise their intended role could be considered as the main 'coping strategies' (see the section on HRD strategies, above). However, some specific (extra) coping strategies were also encountered.

Communication seems to be the key word in these coping strategies. It is essential to make sure the organisation understands the (new) role of HRD, the intentions of the HRD department, what is expected of managers and employees (and why), the new vision on learning (broader than the old classroom approach) and has the necessary information on learning opportunites. This understanding and information is very important for managers and employees to be motivated to implement the changes and to bring about a fruitful partnership between HRD professionals, managers and employees.

More specifically, the following communication strategies were found:

- Communication directed at *changing the view on (the need for) learning*: For instance, it was found that all French case organisations pay attention to sharing knowledge and communication improvements in order to let employees know why change is necessary, why learning plays an important role in the change process of the organisation and that learning takes place not only by following courses, but also by learning from each other. If this communication succeeds in changing attitudes towards learning, they might serve to increase motivation for learning, as well as enhance the creation of a learning culture and promote knowledge sharing.

- Initiatives to *increase communication or even co-operation with managers* and employees to direct HRD initiatives more closely to their needs. For instance, the Italian software company Datalogic has adopted direct horizontal communication with line management as one of its main coping strategies. As is normal for middle-sized companies, new emergencies and changes are rather frequent. The HRD department deliberately adopts a very flexible approach and a listening attitude, which leads to teamwork between managers and HRD practitioners. One could say that the traditional distinction between line and staff is overcome. Such strategies can be expected to create goodwill and motivation. The Dutch building company KIBC found that improving communication and information flows are both very useful in decreasing resistance and increasing motivation for learning.
- *Providing information* on the position, roles and responsibilities of the HRD department, on learning needs and on learning possibilities. This might provide an antidote to the inhibiting factor of lack of information and might thus serve to increase motivation for learning and for actively participating in the renewed HRD function.

Other coping strategies were also found. These include:

- Measures to *reduce the workload of HRD professionals*, and thus tackle the problem of a lack of resource, such as recruiting new HRD professionals, delegating responsibilities to line managers, and providing a training programme for those managers and increasing efficiency of HRD work methods (a more clear definition of HRD roles and tasks to avoid double work).
- Measures which can be seen as efforts to *underline the professional approach* of the HRD professionals, and to make sure the organisation has a positive approach to the HRD function, which might increase the motivation to adopt new HRD practices, namely: showing added value of the HRD department, a careful planning of HRD activities and policy, and a critical evaluation of the effects of HRD.
- Efforts to ensure that a lack of *learning possibilities* does not hinder the change process, such as continuously updating the supply of HRD initiatives or increasing possibilities for knowledge sharing and informal learning.
- Strategies that are probably meant to *increase motivation for learning in the workforce*, by bringing in 'fresh blood', and making sure (through the recruitment process) that new workers are motivated for learning, application of new selection criteria in recruitment, and redeployment of some employees.

• Activities that serve to provide the HRD professionals with a '*sounding board*', and with new ideas for initiatives within their own companies, for instance, networking with other organisations that are implementing the learning organisation concept.

Summary

In summary then, this research points to changing conditions affecting businesses across Europe, and which lead to the formulation and implementation of new business strategies. Responding to the same conditions, and those new strategies, HRD departments and practitioners are developing new visions of their role. While success in achieving those visions is variable across the HRD departments studied in this project, and while it is also true to say that traditional training and development activities still figure prominently in HRD policy and practice, there are signs that significant changes occur, and will continue to occur, across Europe. Chapter 12 examines some of the implications of this changing scene.

12 Reflections and discussion

Sally Sambrook and Jim Stewart

This final chapter has three related aims. First, we consider the implications of the findings from this two-year research project in terms of their relevance and utility in developing a European model of HRD. Second, having reported the results of a pan-European research project exploring the connections between HRD practices and lifelong learning in learning-oriented organisations, here, we wish to engage in a critical examination of the concepts of HRD, learning-oriented organisations and lifelong learning. Third, we examine the potentialities and limitations of collaborative and comparative research based on the experience of this project.

Each of these aims will be dealt with in turn, with major attention being given to the first two items. We do not intend to conduct a detailed examination of comparative research. However, several issues of relevance and interest to those engaged in such research arise out of achieving the first two aims, and these will be identified and briefly discussed later in the chapter.

Implications

One aim of the project, as discussed in the section on 'A European outlook on HRD?' in Chapter 2 was to explore the extent to which HRD practices in Europe differed from those in the USA and Japan. There is a danger that this implies a universal American or Japanese model, and, from the differences found in the literature review, this was not the case. It also implies the existence of a 'European' model of HRD.

A European model of HRD?

As was explained in Chapter 2, results from this study suggest that there is no distinctive European model of HRD. Various attempts were made to find differences between organisations in each of the dimensions. The organisations were categorised according to the selection matrix described in Chapter 3. No significant differences were found between economic sector (service or industry) nor production type (customer orientation or mass production). This suggests that the type of organisation does not influence how the HRD role is envisaged, nor the strategies employed to implement HRD activities, nor the inhibiting/supporting factors. However, although no differences were found among organisational types, Poell and Chivers (1999) did find differences in their research when types of *work* were analysed.

The research findings were also analysed for differences across the various European countries. In other words, is there a European perspective on the concept of HRD in the organisations selected? However, this was difficult to answer because cultural, political, jurisdictional and other related factors, which could account for national differences, were not included in the study. The only nation-specific finding was the existence of the Investors in People programme in the United Kingdom, in which all British case studies participated. So, at this stage, we conclude that there is no one single European model for HRD, and that there are subtle but meaningful differences as to the philosophies, strategies, and practices on HRD across the countries in the study.

The role of HRD professionals – new skills and strategic challenges

The discourse of strategic HRD (Sambrook, 1998) suggests that human assets are becoming the most important wealth of an organisation if they are effectively nurtured and if their potential is efficiently developed and exploited. Yet, evidence from literature and this research suggests that, currently, HRD is generally not very well integrated into the corporate strategies of many organisations. Therefore, it is not seen as a viable mechanism for achieving competitive advantage. HRD is often seen more as a cost than an investment and considered merely as a means of overcoming specific skill shortages (Garavan, Heraty and Barnicle, 1999; Barham and Rassam, 1989). To overcome this, HRD functions need to increase their strategic orientation in order to become involved in strategic processes, and HRD professionals are challenged to continuously evaluate and redefine their activities in order to meet these strategic requirements.

HRD role and strategies must be reconsidered in the future from a learning perspective instead of the classical training/teaching perspective, as is still often the case. This implies a much broader role for, and greater importance of, the HRD function. However, such a change requires knowledge and understanding of the concept of the learning organisation, a concept that is still largely emergent and confused with other concepts. HRD practitioners and senior managers need to talk the same language of 'learning organisations'. Senior managers need to be aware of and understand this emerging concept, which appears to be an increasingly important element of competitive strategy. Understanding and implementing (or enacting) the learning organisation concept in the corporate environment suggests significant changes in leadership and organisational structures and cultures. It also seems important that HRD practitioners learn the language of business and strategy if they are to become involved in strategic issues, that is, if they are invited to contribute to the formulation of the overall organisational strategy. This suggests the need to develop a common language (or discourse) among organisational members (Sambrook and Stewart, 2000). However, HRD *activities* must more closely 'fit' corporate *articulations*. As similar research in the United Kingdom suggests, there is a need to align discourse and action (Sambrook, 2000).

As structures and cultures change, so do HRD practices and roles. Instead of trainers, HRD practitioners now become consultants, who also have to manage the link between their activities and company strategy. This requires a totally different set of skills, and attitudes, as this is more a 'behind the scenes' rather than an 'on stage' role. Yet, this study revealed only one company that explicitly engaged in deliberately increasing the skills of HRD professionals. Also, as structures and cultures change, HRD practitioners need to be aware and take care of the internal development of the HRD function. There are risks of losing power, and even the disappearance of the HRD function. To help overcome this, HRD professionals need to clearly identify their contribution to the organisation. However, there is still little evidence to indicate HRD's added value to the business, and investments in the function are still very much made as an 'act of faith' (Garavan *et al.*, 1999).

The study shows that the development of human resources is not a prerogative of HRD professionals. Increasingly, HRD is becoming the responsibility and business of line managers. A key reason for this relates to new ways of organising firms. Research findings suggest a diffusion of organisational structures away from functions to processes. Line managers responsible for these processes, or parts of them, require the ability to flexibly manage the resources at their disposal in view of specific dynamic exigencies of the processes (versus the relatively static exigencies of functions). This implies that managers are both more able and increasingly expected to manage their human resources, including their development. As a result of this, the decentralisation processes require specific forms of local governance of knowledge and competencies, as opposed to the traditional and centralised position of HRD. Thus, HRD activities become diffused throughout the organisation.

The role of managers

Our research findings support the view that managers fulfil a key role as HRD practices change. For instance, they are expected to perform assessments and needs analyses, work on development plans for their staff, motivate employees to learn and manage the workplace as a place fit for learning. But it was also confirmed that it is sometimes difficult for managers to fulfil this active role, either because of their work load, lack of affinity with HRD tasks or a lack of skills in this field. This suggests the need to explore further the changing responsibilities for HRD, and, in particular, what is expected of managers, and what remains (or becomes) the role of specialist practitioners. Role ambiguity is widespread, and this serves only to confuse the issue. One possibility is that the HRD function will vanish, as learning issues are more and more integrated with general management. Or, a different (strategic, supportive, consulting) role will emerge for HRD professionals. However, as Horwitz observes: 'The HRD literature is somewhat normative and rhetorical in exhorting line managers to take responsibility for training and development. The reality is that this is the exception rather than the norm'. (Horwitz, 1999: 188). Horwitz also notes that the delegation of HRD responsibilities carries problems and risks. For instance, line managers are not specialists in people development and ownership of HRD responsibility may not be part of their performance objectives, which often consider more bottom-line financial and short term objectives. If responsibility for HRD is to be genuinely integrated in line managers' roles, it is essential that both parties jointly reach agreement on mutual expectations and find solutions for practical as well as more fundamental problems in this respect (see, for instance, Ellinger, Watkins and Bostrom, 1999 for a study on how managers perceive their own role as learning facilitators).

Once agreed, there is then the need to consider how to develop both managers and HRD practitioners for their new roles. Research has shown how managers lack preparation for their new human resourcing responsibilities (Cunningham and Hyman, 1999: 18). However, sending managers on training courses to develop these new HRD skills might not be successful, as previous research has shown that managers do not necessarily learn from training (Antonacopoulou, 1999). One approach might be to involve managers in HRD, with the aim of changing their own views on learning and increasing their motivation to support the learning of others. HRD professionals from the case study organisations tried to realise this attitude change by actively supporting managers in their new tasks. Another, long-term approach might involve incorporating HRD skills in all management development programmes if HRD is to become an integrated part of business. The ways in which managers support their staff in learning could then also become an issue in performance appraisals and management career planning. This would require careful examination of the existing provision for professional development of both managers and HRD specialists.

The role of employees

As HRD practices evolve to further involve managers, employees also have increasing involvement. Our research findings suggest that *employee* motivation to learn can be a key factor influencing learning in organisations. If employees are not motivated to learn, this imposes a serious inhibiting factor to realising new work practices. If individual employees do not see the importance of learning, they often fail to take the opportunities offered. An important element of motivation is the appreciation of more informal ways of learning and development, and a sense of personal responsibility for their own learning. This means a considerable shift from the traditional views employees (tacitly) hold on learning. HRD professionals from the case study organisations were found to be actively trying to change these views of learning as a classroom, teacher-led activity. It would be worthwhile to explore ways in which this attitude change can be brought about (e.g. by adopting different HRD practices, but also by targeted HRD interventions and work methods). One attempt to increase motivation, also found in some of the companies from this project, is to provide training credits and provide career guidance. As Chaplin stated,

> Companies should ensure that all learning achievements by their staffs are recognised by publicity, appropriate promotion and reward. Such measures will motivate other members of the workforce to become involved in lifelong learning.
> (Chaplin, 1993: 92)

A critical examination of the concepts of HRD, learning-oriented organisations and lifelong learning

The project as a whole, and this discussion so far, assumed an unproblematic status for the key concepts in the research. While we accept and support the value of this, we also think it is important to acknowledge the tensions arising from the contested nature and meaning of these concepts. This section, therefore, provides a brief critical examination of the terms HRD, learning-oriented organisations and lifelong learning. This is included to provide a means of evaluating the validity and utility of the research findings. We will, though, return to our own position at the end of the chapter.

The project sought to produce descriptive accounts of the connections between lifelong learning and HRD practices in learning-oriented organisations. In particular, it was concerned with the changing role(s) of HRD professionals. One finding from the UK research, supported by cases in other countries, is that there is a 'mismatch' between the language of the project and that used in work organisations. For example, the term HRD was used in only one of the UK organisations in a formal way, and that was only in the job title of the HRD manager. All other professional practitioners had titles with either 'training' or 'training and development' and the function itself was formally referred to in company documents as 'training and development'. Staff members interviewed across a cross-section of levels and functions invariably used the short-hand expression 'training department'. The same was true of the other case study organisations and, outside of company documents, the terms 'learning organisation' or 'learning-oriented' are part of the language of few professional practitioners and senior managers. So, those terms cannot be said to be used consistently within the case study organisations, or even among those groups who are actively promoting their application and seeking their claimed benefits. In addition to this 'mismatch', there are additional and related problems with the concepts.

Human resource development (HRD)

The term HRD can, in some ways, be compared with HRM (McGoldrick and Stewart, 1996; McGoldrick, Stewart and Watson, 2001; Sambrook, 1998). Both have their origins in the USA and have stimulated debate around their meaning, especially when contrasted with more traditional and established terms such as personnel and training (Stewart, 1992; Stewart and McGoldrick, 1996).

The research of one of the present authors provides additional evidence of the 'mismatch' noted above, and attempts to account for the growth in use of the term by academics (Sambrook, 1998). One potential explanation of both these phenomena is that suggested in relation to HRM by Legge (1995), and that is the interests of academics and their careers (Sambrook and Stewart, 1998a). However, what can be argued is that HRD is an emerging term that has yet to gain universal acceptance in professional practice and still lacks a shared meaning or definition, even among those communities who regularly use it to frame and denote a particular approach to that practice (Sambrook and Stewart, 1998b; Stewart, 1999; Stewart, McGoldrick and Watson, 2001).

Lifelong learning

While use of the term 'lifelong learning' can be traced to the 1970s (Tjepkema *et al.*, 1999), in common with HRD, its currency is relatively recent. Of particular relevance to this project is the fact that 1996 was proclaimed by the EU to be the official European Year of Lifelong Learning, and have now published a 'Memorandum of Lifelong Learning' (http://www.europa.eu.int/comm/education/life/memoen.pdf).

As currently formulated (Gass, 1996; OECD, 1996; DfEE, 1998), the concept has a significant focus on formal opportunities for education, training and development and associated structural provision of resources. However, such formulations downplay the validity and potential application of theories of learning which suggest that individual learning is both inevitable and continuous (see Stewart, 1999; Burgoyne, 1997). That being the case, application of the concept in the context of work organisations will tend to downplay the role and significance of 'implicit learning' (Chao, 1997), 'incidental learning' (Marsick and Watkins, 1997) and 'informal/ accidental learning' (Mumford, 1997).

An additional problem with the concept as currently formulated is that at the same time as downplaying certain theories of individual learning, there is an emphasis on the individual as the 'learning unit'. This has the consequence of downplaying the social nature of learning and theories such as 'situated learning' which seek to locate learning in social processes (see Fox, 1997; Elkjaer, 1999). Such theories can be argued to be of particular interest and relevance when considering the concept of 'learning organisations'. However, that concept itself can also be problematic.

Learning organisation

The concept of 'the learning organisation' has been criticised in both the professional (Sloman, 1999) and academic literature (see Easterby-Smith *et al.*, 1999).

One element in the critique of the idea of 'learning organisations' is the necessary connection of the concept with that of 'organisational learning'. There have been significant and influential attempts to theorise this concept and study its application in work organisations (see, for example, Moingeon and Edmondson, 1996; Nonaka, 1996; Dixon, 1999; Argyris, 1999). These attempts though have been subject to recent criticisms and claims that satisfactory theories have yet to be formulated (Prange, 1999; Elkjaer, 1999). To the extent that the idea of 'organisational learning' remains problematic, the idea of 'learning organisations' cannot be said to be capable of operationalisation in any meaningful sense; certainly not in a way which allows unproblematic research into its application. In any case, as with HRD, the existence of competing and incommensurable formulations of the concept (see for example Senge, 1990; Pedler *et al.*, 1996; Swieringa and Wierdsma, 1992) suggests significant difficulties in researching the concept.

A robust defence of the concept has recently been published by one of the leading theorists, which provides a reasoned response to many of these points (Burgoyne, 1999). However, our conclusion is that the concept remains problematic. An emerging issue is that of the connection of 'learning organisation' with ' knowledge management.'

The latter is argued by some (Scarborough, Swan and Preston, 1999) to be replacing the former as a focus of academic and organisational interest. This argument might be supported by the proliferation of books on the subject (see, for example, Rumizen, 2001; Howe *et al.*, 2001). It is, in any case, clear that the concept of learning organisation remains contested (which may in itself be a reason why not all organisations in this study use the term explicitly).

Discussion

Based on this brief analysis we can conclude that researching the relationships and connections between the three concepts would be, in any circumstances, an ambitious project. We do not have to employ critiques from 'critical management' (Alvesson and Willmott, 1996), or postmodernism (Alvesson and Deetz, 1996) or indeed to employ the tools of discourse analysis (Sambrook and Stewart, 1998a; Oswick *et al.*, 1997) to problematise the concepts. There are additional characteristics of this project which raise additional issues for design and conduct of research. These are discussed in the next section.

Implications for comparative and collaborative research

The issues arising from this project that we wish to discuss can be considered under the two headings of 'comparative' and 'collaborative'.

Comparative research

The previous section has established the problematic status of the concepts. In particular, the 'mismatch' of language use between academics and those studied in work organisations raises issues concerning the extent to which valid comparisons can be, or are being, made. However, this is just one facet of language use. There are potential and actual differences in the meaning attached to conceptual terms among academics, and among individual employees within and across work organisations (Sambrook, 1998). A particular example of the former in this project is the matrix of organisation types devised and proposed by the German partners. They proposed a dichotomy or continuum of 'mass production' versus 'customer orientation' to organise the case study organisations concepts with potentially multiple connotations and meanings, and the 'choice' was in fact rejected by the participating UK case study organisations. As the UK partners in the project, we applied an interpretation negotiated as acceptable with representatives of the organisations in order to 'allocate' each to one of the four cells. However, while this interpretation was communicated to the project management team and the other partners, it remains probable that, across the twenty-eight cases, organisations have been allocated to cells in the matrix against varying understandings of the dimensions and associated criteria. As well as having implications for making valid comparisons, this example also illustrates issues for collaborative research (see below).

Conceptual understanding and meanings attached to conceptual terms is an issue which is likely to be compounded in international research. The obvious problem of differences in national languages and the need for translation is probably only the tip of the large iceberg of different understandings, varying interpretations and multiple meanings associated with cross-national research. A simple illustration here is the search for examples of 'good practices'. Some of those selected appear in the text boxes in the country-specific chapters. However, what might be considered 'good' in varying cultural contexts is of itself problematic. In attempting to overcome this, the project team elaborated the meaning of 'good practice' through the use of concepts such as 'interesting', 'novel' and 'innovative'. However, given different cultural traditions and their effects in influencing and shaping approaches to professional practices, what might be considered 'innovative' in one context may well be considered established or normal practice in another. So, valid comparisons again become questionable.

Collaborative research

The issues discussed so far have obvious implications for collaborative research across national boundaries. There are though two issues associated with collaborative projects worth examining which arise irrespective of the comparative focus.

The first issue is that of communication within the team of researchers. Advances in information and communications technology might be thought, or argued, to have overcome many difficulties associated with this issue. Our experience, though, is that face-to-face discussion and debate remains the most satisfying, productive and effective process in conducting collaborative research. This project had a small and limited number of partner meetings. There was, therefore, a heavy reliance on e-mail and fax as methods of communication. In addition, much of the communication was channelled through the project management team and there was, therefore, little direct communication between the project partners. One consequence of this process was that the management team become, of necessity, arbiters of the various and varying views being expressed. This can be considered a legitimate role given their responsibility for managing the research process, and we would endorse that view. We do though believe that, at times and in relation to some of the questions and issues that inevitably occur in the conduct of research, being placed in the role of arbiter is an unfair burden, and that full participation of all partners in decisions is the ideal process. It is in relation to such times and questions that problems of communication become more sharply focused.

The second issue is that of variability in methodological orientation. This is an added complication to variability in meanings attached to conceptual terms, though the two can of course be related. In this study, the overall research design was produced by the project management team and partners were invited to participate. That being the case, significant differences in methodological position would have lead, presumably, to declining the invitation, and therefore, little or no problems in relation to methodological decisions. However, the often claimed broad methodological distinctions and disputes (Easterby-Smith *et al.*, 1991; Gill and Johnson, 1997) deflect attention from less obvious though significant epistemological nuances (see, for example, Benton and Craib, 2001). There remains therefore the potential for disagreement around the appropriateness of particular methods and their application, and, perhaps more importantly, the status of research data and the claims that they might support. There is, of course, a direct connection here with the first issue in that open debate can and will resolve any disagreements that might arise. With limited opportunities for such debate though the issue can be more significant. Although limited, we can say that in this project the partner meetings were both enjoyable and productive, and they enabled most, if not all, differences to be amicably resolved. This might not though be the experience of all participants in other collaborative projects.

Final thoughts

Having critiqued both the content and the process of this project, we have now achieved the aims of this chapter. Returning to our original position, we conclude with some final thoughts on the potential implications of the findings. They do suggest that opportunities for lifelong learning are being developed within the organisations and European countries studied, and that HRD professionals have a key role in promoting and supporting lifelong learning. The case studies indicate that there are many organisations in Europe that are attempting to embrace the concept of the learning organisation in creating opportunities for lifelong learning. They have demonstrated that the concept can be powerful and capable of application, although they also experienced factors that hindered the implementation of the concept. However, a note of caution should be made as to the relationship between the observed changes in HRD tasks and interventions and the concept of the learning (oriented) organisation. For example, Raper, Ashton, Felstead and Storey (1997) also recognised the great interest in learning at the organisational level but wondered if becoming a learning organisation was the motive for changes in the process of learning at work. Trends that were identified in training practices in organisations were, for instance, the declining use of external training, and the increased use of internal training, especially on-the-job training, planned work experience and the use of coaching. These trends are in tune with important characteristics of the concept of the learning organisation, but often the motive for changes in employee learning were not so much support for becoming a learning organisation, but rather the wish to cut down on training budgets and a scaling down of central training departments. Restructuring of organisations, the devolution of responsibility for training to line managers or supervisors, changes in product markets, the introduction of quality programmes in the organisation, introduction of new technologies and changes in product and technical knowledge also appeared to be driving forces for organisations to change the learning process at work. These drivers for change seem to be related more to product market and technological change rather than any significant support for a new learning philosophy (Raper *et al.*, 1997).

There is also the problematic issue of language – and whether there is yet a common language (or discourse) between researchers and practitioners. Whilst the project has focused on the role of HRD practitioners in learning-oriented organisations, it has become apparent that many practitioners do not adopt the term HRD and do not speak of their organisations as being learning-oriented. However, their roles are indeed characteristic of what is commonly described as HRD, and their organisations do indeed display many of the features associated with learning (oriented) organisations, at least as they were defined for the purposes of this project. The issue of language and terminology is an important one, not least in advancing theory *and* practice. There are obvious dangers in theory building being too far ahead of practice, which can be a consequence of esoteric and obscure language. Meanings and definitions must, therefore, be further explained and shared if academics and practitioners are to learn from each other and together.

To finally conclude, this two-year study, involving almost 200 organisations across seven European countries, has found empirical evidence of a changing role for HRD professionals and an increasing responsibility for HRD activities amongst managers and employees. A key reason for pursuing the learning (oriented) organisation concept is to enhance competitiveness. With these factors in mind, there is a need for HRD professionals to ensure the development of a strategic role, to clarify their functional role, develop the new skills required of these changes, and more clearly demonstrate their value and contribution to organisational success.

Bibliography

Alvesson, M. and Deetz, S. (1996) 'Critical theory and postmodernism approaches to organisation studies', in S.R. Clegg *et al.* (eds) *Handbook of Organisation Studies*, London: Sage.

Alvesson, M. and Willmott, H. (1996) *Making Sense of Management: A Critical Introduction*, London: Sage.

Ansoff, H.I. (1987) 'De evolutie van de strategische besluitvorming: van ondernemerschap naar multi-dimensionele strategie', *Handboek voor managers* [*Handbook for Managers*] 3, 21:201–226.

Antonacopoulou, E.P. (1999) 'Training does not imply learning: the individual's perspective', *International Journal of Training and Development* 3, 1:14–33.

Argyris, C. (1992) *On Organisational Learning*, Cambridge, MA: Blackwell.

—— (1999) *On Organisational Learning* (second edition) Oxford: Blackwell.

Argyris, C. and Schön, D.A. (1978) *Organisational Learning: A Theory of Action Perspective*, Reading: Addison-Wesly.

Barham, K. and Rassam, C. (1989) *Shaping the Corporate Future: Leading Executives Share their Vision and Strategies*, London: Unwin Hyman.

Benton, T. and Craib, I. (2001) *Philosophy of Social Science: The Philosophical Foundations of Social Thought*, Basingstoke: Palgrave.

Bomers, G.B.J. (1990) 'De lerende organisatie: de enige zekerheid voor organisaties is permanente verandering', *Harvard Holland Review* 68, 22:21–31.

Brandsma, J. (ed.) (1997) *Een leven lang leren: (on)mogelijkheden en perspectieven.* [*Lifelong Learning: (Im)possibilities and Perspectives*], Enschede: University of Twente, OCTO.

Burgoyne, J. (1997) 'Learning: conceptual, practical and theoretical issues', British Psychological Society Annual Conference, Herriott-Watt University, Edinburgh, April 1997.

—— (1999) 'Design of the times', *People Management* June.

Carnevale, A.P. (1991) *America and the New Economy: How New Competitive Standards are Radically Changing American Workplace*, San Francisco: Jossey-Bass.

Chao, G.T. (1997) 'Organisation socialisation in multinational corporations: the role of implicit learning', in C.L. Cooper and S.E. Jackson (eds) *Creating Tomorrow's Organisations*, Chichester: John Wiley.

Chaplin, T. (1993) 'The roles and strategies of business corporations', in Combey and Doherty (eds) *Lifelong Learning for European Business: The Strategic Investment*, Conference report ELLI.

Cunningham, I. and Hyman, J. (1999) 'Devolving human resource responsibilities to the line: beginning of the end or a new beginning for personnel?' *Personnel Review* 28, 1/2:9–27.

De Geus, A.P. (1988). 'Planning as learning: at Shell, planning means changing minds, not making plans', *Harvard Holland Review* 66, 2:70–74.

DfEE (1998) *The Learning Age: A Renaissance for Britain*, London: HMSO.

Dixon, N. (1999) *The Organisational Learning Cycle* (second edition), Maidenhead: McGraw-Hill.

Drucker, P.F. (1995) *Managing in a Time of Great Change*, New York: Truman Valley.

Easterby-Smith, M., Burgoyne, J. and Araujo, L. (eds) (1999) *Organisational Learning and the Learning Organisation*, London: Sage.

Easterby-Smith, M., Thorpe, R. and Lowe, A. (1991) *Management Research: An Introduction*, London: Sage.

Elkjaer, B. (1999) 'In search of a social learning theory', in M. Easterby-Smith *et al.* (eds) *Organisational Learning and the Learning Organisation*, London: Sage.

Ellinger, A.D., Watkins, K. and Bostrom, R.P. (1999) 'Managers as facilitators of learning in learning organisations', *Human Resource Development Quarterly* 10, 2:105–125.

Fiol, C.M. and Lyles, M.A. (1985) 'Organisational learning', *Academy of Management Review*, 10, 4:803–813.

Fox, S. (1997) 'From management, education and development to the study of management learning', in J. Burgoyne and M. Reynolds (eds) *Management Learning: Integrating Perspectives in Theory and Practice*, London: Sage.

Garavan, T., Heraty, N. and Barnicle, B. (1999) 'Human resource development literature: current issues, priorities and dilemmas', *Journal of European Industrial Training*, 23, 4/5: 169–179.

Gass, R. (1996) *The Goals, Architecture and Means of Lifelong Learning: European Year of Lifelong Learning*, background paper issued by the European Commission, Luxembourg: Office for Official Publications of the European Communities.

Gill, J. and Johnson, P. (1997) *Research Methods for Managers* (second edition), London: Paul Chapman Publishing.

Honold, L.J. (1991) 'The power of learning at Johnsonville Foods', *Training* 28, 4:55–58.

Horwitz, F. (1999) 'The emergence of strategic training and development: the current state of play', *Journal of European Industrial Training* 23, 4/5:180–190.

Howe, M.A., *et al.* (2001) *The Decision-Makers' Guide to Knowledge Management: How to Implement a Knowledge Management System in Your Organisation*.

Imai, M. (1986) *KAIZEN: het stap voor stap bezig zijn met verbetering van een produkt of dienst.* [*KAIZEN: Step by Step Improvement of Processes and Services*] Deventer: Kluwer.

Kessels, J.W.M. (1995) 'Opleiden en leren in arbeidsorganisaties: het ambivalente perspectief van de kennisproduktiviteit', *Comenius* 15, 2:179–193.

Keursten, P. (1995) 'De opkomende kennis economie: kansen en vragen voor opleidings professionals', *Opleiding & Ontwikkeling* [*Training & Development*] 8, 6:5–9.

Kim, D. (1993) 'The link between individual and organisational learning', *Sloan Management Review*, Fall: 37–50.

Laiken, M. (1993) 'From trainer to consultant in 5 (not easy!) steps', *Performance and Instruction*, November/December:32–36.

Legge, K. (1995) *Human Resource Management: Rhetorics and Realities*, Basingstoke: Macmillan.

Leonard-Barton, D. (1995) *Wellsprings of Knowledge: Building and Sustaining the Sources of Innovation*, Boston: Harvard Business School.

Leys, M., Wijgaerts, D. and Hancké, C. (1992) *Van leren op de vloer tot lerende organisatie: zeven Europese bedrijven het bedrijfsopleidingsbeleid voorbij?* [*From Learning in the Workplace to Learning Organisations: Seven European Companies Move Beyond Training Policies?*] Brussels: SERV-Stichting Technologie Vlaanderen.

Marsick, V.J. and Watkins, K.E. (1997) 'Lessons from informal and incidental learning', in J. Burgoyne and M. Reynolds (eds) *Management Learning: Integrating Perspectives in Theory and Practice*, London: Sage.

McGill, M.E. and Slocum, J.W. (1994) *The Smarter Organisation: How to Build a Business that Learns and Adapts to Marketplace Needs*, New York: Wiley.

McGoldrick, J. and Stewart, J. (1996) 'The HRM-HRM nexus', in J. Stewart and J. McGoldrick (eds) *Human Resource Development: Perspectives, Strategies and Practice*, London: Pitman Publishing.

McGoldrick, J., Stewart, J. and Watson, S. (2001) 'Researching HRD: philosophy, process and practice', in J. McGoldrick, J. Stewart and S. Watson (eds) *Understanding Human Resource Development: A Research-Based Approach*, London: Routledge.

McLagan, P. (1996) 'Great ideas revisited: competency models and creating the future of HRD', *Training & Development*, January: 60–65.

Miles, M.B. and Huberman, A.M. (1981) *Qualitative Data Analysis: A Sourcebook of New Methods*, London: Sage.

Mintzberg, H. (1979) *The Structuring of Organisations: A Synthesis of the Research*, Englewood Cliffs: Aspekte.

Moingeon, B. and Edmondson, A. (eds) (1996) *Organisational Learning and Competitive Advantage*. London: Sage.

Morgan, G. (1990). *De nieuwe manager: ontwikkeling van managementvaardigheden voor een wereld in beweging* [*The New Manager: Management Skills for a Turbulent World*] Schiedam: Scriptum.

Mumford, A. (1997) *Management Development: Strategies for Action* (third edition), London: IPD.

Nonaka, I. (1991) 'The knowledge-creating company', *Harvard Business Review* 69, 6:96–104.

—— (1996) 'The knowledge-creating company', in K. Starkey (ed.), *How Organisations Learn*, London: International Thomson Business.

Nonaka, I. and Takeuchi, H. (1995) *The Knowledge-Creating Company: How Japanese Companies Create the Dynamics of Innovation*, New York/Oxford: University Press.

OECD (1996) *Lifelong Learning for All*, Paris: OECD.

Onstenk, J. (1994) *Leren en opleiden op de werkplek: een verkenning in zes landen* [*Learning and Training in the Workplace: An Exploration in Six Countries*] Amsterdam: A&O.

Oswick, C., Keenoy, T. and Grant, D. (1997) 'Managerial discourses: words speak louder than actions', *Journal of Applied Management Studies* 6, 1.

Pascale, R.T. (1990) *Managing on the Edge: How Succesful Companies Use Conflict to Stay Ahead*, London: Viking.

Pawlowsky, P. and Bäumer, J. (1996) *Betriebliche Weiterbildung: Management von Qualifikation und Wissen* [*Personal Development Within Corporations: Management of Quallifications and Knowledge*] München: Beck.

Pearn, M., Roderick, C. and Mulrooney, C. (1995) *Learning Organisations in Practice*, London: McGraw-Hill.

Pedler, M., Boydell, T. and Burgoyne, J. (1991) *The Learning Company: A Strategy for Sustainable Development*, Londen: McGraw-Hill.

—— (1996) *The Learning Company* (second edition), Maidenhead: McGraw-Hill.

Pinchot, G. and Pinchot, E. (1994) *De ondergang van de bureaucratie en de opkomst van de intelligente onderneming* [*The Fall of Bureaucracy and the Rise of the Intelligent Company*] Amsterdam: Contact.

Poell, R. and Chivers, G. (1999*) HRD consultant roles in different types of organizations*, paper presented within the AHRD/VETNET strand of the European Conference on Educational Research (ECER), Finland: Lahti, September 1999.

Prange, C. (1999) 'Organisational learning: desparately seeking theory?', in M. Easterby-Smith *et al.* (eds) *Organisational Learning and the Learning Organisation*, London: Sage.

Quinn, J.B. (1994) *Intelligente ondernemingen: een nieuw model voor een nieuwe tijd* [*Intelligent Enterprises: A New Model for a New Era*] Amsterdam: Contact.

Raper, P., Ashton, D., Felstead, A. and Storey, K. (1997) 'Toward the learning organisation? Explaining current trends in training practice in the UK', *International Journal of Training and Development* 1, 1:9–21.

Robinson, D.G. and Robinson, J.C. (1995) *Performance Consulting: Moving Beyond Training*. San Francisco: Berrett-Koehler.

Rumizen, M.C. (2001) *Complete Idiot's Guide to Knowledge Management*, London: Alpha Books.

Sambrook, S. (1998) 'Models and Concepts of Human Resource Development: Academic and Practitioner Perspectives', (unpublished) doctoral thesis, Nottingham Business School, The Nottingham Trent University.

—— (2000) 'Talking of HRD,' *Human Resource Development International* 3, 2:159–178.

Sambrook, S. and Stewart, J. (1998a) 'HRD as a discursive construction', paper presented at the Leeds-Lancaster Conference on Emergent Fields in Management, University of Leeds, Leeds.

—— (1998b) 'HRD as a discursive construction', paper presented at Professors Forum, IFTDO World Conference, Trinity College, Dublin.

—— (2000) 'Factors influencing learning in European learning oriented organisations: issues for management', *Journal of European Industrial Training* 24, 2/3/4:209–219.

Scarbrough, H., Swan, J. and Preston, J. (1999) *Knowledge Management and the Learning Organisation: The CIPD Report*, London: CIPD.

Senge, P.M. (1990). *The fifth discipline: the art and practice of the learning organisation*. New York: Double Day Currency.

Senge, P.M., Roberts, C., Ross, R.B., Smith, B.J. and Kleiner, A. (1994) *The Fifth Discipline Fieldbook: Strategies and Tools for Building a Learning Organisation*, Londen: Nicholas Brealy.

Sloman M. (1999) 'Seize the day', *Learning Centre, People Management* 5, 10.

Stahl, T., Nyhan, B. and d'Ajola, P. (1994) *De lerende organisatie: een nieuwe visie op Human Resource Development* [*The Learning Organisation: A New Vision for Human Resource Development*] Brussels: European Commission.

Stewart, J. (1992) 'Towards a model of HRD', *Training and Development* 10, 10.

—— (1996) *Managing Change through Training and Development*, London: Kogan Page.

—— (1999) *Employee Development Practice*, London: FT Pitman Publishing.

Sugarman, B. (1998) 'The learning organisation: implications for training', in S.M. Brown and C.J. Seidner (eds) *Evaluating Corporate Training: Models and Issues*, Norwell: Kluwer Academic.

Stewart, J. and McGoldrick, J. (eds) (1996) *Human Resource Development: Perspectives, Strategies and Practice*, London: Pitman Publishing.

Swieringa, J. and Wierdsma, A. (1992) *Becoming a Learning Organisation: Beyond the Learning Curve*, Amsterdam: Addison-Wesley.

Ter Horst, H.M., Mulder, M., Tjepkema, S. and Scheerens, J. (1999) *Future Challenges for Human Resource Development Professionals in Europe. Part II: A Literature Review on Differ-*

ences in Outlook between European, US and Japanese HRD Departments, project report, Enschede: University of Twente.

Ter Horst, H.M. Tjepkema, S., Mulder, M. and Scheerens, J. (eds) (2000) *Glimpses of Changing HRD Practices in Learning-Oriented Organisations Throughout Europe: Practitioner's Book*, project report, Enschede: University of Twente.

Tjepkema, S. and Wognum, A.A.M. (1995) *Van opleider naar adviseur? Taakgebieden van opleidingsfunctionarissen in leergerichte organisaties* [*From Trainer to Consultant? Roles and Tasks of HRD Professionals in Learning Oriented Organisations*] Enschede: University of Twente.

—— (1996) 'From Trainer to Consultant? Roles and Tasks of HRD Professionals in Learning Oriented Organisations', paper presented at ECLO conference 'Growth through learning', Copenhagen.

Tjepkema, S. (1993a) *Profiel van de lerende organisatie en haar opleidingsfunctie* [*Profile of the Learning Organisation and its HRD Function*] Enschede: University of Twente.

—— (1993b) 'Inrichting van de opleidingsfunctie in een lerende organisatie: de aanpak van zes Nederlandse bedrijven' ['Organisation of the HRD function in a learning organization: the approach of six Dutch companies'] (unpublished) MSc thesis, Enschede: University of Twente.

Tjepkema, S., Ter Horst, H.M., Mulder, M. and Scheerens, J. (eds) (1999) *Future Challenges for Human Resource Development Professionals in Europe. Part I: Results of Case Studies in 28 companies on Lifelong Learning in Learning-Oriented Organisations*, project report, Enschede: University of Twente.

—— (2000) *Future Challenges for Human Resource Development Professionals in Europe. Part IV: Results of a Survey in Learning-Oriented Organisations in Seven Countries in the European Union*, project report, Enschede: University of Twente.

Van den Broeck, H. (1994) *Lerend management: verborgen krachten van managers en organisaties* [*Learning Management: Hidden Powers of Managers and Organisations*], Schiedam: Lannoo/Scriptum.

Van der Krogt, F.J. (1991) 'Aansluitingsstrategieën en opleidingsactiviteiten in verschillende organisatietypen', *Opleiding & Ontwikkeling* [*Training & Development*] 4, 7:3–15.

Watkins, K.E. and Marsick, V.J. (1993) *Sculpting the Learning Organisation: Lessons in the Art and Science of Systemic Change*, San Francisco: Jossey-Bass.

Winslow, C.D. and Bramer, W.L. (1994) *Future work: putting knowledge to work in the knowledge economy*, New York: The Free Press.

Yin, R.K. (1984) *Case Study Research: Design and Methods*, London: Sage.

Index

References to tables are in bold type, and appear after the main sequence of page references e.g. 169, 171, **41**, **42**